"*Without a doubt, the most illuminating and significant book on the Thompson River. A fascinating read.*"

—**Chris Harris**, author and publisher, *Flyover*

"*I've rafted the Thompson with Bernie, listened to his stories, and read his previous book. This book is a superb accumulation of four decades of rafting, research, storytelling, and writing. I enjoyed every page.*"

—**Murphy Shewchuk**, author and publisher, *Cariboo Trips and Trails*

"*There is satisfying depth and range of information in Bernie Fandrich's new book, British Columbia's Majestic Thompson River. The history, geology, botany, hydrology—Bernie never misses an opportunity to present all this with great humour. He obviously loves this river—and so will you.*"

—**Bruce Batchelor**, author, *Yukon Channel Charts*
and *Nine Dog Winter*

"*I have rafted the historic Thompson River many times and can attest that no one has more knowledge of the river than Bernie Fandrich does. His excellent book delivers a unique insight into the history of British Columbia's Interior.*" "

—**David Gregory**, editor, Okanagan Historical Society Reports

"*Bernie Fandrich is one of a very small group of flyfishers who has fished every drift and slick on the Thompson—not once but many times. In his book he divulges no fishing secrets, but he reveals everything that you need to know about the river.*"

—**Gordon Milne**, Superintendent of Schools (retired)
and fellow flyfisher

British Columbia's

MAJESTIC THOMPSON RIVER

KM-by-KM Guide, Events, and Tales

To Bill

Delight in the river

Bernie Fandrich

Bernie Fandrich

British Columbia's Majestic Thompson River

Nicomen House Publishing
PO Box 30
Lytton, BC V0K 1Z0

www.berniefandrich.com info@berniefandrich.com

Editing by Arlene Prunkl
Cover and Interior Book Design by Jessica Thomson

Library and Archives Canada Cataloguing in Publication

Fandrich, Bernard
British Columbia's Majestic Thompson River : km-by-km guide, events, and tales / Bernie Fandrich.

Includes bibliographical references.

ISBN 978-0-9917345-0-4

1. Thompson River (B.C.)—Description and travel. 2. Thompson River Valley (B.C.)—Description and travel. 3. Thompson River Valley (B.C.)—History. I. Title. II. Title: Majestic Thompson River.

FC3845.T56F36 2013 917.11'72 C2013-900461-0

First Printing, 2013

A man of wisdom delights in water — Confucius

Acknowledgements

A few years ago, my daughter Meghan scanned my previous book, *Rafting in BC*, that I had co-authored with Doug VanDine two decades earlier, and she presented a digital copy to me as a Christmas gift. Her hidden agenda was to encourage me to write a new book about the Thompson River.

Meghan was the primary catalyst for the writing of this new book, and her early copy editing turned a rather disjointed manuscript into something readable. Her consistent comment was, "That's really good, Dad. You're a great storyteller. Keep writing."

My friend Paul Bucci visited for a few days early in the process, and together we sat down and penned the opening chapter of the first descent of the Thompson by Governor Simpson in 1828. Paul's visit helped launch the direction of the book.

About the time I thought it was publishable, I asked one of my fishing companions, Bob Tyrrell (owner of Orca Book Publishers), to read it and give me his candid opinion. "The manuscript is well written and contains lots of interesting information, but there are a number of issues…" His recommendations all made sense and I felt compelled to carry them out.

Arlene Prunkl did the final editing and, later, the proofreading of the manuscript. Arlene liked my sense of humour and encouraged me to use it. The improvement was remarkable, and a polished new work emerged, something eminently readable and sprinkled with light-hearted humour.

With the changes finally implemented, graphic artist Jessica Thomson (a former Kumsheen Resort photographer) completed the manuscript's layout and added a much-needed touch of class to book's appearance. She endured my constant changes: "Sorry, Jessie, but I think this photo is just a tad better," or "Sorry, Jessie, but I decided this chapter wasn't very good so here's a new one."

Finally, I need to thank my wife, Lorna, for enduring my occupation of the kitchen table for a few years. On rare occasions, I would remove the mountains of books, photos, and computers so we could sit down to a normal meal. Otherwise, the sunroom had to do. My reassurance that "it's almost done" dragged on for a long time.

To these key people and everyone else who helped in some way, I give my heartfelt thanks.

Contents

Stops, Pit Houses, "Indian Hunting Grisly," Double-Headed Snake, Ashcroft Manor, Buffalo George, Thompson Indian Burial Customs, Golden Eagles, Osprey, The Roaring Landslide of 1880, Horse Ferry, Kamloops Lake Salmon Fossils, A Desert Climate, Conclusion

SAVONA TO LYTTON
117.0 KM - 0 KM

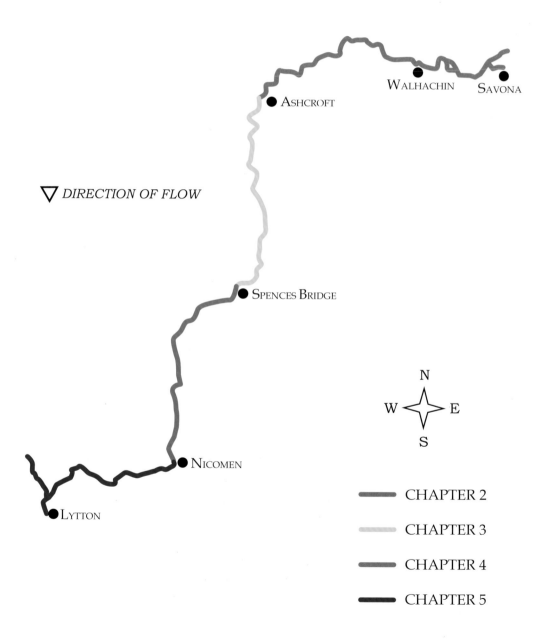

DIRECTION OF FLOW

WALHACHIN

SAVONA

ASHCROFT

SPENCES BRIDGE

NICOMEN

LYTTON

N
W · E
S

— CHAPTER 2
— CHAPTER 3
— CHAPTER 4
— CHAPTER 5

Introduction

The Thompson is no ordinary river: its beauty can astound you and its power can zap you in minutes. Forty years of my life are interwoven with this majestic river. For four decades, I have travelled its rapids, hiked along its shores, marvelled at it from the highway, and studied its history.

Ever since my very first eight-mile rafting trip from Spences Bridge to Goldpan Provincial Park on June 10, 1973, I have continued to discover that this is no ordinary river. The first trip, rafted at high water, instilled in me a huge sense of respect and awe for the Thompson. The respect, admiration, and sometimes even fear have never left me.

That first year, as spring flowed into summer and the water level receded, I realized that a new river was emerging. Boiling rapids disappeared and new ones crept to the surface. I liked the river much more when the water level was lower and warm water replaced the melting snow.

In the fall, yet another river showed itself. Stunning in every respect, the rapids morphed into the most amazing stretches of whitewater imaginable. The river also hosted millions of salmon, hundreds of anglers, and myriad birds and wildlife feeding on the dead salmon. I was smitten by this majestic river. Little did I know that our special relationship would continue for more than four decades.

Ten years later, with Doug VanDine, a geological engineer, I co-authored a book about the Thompson River between Ashcroft and Lytton. My role was to write about ten years of running the river, and Doug wrote primarily about the fascinating landforms and landslides along the Thompson Valley.

Rafting in British Columbia: Featuring the Lower Thompson River was primarily a guidebook between Ashcroft and Lytton. It was purchased by thousands of rafting enthusiasts and kayakers to help them navigate the river, to learn the names of the rapids, and to add value to the river experience by reading stories about the river, the rapids, and the geology.

Three decades have passed since the first book, and it is time for another. A much different book has emerged. While it still includes fascinating river stories, it now also introduces the reader to a host of other events along the Thompson.

For example, as a pioneer of the whitewater rafting industry in Canada, I was surprised to discover that the first descent of the Thompson occurred almost 150 years before my own scary first descent. The event was witnessed only by indigenous people, a few fur traders, and the wild animals living here in 1828.

The best river guide in Canada, Jean Bernard, led that first descent. The expedition included 14 men in two canoes and a heavy slug of a boat manufactured for the express purpose of running the river from Kamloops to Lytton. It's a fascinating story, and that's where this book begins its journey.

The story of the first descent is followed by four chapters that feature a kilometre-by-kilometre description of the river from Savona to Lytton, a distance of 117 kilometres.

One of the Thompson's neglected jewels, the stretch of river from Savona to Ashcroft, is described in Chapter 2. You will learn about the rapids, read about the interesting things that happened along the river, and of course view some photographs as we journey from one landmark to the next through a delightful interior desert.

You may be inspired to chat with your friends, dig out your canoes and paddles, grab your fly-fishing rod, and spend a day or two floating this enchanting segment of river when you've completed Chapter 2.

Chapter 3 begins at Ashcroft, and we float downriver to Spences Bridge through a series of landslides and a wonderfully scenic landscape. This is a naturalist's heaven. On one trip through this section, several naturalists on board identified more than 45 species of birds.

Of course, we can't forget the rapids, especially in Black Canyon. The 150-million-year-old canyon is spectacular and is only visible from the river. Leading up to it is the biggest rapid on the upper river; it's like a storm before the calm.

We move downriver in Chapter 4 and journey between Spences

Bridge and Nicomen. Although the most popular day voyage on the river goes from Spences Bridge to Lytton, we've divided the 40 kilometres into two sections. The whitewater in the first half is not as extreme as it is from Nicomen to Lytton, so to compensate for the somewhat reduced river excitement, you'll read more stories.

Chapter 5 begins at Nicomen, only 16 kilometres from Lytton. This km-by-km chapter leads you through the wildest, the best, and the most consistent stretch of whitewater on the Thompson.

You'll learn all the rapid names, and if a good story is associated with the name, you'll hear the story. Most stories are true but a few are, well, fantasies.

We abandon the km-by-km descriptions in Chapter 6 and go ashore to examine some plants that have learned to live with very little water and lots of sunshine. By no means an exhaustive list, some of the more common flora is described (and a few less common types too), and usually a noteworthy story is attached. All of the remaining chapters focus on the peripheral events and features that have made the Thompson River what it is today.

In Chapter 7, learn some surprising things about Lytton, probably the oldest continuously inhabited settlement in North America. Focusing on what happened here in the first few years after Simon Fraser arrived in 1808, the chapter ends with an intriguing story about a Chinese Joss Temple.

In Chapter 8, we examine the towns that sprung up along the Thompson. Two of them, Walhachin and Nicomen, are no longer towns but remnants still exist; in both cases, their stories are captivating.

In Chapter 9, read a mixture of snippets about events that are river-related. From the discovery of gold on the Thompson River upstream from Lytton, to the history of inflatable boats, to the first recorded fly-fishing episode in BC, ten intriguing episodes won't hone your paddling skills but will ensure you are a better-informed paddler.

River-related events are followed by a series of pieces about events that took place somewhere near the river. In Chapter 10, you'll discover details of the Fraser Canyon War, learn about camels that trudged along the Cariboo Wagon Road, and read two versions of the Bonaparte Murder.

A book could probably be written about each one of a hundred different characters who influenced events along the Thompson. Chapter 11 includes a brief look at five colourful figures, one First Nations chief and four others, who played a role in momentous events—or were just interesting characters.

This book wouldn't be complete without reference, in Chapters 12 and 13, to the construction of the Canadian Pacific Railway through the Thompson Valley, the influence of the Chinese railway workers, and the effect that the railway had on the communities along the river.

Chapter 14, our last chapter, is an assortment of stories and information included to make your river trip more interesting. For example, did you know that at one time the headwaters of our river were located near Hell's Gate, about 40 kilometres south of Lytton? Did you know that explorer David Thompson never laid eyes on the river he was named after?

Many more details, stories, and episodes could have been included in this book, but I wanted to create something light for you to carry with you on the river. My intention was to share stories with you, to tell you about some of the funny and not-so-funny events that have happened to others and me during my 40-year relationship with "my" river.

By broadening my story to include some of the river's historical moments, I hope to add value to your Thompson River experience. Simply put, I would like you to appreciate, admire, and be more mindful of the river you are rafting, canoeing, fishing, standing beside, or watching.

In this book, I have used a mixture of metric and imperial measures. For the more distant historical content, I have used miles and feet, etc., since that was what I found in my research. For more recent history and for the present day, I have used metric measures, the Canadian standard since the early 1970s. As well, throughout the book, I frequently use the terms native and First Nations; these terms are used to refer to the indigenous people of the area rather than the term Indian, which is now considered outdated or offensive by some in Canada. In fact, even the term native is still controversial today. Some sources say it should be capitalized, others not. Even the Canadian Oxford Dictionary seems to be on the fence and thus allows both ways.

If your understanding has broadened because you held *British Columbia's Majestic Thompson River* in your hand, then I'm pleased that I shared my thoughts and experiences with you.

After all, the Thompson is no ordinary river.

Shooting the rapids of a treacherous river

First Descent of the Thompson River

It started, as many great things do, as an adventure in capitalism. Hudson's Bay Company governor George Simpson, a short, intense, balding man, stood on the banks of British Columbia's Thompson River in October of 1828, preparing for the waterway's first ever descent.

To his right would have been the tall, heat-baked hills of Kamloops, with towering black rocks and tall spires of white clay. To his left were hills covered in bunch grass, their brown blades speckled with water from an uncharacteristic fall rain.

Driving Simpson's haste was a powerful mix of fear, ego, and greed. As the new governor of the largest company in North America, Simpson was in a desperate race to preserve the Hudson's Bay's dominance of the fur trade. The United States, then only slightly more than 50 years old, was beginning to flex its nascent muscles, threatening to establish a border that would remove the Bay's access to the mouth of the Columbia River, killing a vital trade route that would block the company's entire western fur trade.

With a bagpipe wailing and smoky muskets firing in salute, Simpson had arrived in Fort Kamloops after a desperate dash from York Factory on Hudson Bay, an incredible distance of 2,997 miles travelled by water and by land in just 62 days.

As Canada's most powerful captain of industry, Simpson had set in motion an audacious scheme. The Hudson's Bay Company already had a well-established route from York Factory to Fort Alexandria on the Fraser River south of modern-day Quesnel. What Simpson desperately needed was a navigable water route from Fort Alexandria to the coast above the 49th parallel and free of American interference.

There were just two options: use the Fraser River, described by its discoverer as unnavigable, or use a route by horseback to Kamloops and then watercraft on the untried Thompson River, on to the Fraser, and down to Fort Langley.

Although Simon Fraser had described his eponymous river as too treacherous to navigate, Simpson had his doubts. Fraser had run the river during high water in the dangerous spring and summer seasons. Was the Fraser navigable in early fall, when the water was lower? Simpson didn't know, so he launched a grand experiment. Not only would he order a trusted lieutenant, James Murray Yale, down the Fraser River from Fort Alexandria, but Simpson would try the Thompson route himself in a bid to see which one was better.

Simpson Departs Kamloops

Simpson left Kamloops on October 6, 1828, at 4 p.m. with two canoes and a "miserable Thompson River boat" that had been built just six days before. With 14 men and former Fort Kamloops' chief trader Archibald McDonald, Simpson paddled down the azure waters of the Thompson, past the lush green shores on his right, and on to the still, deep waters of Kamloops Lake. It wasn't an easy trip. The wind was blowing hard and the heavy new boat was a beast to move, using up to 12 paddlers and sails when possible while the canoes could get by with just two men apiece.

Pulling up to the lake's flat gravel shores, Simpson broke for the evening. At 4 a.m., Simpson's crew began struggling again down the lake and, despite calm weather, made only about 16 miles by breakfast at 7:45.

Unpleasant Travelling Companion

At Savona, Simpson took the time to harangue a small group of natives. His voice soaring with dramatic oratory, Simpson urged the group to be friendly while plying them with small gifts of tobacco and trinkets.

At its peak, the Hudson's Bay Company controlled three million square miles of territory. The massive fur-trading giant in Canada's dangerous wilderness was never a place for weaklings, but even by Bay standards, Simpson was a driven man. Work days generally started at 1 a.m. Some 30 minutes later, the voyageurs would be on the river, stopping only for two short food breaks in 18 hours of labour before making camp.

Simpson was an unpleasant travelling companion, lashing out at his crew, attacking them for misdemeanours as petty as not singing loudly enough as they paddled. Perhaps their one glass of wine during their ten-minute lunch made the day pass faster. Perhaps it did not.

Downriver to Nicomen

The Thompson takes on an even more luminous shade of blue as it exits Kamloops Lake, the river silt having been deposited in the deep lake's warm waters.

Without stopping to scout the rapids, Simpson and his crew headed downriver, plunging into Black Canyon a few miles below present-day Ashcroft.

Sweeping past its dark cliffs hundreds of yards high, with hundreds of birds soaring even higher than that, the crew would have been intent on their first taste of the Thompson's major rapids. Dodging rocks and fighting conflicting currents, Simpson's crew passed through without mishap, holding tight to the river's right shore. The Thompson flowed faster there and the rapids grew bigger and stronger. Still, without pause, the paddlers ran the river, hitting Martel Rapids at 3:45 p.m. about eight miles above Spences Bridge and Orchard Rapids after that. Some 30 minutes later, they passed the mouth of the Nicola River, stopping for the day about five miles later at an area near the flat at Big Horn.

The Thompson has been running along its current route since the last glacial age more than 20,000 years ago, and through the passage of time, nature's little ironies form.

One of these is the Frog, a massive boulder that bisects the river's flow. Thousands of years of erosion have made the glistening black rock resemble a frog, one that squats with its back against the river's ferocious force.

The next morning, Simpson arose uncharacteristically late, no doubt wanting to wait for daylight before hitting the water at 6 a.m. and running "three strong rapids to [Nicomen]…all without examination by seven."

Danger: Devil's Gorge Ahead

Simpson stopped at the Nicoamen River to scout the Devil's Gorge and its major rapids. Cascading from a narrow chasm, Nicoamen Falls plunge 100 feet to the river bed below before flowing to the Thompson a short distance away.

Simpson, the hard-driving business administrator bent on protecting his fur empire, makes no mention of the Frog or its surging rapids. Nor does he notice an opportunity worth millions of dollars. Unknown to anyone, a vast store of gold lay hidden in the gravel under his feet, the discovery of which would spark Canada's largest gold rush only 30 years later.

Simpson, however, had more immediate concerns on his mind. He knew from a messenger at Kamloops that James Murray Yale had made it through some of the worst rapids on the Fraser, but he had no clear idea of Yale's ultimate fate.

And below Simpson in the roaring whitewater were the worst rapids of the Thompson; they would later be named the Jaws of Death.

Simpson's Descent through the Lower Gorge

For all Simpson's power and his autocratic personality, the Hudson's Bay governor was in imminent peril.

Hidden rocks caused boils on the Thompson. Whirlpools twisted, threatening to spin and flip the boats. Water flowing over huge boulders and bedrock forced holes to open on the surface.

Chief trader Archibald McDonald recorded his journey with Simpson through the Jaws of Death: "We were nearly swamped, for in three swells we were full to the thafts [thwarts or horizontal braces across the canoe] and the danger was increased by the unavoidable necessity of running over a strong whirlpool while the boat was in this unmanageable state."

At high water, waves exploded up to five yards high in this treacherous stretch of river. At low water, Simpson was still faced with huge careening waves for 200 yards. This is the heart of the Thompson's whitewater—a series of 12 or more rapids, depending on water levels, before safe harbour at Lytton.

Perched in the comparative manoeuvrability of a canoe, Simpson's ride was dangerous, but nothing compared with the sluggish river boat that would have been at the full mercy of the current.

The three boats pitched their way down the river, the crews struggling to keep upright and in control. The dangers were many: swamping the boats (which they did), flipping and capsizing, breaking their crafts' spines on submerged hazards, being catapulted out of their boats by the river's sudden drops and heaves, or simply being smashed to pieces on the rocks and cliffs that were present almost every inch of the way.

Many voyageurs didn't know how to swim, and the few who did stood little chance of surviving in the Thompson's cataracts. What's more, the potential loss of equipment and provisions could mean that their expedition was doomed.

Simpson's voyageurs prevailed, however, and in just over 60 minutes, the crew had passed over the biggest challenges the river had to offer.

"Left this place at eight, and in another hour, after running the worst place, arrived at the Grand Forks, where we were much gratified to find Mr. Yale and our people quite safe and well," wrote Archibald McDonald, Simpson's travelling companion and the newly appointed chief trader for Fort Langley. "This meeting is rendered still more interesting from the circumstance of both parties descending rivers that were never ran *sic* before [that is to say dangerous parts not run before], and that were always considered next to impossible."

Simpson and his crew had a right to assume a self-congratulatory tone after surviving a first descent of such a treacherous river.

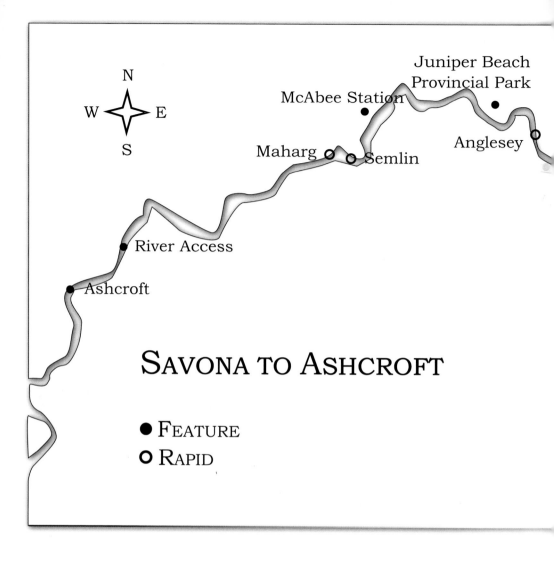

Juniper Beach
Provincial Park

McAbee Station

Maharg ○ ○ Semlin

Anglesey

River Access

Ashcroft

SAVONA TO ASHCROFT

● FEATURE
○ RAPID

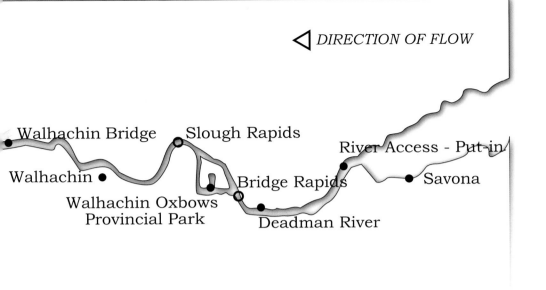

Walhachin Bridge   Slough Rapids

River Access - Put-in

Walhachin •

Bridge Rapids   • Savona

Walhachin Oxbows
Provincial Park

Deadman River

Savona to Ashcroft: *117.0 km to 80.7 km*

Savona
50°45'10.03"N, 120°50'34.43"W

Savona (current pop. 650) began as a modest Hudson's Bay Company trading post on the north side of Kamloops Lake, near the outflow of the Thompson.

The town was originally called Savona's Ferry, then Savonas, then Van Horne (for a short period only, as Sir William Cornelius Van Horne, a CPR bigwig, apparently thought having his name attached to the tiny community was far beneath his dignity), and is now Savona.

François Saveneux (Savona), a former HBC employee, operated a one-horse ferry here between 1858 and 1862. He launched the operation when the increasing traffic up the Fur Brigade Trail needed an efficient way to cross the lake.

By 1865, the village was even busier: the Colonial government had allowed a contract for the construction of a wagon road from Cache Creek to Savona to aid the hordes of gold seekers who were flooding into the area. The wagon road ended at Savona. To continue to Fort Kamloops and beyond, it was necessary to travel by boat or along the winding Fur Brigade Trail.

The *Marten*, the first sternwheeler on Kamloops Lake, was assembled in Savona in 1866 for the transport of passengers and freight. Other communities sprang up along the rivers and lakes with the discovery of gold in the region, and the *Marten* served them all.

François Saveneux died in 1862; his wife and his brother-in-law Joseph Bourke ran the lucrative ferry business until 1870, when the government took over its operation. Saveneux's one-horse ferry was soon replaced by a large, flat-bottomed reaction ferry (described in Chapter 9) that was tethered to a cable closer to the mouth of the Thompson. Large sweep oars angled the boat and the current drove it across the river.

Around the same time, gossip broke out that the CPR was coming and would lay its tracks along the south side of the lake. Every community wanted to cuddle the railway back then, so the townsfolk waited for winter, when the lake would freeze. Then, horses pulled all the buildings over the ice to the south side, completely relocating the town.

Savona was booming by 1880, when at least three steamboats had regular schedules from there to Kamloops and points beyond. These shallow-draft boats chugged along rivers and lakes for seven months of the year, navigating from Savona to within 35 kilometres of the north end of Okanagan Lake. River transportation provided an economical way to transport people and commodities from one location to the next. It was a very viable business.

In 1881, the *Peerless*, one of these early paddlewheelers, decided to take a westward journey down the Thompson River from Savona all the way to Spences Bridge. The trip downriver went quickly, but the return trip was a struggle.

Group of friends heads out for a few days on the river

Steelhead Provincial Park
50°45'25.18"N, 120°51'55.21"W

This 38-hectare park is located at the outflow of the Thompson, only a few minutes from Savona. It includes over 240 metres of Kamloops Lake beach and, with around 40 campsites, is a convenient place to camp if you arrive too late to immediately begin your downriver journey. It is also an ideal location for launching your raft or canoe and heading downriver.

A ferry landing and stagecoach depot operated from here at one time, and one of the oldest homesteads in the southern Interior still stands in the park.

The largest section of Steelhead Park is southwest of the Trans-Canada Highway, with over a kilometre of river shoreline. When the park was established in 1995, this undeveloped area was designated a natural environment zone.

The campsite and historic buildings are on the east side of the highway but the river access is on the west side. The park is open from early May until late September.

River Access – Put-in
50°45′16.98″N, 120°52′21.88″W—117.0 KM

This picturesque river segment is not rafted very often but is a relatively popular canoe route. Its appeal is mostly in the region's beauty, the splendour of the water, the history, and the intriguingly dry, desert-like climate. Anglers may say there are no fish in this section of river, but never trust fishermen's tales.

The river flows through an interesting geologic zone, with remnants of the last ice age cut through its banks. It is classic Thompson: wide, beautiful, and deep.

The rapids in this section are mostly Grade 2 with an occasional easy Grade 3. The river's flow varies dramatically between mid-June's high water and late fall/winter's low water.

This river section is not for a casual canoeist or rafter because there are many hazards and rapids that can easily upset a craft. Midstream rescue skills are required, especially in spring and early summer. Always travel with more than one craft, and ensure that participants are capable of implementing a rescue plan.

First Nations have been actively involved in the protection and interpretation of heritage sites and artefacts found within Steelhead Park. This First Nations fishing area contains archaeological evidence that dates back 10,000 years. Should you see fishnets set in the river near the put-in, please respect and stay away from them.

To reach the put-in site from the Trans-Canada Highway, take the dirt road that heads west on the south end of the Kamloops Lake Bridge.

Abandoned CN Tunnel Entrance
50°44′36.22″N, 120°54′9.67″W—114.3 KM

A few minutes after leaving shore, keep your eyes open for an abandoned Canadian National Railway tunnel (the entrances are now filled with glacial silt) above the tracks on river right. Early tunnels through loose glacial lake sediment used wooden timbers as support; when the timbers rotted, the railway often found it easier to realign the rail line than to shore up the old tunnel. That is what happened here.

The mouth of the Deadman River

Deadman River
50°44'39.59"N, 120°55'7.49"W—113.1 KM

The Deadman's somewhat gruesome name (also the Knife, Dead, Defeant, and Rivière du Défunt in old maps and diaries) originated with the murder of a fur trader in 1815. Monsieur Charette, a happy but stubborn clerk and labourer for the North West Company, met with an untimely death here: his travelling companion, a native guide, stabbed him over a nasty disagreement about where to camp for the night.

It was also near here in 1841 that Chief Nicolas assisted the HBC in the capture of the murderer of HBC chief trader Samuel Black. The murderer was shot as he tried to swim across the river.

In the early 1860s, a local native found a small, heavy rock near the Deadman, which, with a map and directions for where to find more heavy little rocks, he sold to the Savona postmaster. Being a latent capitalist who was a bit on the lazy side, the postmaster later sold them both to a naïve visitor for $15.

The story gets twisted and lost, but in the early 1930s the Vidette gold mine opened up in the Deadman Valley and returned over a million dollars to the owners and investors. In 1934, a "village" sprung up around the mine site and more than 125 men were employed in the mine. The two-storey bunkhouse that housed the single men even had electricity (generated from nearby Deadman Falls), flush toilets, showers, and luxuries that didn't hit mainstream until many years later.

There is probably a link between the heavy little rock and the Vidette gold mine, but it is a difficult one to verify.

Some placer-mining activity took place near the mouth of the Deadman as early as 1852. No one struck it rich. A few years later, miners recovered from 25 to 45 cents per day—and for short periods, as much as $1 per day—from gravels lying between the high and low water.

The old Hudson's Bay Brigade Trail followed the lower part of the Deadman River into the Interior, and this route was also used by gold seekers. It is a geologically fascinating valley and is worth exploring for that reason alone.

An interesting feature of the Deadman River delta where it empties into the Thompson is the "kettle holes" that pock the area. These depressions, some over 30 metres deep and 100 or more metres in diameter, are evidence that the delta originally built up over some glacial ice that eventually melted, creating the depressions.

First CN Bridge
50°44′47.51″N, 120°55′28.35″W—112.6 KM

This bridge belongs to the Canadian National Railway and replaces the original bridge that washed out during the 1948 flood. Steel rails from the old bridge still protrude from the river at low water.

Fly fishing downstream from the first train bridge

Bridge Rapids (Grade 2)
50°44'55.29"N, 120°55'29.79"W—112.3 KM

Here, volcanic rock that crops out along river left deflects the river toward the right. This deflection, combined with a slight drop in elevation, creates Grade 2 rapids just below the bridge. At the rapids, a gravel bar splits the river much of the year, and most of the water flows on river left.

Walhachin Oxbows Provincial Park
50°45'30.79"N, 120°56'37.13"W—110.6 KM

This 37-hectare park protects a small remnant of river ecology and was declared a park in 1997. The area consists of gravel and sand deposits and contains cottonwood and willow trees and underbrush, providing a valuable wildlife habitat.

The "oxbow" can only be accessed from the river. Just the entrance is visible, and at low water most of it is dry. The CN line runs through the park and traverses the oxbow with two bridges.

Camping at Walhachin Oxbows Provincial Park – a naturalist's paradise

Slough Rapids (Grade 2)
50°45′34.59″N, 120°56′39.47″W—110.4 KM

Immediately below the mouth of the oxbow, the river is constricted between the high Brassy Creek terrace on river right and the boulder riprap that CN placed along the left bank. The constriction causes these little rapids.

The terrace, previously classified as a glaciofluvial delta, was identified as a terrace in 2004. This is an important reclassification for geologists but not for the cliff swallows that build their nests in the layers of silt that settled out from the silt-rich waters of glacial Lake Thompson.

Glacial silt beds are now the home of bank swallows

Skull Flats
50°45'34.28"N, 120°59'32.73"W

Somewhere on the terrace on the right is the site of an ancient Interior Salish camp and a registered archaeological site. Many artefacts were recovered here, including a human skull, which gave name to the flats.

Created by glacial action 10,000 years ago, the sand terrace is an Aeolian Sand Veneer.

Walhachin
50°45'14.72"N, 120°59'23.88"W

Walhachin is a native word meaning "land of the round rock." This land has a fascinating story to tell.

The town (pop. 100) is still inhabited, with nine or so of the pre-WWI houses remaining; however, most are unrecognizable because their restorations and changes were not historically accurate. Nevertheless, it is worthwhile visiting present-day Walhachin and taking a stroll through its dirt streets. The view of the Thompson is spectacular. A sign on the highway provides direction to the town, and a trail leads up from the river.

Penny
50°45'6.00"N, 120°59'4.24"W

Charles Pennie homesteaded here in 1870 and developed a successful cattle ranch and small orchard. There was a CPR flag stop called Penny here for many years.

Pennie sold his ranch to the B.C. Development Association (the group that developed Walhachin) in 1908. *The Ashcroft Journal* reported that Charles Pennie and a neighbouring rancher, J.B. Greaves, received $200 an acre or $229,400 for their two ranches. That was a considerable sum, especially as land usually sold for as little as $1 an acre. In 1909, a year after Pennie sold his ranch, the station at Penny was renamed Walhachin.

Frederick Niven, one of Canada's leading writers in the 1920s, wrote *Wild Honey*, a story that begins in a place called "Penny's Pit" on the Thompson River. The book, sold as a novel when published, is based on Niven's experiences of travelling with two hobos along the Thompson and Fraser Rivers. It is an interesting story about the good ol' days of train-hopping hobos.

Second CN Bridge and Rapids (Grade 2)
50°45'51.38"N, 121° 0'48.91"W—104.0 KM

The CNR began construction of a line through this area in 1912, 24 years after the completion of the CPR. Being the first comer, the CPR had selected the choice grade; the CNR, then, was left with the less desirable and much more expensive grade on which to lay its track. Be careful when running the bridges, as there often are obstacles between the bridge pylons (especially at low water) and waves and hydraulics downstream of the pylons (especially at high water).

Walhachin Bridge
50°45′51.53″N, 121° 1′55.34″W—102.5 KM

Built in 1911 to connect the townsite of Walhachin to the orchards and road on the north side of the river, this was the first steel bridge in the interior of the province. Other steel bridges soon followed in Ashcroft, Spences Bridge, and Lytton.

It seems that the folks at Walhachin had enough friends in Victoria that the government of the day paid for the bridge. Some things just do not change.

A reaction ferry transported people and supplies across the river before the arrival of the bridge.

Osprey nest on top of one of the first steel bridges in British Columbia

Public River Access
50°45′54.29″N, 121°2′5.31″W—102.5 KM

A narrow strip of land between the CN tracks and the river at the north end of the bridge was set aside in the 1980s to provide the public with river access. Unfortunately, no put-in ramp was developed, but it is possible to launch a light raft or canoe here. The public strip extends from the bridge downstream to the pumphouse, approximately 400 metres.

Anglesey Rapids (Grade 2 to 3)
50°46′21.71″N, 121° 3′40.59″W—100.1 KM

These rapids are named after the Sixth Marquis of Anglesey, the highest-ranking nobleman of Walhachin. One of the primary investors of Walhachin, he built a mansion on the north bank in 1912. It had indoor plumbing with hot and cold running water, patios overlooking the Thompson and the orchards, a concrete swimming pool, and a music room with a grand piano.

Around the bend from Juniper Beach

Juniper Beach Provincial Park
50°46′44.48″N, 121° 4′51.82″W—97.6 km

This is the best and most convenient public river access between Savona and Ashcroft. It is off the Trans-Canada Highway, only a few kilometres west of Savona and 19 kilometres east of Cache Creek.

The park is popular with anglers and anyone needing access to the Thompson. Its flora and fauna are representative of the region, including prickly pear cactus, sagebrush, rabbit bush, and junipers, of course, as well as rattlesnakes, black widow spiders, deer, and a variety of birds such as bluebirds, western tanagers, kingfishers, and osprey. The pine beetle attack of 2007–2008 destroyed most of the park's ponderosa pine trees.

Mauvais Roche Rapids (Grade 2+)
50°47′1.04″N, 121°5′19.56″W—96.8 km

These rapids have a French name that loosely translated means "a rocky but brief experience." Although the origin of the rapids' name is not recorded, it was probably named by early French river runners who worked for the Hudson's Bay Company and travelled the river by canoe. They also named the Bonaparte River.

The rapids have quite a few smooth round river cobbles (otherwise known as rocks) that channel the water, creating enjoyable waves.

McAbee Station
50°46′53.23″N, 121° 8′10.68″W—92.5 km

Standing alone next to the CN rail line on the right is the old McAbee Flag Station. At one time, trains stopped and picked up and dropped off passengers and freight here. The original structure remains and a certain stateliness is still evident, as is the wooden pole antenna that transmitted Morse code messages to trains and other stations along the line.

The McAbee Fossil Beds are beside the Trans-Canada Highway on the bench above the river here. The beds' geology is unusual because it consists of very old lake sediments (over 50 million years old) that contain perfectly preserved plants, feathers, fish, and insects. It was a very windy spot back then, and the plants, feathers, and insects that blew into the lake settled to the bottom and were fossilized.

Fishing and camping near Onion Beach

Onion Beach

50°46′6.98″N, 121°8′35.10″W—91.0 KM

A few very old privately owned log buildings line the shore on river left. They were abandoned for many years but are again occupied.

The adjoining sandbars served as a campsite on our three-day rafting excursions in the 1970s and early 1980s. Among the cobbles between the river and the high-water mark, wild onions grow in profusion; I christened the camp Onion Beach.

Downriver 100 metres or so, a sandbar still provides a convenient riverside rest stop or campsite, but only at low water and only for very small groups. Do not trespass onto the private land that comes to the high-water mark, and be sure to leave behind no trace of your visit.

At very low water, a series of bridge pilings poke out of the water in front of the sandbar. Obviously, a crossing existed here at one time. Perhaps a simple bridge allowed the residents to cross the Thompson to access the CPR Semlin flag stop between 1888 and 1914.

A bridge also would have provided the residents living on the CPR side with easy access to the wagon road between Cache Creek and Savona. It was probably built and mostly paid for by local residents with contributions from the CPR. However, as an influential politician and because his ranch abutted the Thompson, a man named Charles Semlin may have played a role in the bridge's construction.

Semlin Rapids (Grade 2)
50°45′57.81″N, 121° 8′58.51″W—89.5 km

These rapids are named after Semlin, a former CPR flag station, which was named after Charles Augustus Semlin. Born in Ontario in 1836, Semlin left a perfectly good teaching job to come to BC in 1862. He started out as manager of Ashcroft Manor and Ranch; a few years later he bought the Dominion Ranch (located on the Trans-Canada Highway nearby) from Thomas Buis of Lytton, donned his cowboy hat and boots, and began a cattle-ranching empire.

Semlin switched from cows and bulls to politics a year later—a lateral move in the minds of many people—and for 16 years he represented Yale and area as an MLA. In 1898, he became premier of BC. He abandoned politics in favour of ranching again in 1903. Semlin remained a bachelor all of his life.

Maharg Rapids (Grade 2)
50°46′2.33″N, 121°9′26.51″W—89.2 km

Maharg Rapids are only Grade 2 and in most craft are not even noticeable. They are caused by a rock outcropping on the right.

The CPR tracks are on a fragile rail bed 60 metres above the river.

Carefully excavated out of glacial lake silt, an unstable material, the tracks have somehow remained intact since the 1880s.

C.S. Maharg was a CPR superintendent from Scotland who had a section house named in his honour. Nothing remains of the section house, a building that housed a work crew who maintained a few miles of the railway in the vicinity.

Old Maharg Mining Claim
50°45'48.47"N, 121°10'12.11"W—88.5 KM

Keep a lookout on river left for a dilapidated little shed and some timbers perched over the edge of the cliff. These are the only remains of a series of mining claims and activity that dates back to 1898.

More than 100 years ago, 25 metres of hand-dug tunnels followed gold, silver, and copper veins underground. A series of claims continued to be registered on the property. In the 1970s, more than 273 metres of exploratory tunnels crisscrossed through the river's edge and mountains.

In 1977, Vancouver's Bethlehem Copper Corporation claimed 475 hectares and continued the exploration. Because the exploration work was inconclusive and because the proximity to the Thompson River created mining complexities, Bethlehem abandoned its claims.

Rattlesnake Hill
50°45'16.49"N, 121°13'13.53"W

Immediately to the north (river right) of another CN bridge is Rattlesnake Hill, the only named geological feature along the Thompson River between Savona and Ashcroft. The best view of the hill is from the area of the Maharg Mining Claim, looking downriver toward the west.

A few rattlesnakes still inhabit the dry, barren hill. Geologically, the knob consists of ground-up boulders and rocks from the latest glaciation. Sagebrush, rabbit brush, tumbleweed, cheat grass, and a variety of noxious weeds also survive on Rattlesnake Hill.

Wood Preservative Plant

50°45'5.01"N, 121°12'15.80"W—85.2 KM

The Ashcroft Treating Plant treats 600,000 ties and 1.4 million board feet of bridge timber, switch ties, poles, and pilings each year.

Orderly stacks of Douglas fir, hemlock, ponderosa pine, and mixed hardwoods line the shoreline on river left. It takes about a year for the sun and wind to dry the wood, after which it is loaded into huge pressure cookers and injected with creosote and heavy bunker oil under pressure.

Tons of creosote and bunker oil stored within a stone's throw of the Thompson River is a scary thought; however, the plant has operated without mishap since it located here in the 1980s. Ownership of the plant has changed numerous times over the years.

Under certain wind conditions, the pungent smell of creosote sometimes wafts upriver or downriver for several kilometres.

Third CN Bridge

50°44'38.00"N, 121°13'15.43"W—84.0 KM

To avoid laying the tracks on a very unstable silt bed just ahead, the CNR crosses to the south side of the Thompson here. Then, just 2.2 kilometres downstream, it crosses back again.

Fascinating Geology

50°45'13.71"N, 121°14'29.55"W—82.2 KM

Here, an intriguing "collapse" feature occurs in the silt and other glacial lake sediment. This large feature is probably the result of underwater sliding and folding during or shortly after the time of silt deposition. According to Doug Van Dine, a well-known BC geologist, "the depression resulting from the collapse has been in-filled by fine-textured mudflow alluvial fan sediments." Really?

For years, the flat on river left was a popular swimming hole and party spot for Ashcroft youth and adults alike. The collapse feature probably is not the primary attraction. Locals call this area the Slough, and several old-time ranches and farms operated on the flats to the left.

Fourth CN Bridge

50°44′44.20″N, 121°15′7.85″W—81.0 km

The CNR got the short end of the stick when it came to selecting the best grade for a railway bed. This bridge is Proof #4.

In 1862, a robbery and murder apparently occurred in the vicinity of the bridge and the robbers escaped on horseback, their saddlebags loaded with gold that they subsequently buried near here.

Stories abound about miners returning from the Cariboo with their fortunes in gold nuggets and gold dust. They are always brutally robbed and killed, and their gold disappears or hides under a tree or rock somewhere near Lytton, Spences Bridge, Ashcroft, Savona, or…take your pick. Read Chapter 10 for the robbery details and two quite different versions of this story.

River Access

50°44′33.11″N, 121°15′16.66″W—80.7 km

There are few public river access points between Savona and Lytton. This is one of them. You can get to it easily, as it is just a two-minute drive north of Ashcroft along the east side of the Thompson River.

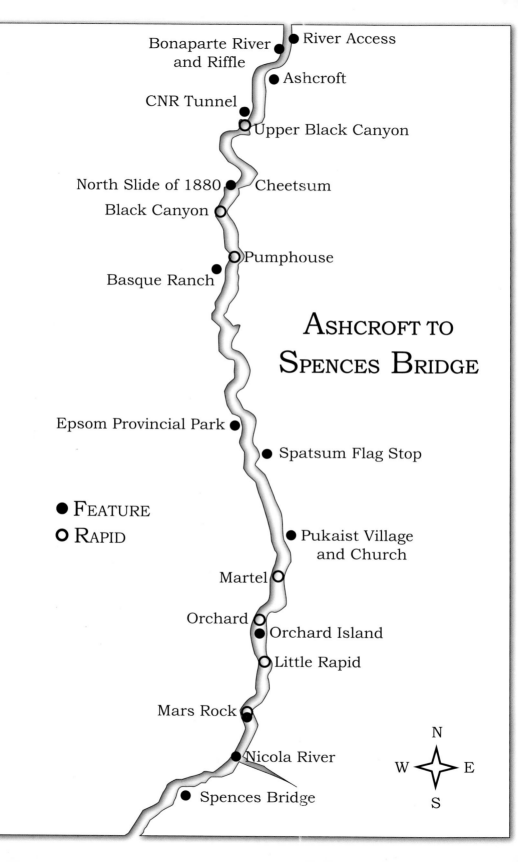

ASHCROFT TO
SPENCES BRIDGE

River Access

Bonaparte River
and Riffle

Ashcroft

CNR Tunnel

Upper Black Canyon

North Slide of 1880

Cheetsum

Black Canyon

Pumphouse

Basque Ranch

Epsom Provincial Park

Spatsum Flag Stop

● FEATURE
○ RAPID

Pukaist Village
and Church

Martel

Orchard

Orchard Island

Little Rapid

Mars Rock

Nicola River

Spences Bridge

N
W E
S

Ashcroft to Spences Bridge: *80.7 km to 39.0 km*

Ashcroft

50°43′27.69″N, 121°16′50.64″W

Four Americans—a cowboy, a prospector, a muleskinner, and a packer—who smelled an opportunity and quickly acted on it founded the town of Ashcroft in 1884.

It was rumoured that the railway was about to be built through the town. The founders pooled their talents and money, and, with ox-drawn freight wagons, brought in everything needed and built the Thompson River Hotel.

Luckily for them, the railway crews arrived the following year, and with them came an instant demand for property and services. Unluckily, the Americans had constructed their hotel next to the reaction ferry near the river instead of on the bustling bench above. No problem: the hotel was simply lifted up, skidded by horses to the flat across from the CPR station, and renamed the Ashcroft Hotel.

A reaction ferry floated people, wagons, and livestock across the river for several years before it was replaced by a bridge in 1886.

To solve the demand for property, Oliver Evans, one of the four American founders, utilized a 66-foot chain that he crudely positioned to mark lots, while his wife and children drove in the boundary stakes. An instant town was "surveyed" and building lots created and sold.

The town took its name from Ashcroft Manor, the English home of the first white settlers in the area, the Cornwall family. Ashcroft flourished as a railway town during the CPR construction. From 1886 until the turn of the century, it was Mile 0, the busy starting point of the Cariboo Wagon Road north.

Dozens of horse-drawn carriages and wagons headed north to the gold fields each day, loaded with mining supplies, cattle, food, mail, and people. They returned with gold, people, and more mail.

The completion of the Pacific Great Northern Railway in 1915, with the driving of the last spike just downstream from Ashcroft, was like driving a spike into the heart of Ashcroft. Steel wheels and iron horses replaced the wagon wheels and warm-blooded horses that had been Ashcroft's mainstay. The metamorphosis converted Ashcroft from a supply centre for the north to an agrarian community, famous for its cannery, disease-free potatoes, sweeter-than-sweet tomatoes, and a variety of other fruits and vegetables.

In the 1960s and 1970s, some of the world's largest open-pit copper mines opened in the Highland Valley to the east, somewhat revitalizing the community.

Today's Ashcroft offers a wonderful setting on the Thompson River, a hot and dry climate, and friendly, small-town folk.

River Put-in Access

50°44′33.11″N, 121°15′16.66″W—80.7 KM

Not that many years ago, most river runners descended the Thompson beginning at Ashcroft rather than Spences Bridge. It was a two-day river trip to Lytton with an overnight camp set up somewhere in the vicinity of Spences Bridge. It was not unusual for hundreds of rafters from Vancouver and the Lower Mainland or Calgary or Washington to set up tents at Murray Creek Falls or along the river for a night of frivolity and fun. Unfortunately, this pattern has changed and participant numbers have declined. Today it's not uncommon to be alone on the river throughout this entire stretch.

Stunning Black Canyon and Black Canyon Rapids are reason enough to run this section of river. Anyone who sees the canyon from the river for the first time is awestruck by the sheer cliffs, roaring river, and a golden eagle catching thermals in the spectacular, 150-million-year-old chasm.

This is just one of several public river access points between Savona and Lytton. You can get to it easily; it is just a two-minute drive north of Ashcroft along the east side of the Thompson River.

Expert canoeists in decked canoes, kayakers, and experienced rafters are the only ones that normally continue past this point, as there is no way to sneak past the boils and whirlpools in Black Canyon, especially at high water. A tour with a commercial rafting company is the best way to see the river beyond here, and the best commercial rafting company is, of course, Kumsheen Rafting Resort in Lytton.

Launching the Kumsheen fleet in 1976 at the Ashcroft put-in

Bonaparte River and Riffle (Grade 2)
50°44'21.35"N, 121°15'32.19"W—80.2 KM

Hudson's Bay Company fur traders named the Bonaparte River to honour Napoleon Bonaparte, who died in 1821. In the 1870s, the Harper brothers built a flour mill at the mouth of this river; it was flooded out when a landslide downstream caused the Thompson River to back up almost 40 kilometres. If you look closely, you can see a signpost on the railway bed near the mouth of the river that shows the height of the floodwaters.

A dam a few kilometres up from the mouth of the Bonaparte diverted water through a turbine that generated electricity for the town of Ashcroft until 1950. A little rapid starts here and is simply a series of waves formed as the Bonaparte pushes into the Thompson.

Panning for gold at the mouth of Bonaparte River

Elephant Hill Park
50°45′7.63″N, 121°17′44.55″W

About three kilometres up the Bonaparte, an eroded riverbank shows layers of gravel and sand deposits that geologists claim came from an ice age about 40,000 years ago. Elephant Hill Provincial Park, to the south of the Bonaparte a few kilometres from the river's mouth, protects the unique geological features and the cattle-free grasslands in this area, one of the driest regions of the province.

Although tough to see from the river, when viewed from a certain angle, the hill takes on the appearance of an elephant. No, there were never any elephants in this area, except perhaps when the circus came to town. Camels, yes. You can walk into the park but no vehicle access is permitted; there are no amenities.

Looking west up the Bonaparte River Valley

Ashcroft Bridges
50°43'36.48"N, 121°16'53.30"W—77.9 km

A reaction ferry crossed the river here from 1883 until 1886, when the first bridge was constructed. That bridge washed away in the flood of 1894 and was replaced as soon as a cable could be stretched across the river. The second bridge remained until 1907, and in 1932, a new steel bridge replaced the third bridge. Road salt eventually ate the bridge's steel girders, weakening it and necessitating its replacement, which is the current structure.

At low water, the bridge piers of the 1907 structure are visible just upstream of the existing bridge.

Black Canyon Slides
50°42'3.83"N, 121°17'29.95"W

For the next nine kilometres, a number of landslides occurred along both sides of the river, especially on river left. Known as the Black Canyon

Slides, they take their name from the canyon that lies nine kilometres downstream from Ashcroft. The banks along this section have been failing for thousands of years, the result of natural wetting of the glacial lake silt and toe erosion by the Thompson River.

In a 20-year period at the end of the 19th century, several major landslides occurred as ranchers irrigated their land above the tracks and the CPR cut into the toe of many slopes to position the railway. In 1899, the CPR took the ranchers to court for causing the landslides. The CPR lost their case in the lower courts, so they appealed to the Privy Council in England. The farmers eventually lost and stopped irrigating above the rail line. Since then, there have been significantly fewer landslides, but they still happen on occasion, especially during torrential downpours.

1897 Slide
50°42′3.83″N, 121°17′29.95″W —74.9 km

The British Colonist described the 1897 landslide on river left as follows:

> *The big gravel mountain one mile below the city [of Ashcroft] had suddenly tired of its place of residence and commenced to move. At one o' clock in the night a large portion of the pine-clad mountain broke off, and started with a rumble like thunder toward the Thompson River… Among the greatest damage to property accruing was the complete destruction of Barne's big granary and 100 tons of wheat stowed within.* (Fandrich, *Rafting in British Columbia*, 23)

Upper Black Canyon Rapids (Grade 2 to 3), CNR Tunnel
50°42′5.74″N, 121°17′41.44″W—74.7 km

These rapids, also known as Tunnel Rapids, begin opposite the CNR tunnel and continue around the corner for 500 metres or so. The whole river comes alive at mid- to high water, and it is difficult to choose which waves will provide the best ride. At low water, the challenge is to determine the main channel in order to avoid the maze of exposed and submerged rocks.

The CNR tunnel, excavated through sandstone, shale, and conglomerate, first opened to rail traffic in 1911.

Old River Banks
50°41'44.59"N, 121°17'40.36"W

The river has pushed its way west in this area, exposing a high bank of sandstone, shale, and conglomerate around 150 million years old. The overall coal-like appearance of the bank is due to the high concentration of carbon in the shale.

1982 Slide
50°41'17.98"N, 121°18'2.37"W—72.2 KM

This very recent landslide, again on river left, occurred in September 1982 after three days of heavy rain. It removed 500 metres of the CPR mainline track, disrupted rail traffic for several days, and reportedly killed an estimated 4,000 young Chinook salmon in the Thompson. The CPR has since carried out work to stabilize the bank.

1886 Slide and Chataway Ranch
50°41'8.39"N, 121°17'39.77"W—71.7 KM

In August 1886 another landslide occurred, again on river left. *The British Colonist* printed this description:

> *Fifty acres slid out several hundred feet and sank fifty feet, the [CPR] rails remaining connected in mid-air. The engine tender and baggage car of the Pacific express went off the embankment. The engineer was scalded and the fireman hurt.* (Fandrich, 25)

The land you can see above this slide is part of the Chataway Ranch, one of the older and larger ranches in the area.

North Slide of 1880 and Cheetsum Rapids (Grade 2 to 2+)

Landslide: 50°40′25.55″N, 121°18′6.06″W
Rapids: 50°40′21.04″N, 121°18′17.71″W—69.7 km

Cheetsum Rapids result from remnants of the largest of the Black Canyon slides on river left. The North Slide of October 1880 completely blocked the river for nearly two days. Newspaper accounts estimate the dam was not less than 150 feet high, and for some time after, the bed of the river downstream was perfectly dry. Natives who witnessed the drying rushed to the riverbed and scoured the cracks and crevices for gold nuggets. Chinese construction workers seized the opportunity to harvest fish that floundered on the newly exposed gravel bars and rocks.

Upstream, the river flooded the benches now occupied by Ashcroft and floated Harper Brothers' gristmill at the mouth of the Bonaparte River right off its foundation. Today, a sign on the railway at the mouth of the Bonaparte marks the height of the water in 1880.

The river eventually overtopped the temporary dam and cut a course through the landslide debris.

Cheetsum Rapids do not demand the greatest expertise to negotiate safely. They form as the river slides over soccer-ball-sized cobbles on the left and rumbles down a slight incline, picking up speed as it travels and creating some playful waves.

CPR Tunnel Entrance

North Entrance 50°39′57.81″N, 121°18′34.39″W
South Entrance 50°39′52.93″N, 121°18′32.08″W—69.3 km

The CPR has a short tunnel on river left.

Black Canyon Rapids (Grade 3 to 5)

50°40′9.37″N, 121°18′33.37″W—68.7 km

These are primarily medium to high water rapids and the largest between Savona and the Frog Rapids. The river takes a sharp turn to the right, pushing the water over a rock ledge, deflecting it, and creating a series of large compression waves. Sometimes, they are the largest on the entire river, rivaling the Jaws of Death Rapids.

A back eddy usually forms on river right, and large motorized rafts can catch the eddy and run the rapids repeatedly.

Big ride in Black Canyon Rapids

Black Canyon, Fifth CN Bridge and Tunnel, Eagles and Swallows

CNR Bridge 50°39′55.34″N, 121°18′42.18″W

CNR Tunnel South Entrance 50°39′56.31″N, 121°18′43.06″W

Black Canyon 50°39′49.62″N, 121°18′47.38″W—68.6 KM

Black Canyon's name originates from the spectacular dark-coloured 150-million-year-old sedimentary rocks bordering both sides of the river.

The CPR Annotated Time Table (1906) describes this area as follows:

> *Three miles beyond Ashcroft the hills press close upon the Thompson River, which cuts its way through a winding gorge of almost terrifying gloom and desolation, fitly named Black Canyon.*

Just upstream of the Black Canyon Rapids, on river left, are remnants of the original 1883 CPR trestle. The CPR and CNR now use tunnels to pass through these steep canyon walls. The CNR tunnel on river right collapsed in 1914, delaying the opening of the Great Northern Railway; the extra financial burden of clearing the tunnel contributed to the bankruptcy of the GNR.

A major high-water hazard, the canyon swirls and boils with powerful eddies and large whirlpools. The river runs straight into the canyon wall and then pushes back on itself. It exits to the left, 90 degrees from where it enters the canyon. Motorized rafts sometimes have to use full power to maintain control and avoid the bedrock on river left. It is impossible to skirt or portage around the canyon.

At low water, Black Canyon is a beautiful, easy drift with a stunning view of the ancient sedimentary rocks and cliffs. A golden eagle nest is perched on the canyon wall, and hundreds of rock doves (excellent eagle fodder) and cliff swallows live here.

Bald eagles in Upper Black Canyon

Railway Defences
50°39′45.50″N, 121°18′25.19″W—68.2 KM

The river shoots out of Black Canyon and smacks against the east bank before turning southward again. To protect the CNR and CPR tracks from being undermined by soil erosion, the railways constructed two groins, dyke-like structures built into the river at an angle to deflect the current away from the tracks. Several high-water events recently necessitated substantial upgrades to the groins.

Slide within a Slide within a Slide
50°39′51.23″N, 121°18′26.91″W

The second-largest and perhaps the longest slide in the area consists of a small slide within a larger slide, within a still larger slide, all three of which occurred prior to 1900 on river left. The slide debris follows along the river for almost two kilometres.

Barnard Creek
50°39′26.76″N, 121°18′16.07″W—67.7 KM

Barnard Creek on river left flows through the centre of the slide. The creek derives its name from Francis Barnard, the entrepreneur who started the Barnard British Columbia Express Company.

Maps from the early 1800s refer to this creek as Nelson Creek. It was originally named after Horatio Nelson, Britain's greatest naval hero, who is best known for his epochal victory and tragic death at the Battle of Trafalgar in 1805. It is likely that Nelson Creek appears on early maps to even the score between Nelson and Napoleon's Bonaparte River.

Pumphouse Rapids (Grade 2 to 3) and Basque Ranch

Rapids 50°38'42.39"N, 121°18'7.71"W

Basque Ranch 50°38'5.32"N, 121°18'40.34"W —66.2 KM

Perched on a cliff ledge just above the water on river right, a pumphouse marks the beginning of these rapids. The waves are straightforward, and no obstacles exist except a huge rock partway through the rapids on river left of centre that creates big waves at high water and a big hole as the water drops. Watch for it, and treat it kindly and with respect.

The pump provides irrigation for the hay fields of the Basque Ranch on the river terraces to the west. Antoine Minnbarriet, a French Basque nobleman whose name was given to Minnbarriet Creek upriver immediately above Black Canyon on river right, founded the 303-hectare Basque Ranch in the 1860s. Currently, Cook's Ferry Indian Band owns and operates the ranch.

Just downstream from the pumphouse on river right, a curious series of steps leads up the bank. Local legend says these steps were used by early Chinese gold miners to transport gold to the top of the bank.

Looking north at Basque Ranch and the Thompson River valley

Cornwall Hills (left) and Highland Valley Mines pumping station

View of Red and Cornwall Hills
50°39'15.96"N, 121°20'19.17"W

Red Hill, also known as Oregon Jack Hill, separates the river from the Trans-Canada Highway. It derives its name from the eye-catching red, yellow, and brown colours often associated with gold-bearing volcanic rock.

To the west, the Cornwall Hills, named after the Cornwall family, are the highest peaks in the area at 2,040 metres. They consist of 300-million-year-old limestone—the oldest rock in the region—that resists weathering better than any other mineral in the area. A lookout on top of these hills is accessible by vehicle, and the view on a clear day is stunning.

Osprey Nest
50°37'34.32"N, 121°18'52.13"W—63.9 KM

An endangered species in BC in the 1960s, ospreys have made a dramatic recovery. In 1974, there was only one nest along the river, and it straddled a snag partway up the bank on river right. Every year, the adult birds returned to the same nest, added more twigs, branches, and bailer twine that they found in the alfalfa fields overlooking the river. Eventually, their offspring built nests of their own along the river, both downstream and upstream from their family home.

Osprey can live more than 30 years, so there are now dozens of nests along the river between Savona and Lytton. During a late-August raft trip around 25 years after spotting the first nest, I noticed that a young osprey was still in its nest, long past when it should have already been flying freely. I watched its parents come with food; the youngster tried to leave with them but could only lift off a few metres from the nest. A bundle of bailer twine wrapped around its leg anchored it firmly to the nest.

A few days later, the young osprey was dead, dangling from the nest by one leg. The snag has since collapsed and the original nest has disintegrated.

Osprey numbers have increased from one pair to dozens along the river

Asparagus Island
50°37'20.45"N, 121°18'50.98"W—63.4 KM

During spring runoff, the river fills a channel, creating an island. As the water level drops, the island becomes part of the mainland again.

In our early days of rafting, this was always our lunch stop on the first day of a two-day trip between Ashcroft and Lytton. Asparagus grows wild on this island in the spring, and we would harvest as much as possible for a gourmet dinner the same evening.

Oregon Jack Creek
50°37'11.66"N, 121°18'58.83"W 63.2 KM

"Oregon Jack" was actually John Dowling, a native of Oregon state who moved to this area in the 1860 and kept a roadside hotel along the Cariboo Wagon Road. He reportedly was "a pleasant man who hasn't been sober since he arrived" (Fandrich, 29).

The creek is barely noticeable where it enters the Thompson but is a marvel of geography and First Nations history in its upper reaches. It originates in the Cornwall Hills west of Ashcroft. The Oregon Jack Provincial Park protects a limestone canyon and waterfall (the Notch) as well as the old-growth Douglas fir and Engelmann spruce, alpine tundra meadows, and stands of aspen along the creek above the falls.

For thousands of years, First Nations people frequented this important area for ceremonial, spiritual, and food-gathering activities. Rock pictographs, culturally modified trees, and an important Three Sisters rock shelter are all within the park.

Archaeologists have discovered evidence of First Nations activity here that goes back over 8,400 years, making it one of the oldest archaeological sites on the Interior Plateau. It is interesting to note that the people who camped here more than 5,000 years ago left behind evidence of their big-game hunting skills as well as their salmon-fishing abilities.

Black bears, mule deer, moose, a variety of other predators, as well as waterfowl in the marsh wetlands are all residents of the area.

Just downstream from the confluence of the little Oregon Jack Creek and the Thompson, a tilted block of glacial lake silt sits near the top of the bank. Geologists estimate that this tilting occurred near the end of the glacial period 10,000 years ago.

Basque Siding
50°37'6.93"N, 121°18'16.40"W

Usually the CPR and CNR travel on opposite sides of the river, but here they run parallel to each other on river left. A siding (an extra set of tracks so two trains can pass or cars not in use can be parked) at Basque allows trains access between railways.

Sixth CN Bridge
50°36'21.03"N, 121°18'46.74"W—61.4 KM

Although bridges are costly to construct, the CNR had no choice but to build another since the CPR owned the land on the other side of the river.

Railcar Riffle
50°36'9.26"N, 121°18'10.75"W—60.7 KM

Quite a few years ago, a train derailment near the CNR bridge dislodged a convoy of coal cars, some of which somersaulted into the river. One car bounced downstream a few hundred metres and remains anchored on the river bottom below seven to ten metres of water. At low water, a smooth dip and curl on the surface mark the submerged car.

Ancient Slide
50°35'12.97"N, 121°18'21.29"W

The large landslide on river left is much older than the Black Canyon slides, perhaps even thousands of years older. It begins one kilometre downstream of Railcar Riffle and extends for more than a kilometre.

Canadian Northern Railway's Last Spike
50°34'35.31"N, 121°18'9.92"W

The last spike for the Canadian Northern Railway was driven here on January 23, 1915. Plagued with financial difficulties from the start, the CNR had no choice but to construct its tracks on the difficult, more expensive grades. Immediately after the last spike was driven, a tunnel at Black Canyon collapsed, delaying the opening of the rail line by several months.

A highway sign reminds us of the Canadian Northern Railway's last spike

Epsom Provincial Park
50°34'31.65"N, 121°17'57.56"W—57.2 km

The best access to the undeveloped 102-hectare Epsom Park on river right is from the river. The park is set aside for future development and provides rough access to the Thompson from the highway. It is a beautiful spot and makes a great informal campsite when floating the river.

Epsom Provincial Park offers excellent river camping

River Terraces and Bridge Remains
50°34′6.51″N, 121°17′59.89″W—56.3 KM

On both sides of the river are prominent river terraces, the tops of which were once the bottom of Glacial Lake Thompson. The lake drained suddenly about 10,500 years ago, and the Thompson River has eroded down to its present level since then.

When the flow is very low, old bridge pilings are visible in the river. Oddly enough, no record of a bridge remains, yet someone obviously built one here many years ago.

On the east side of the river were once a CPR flag stop called Spatsum and a large population of indigenous people at Pukaist. The Cariboo Wagon Road was on the west. The bridge would have linked the residents on both sides of the river, allowing access between the railway and the Cariboo Wagon Road. Perhaps the railway provided financial or other assistance for the bridge's construction. Perhaps it did not.

At low water, old bridge piers protrude through the surface

Coarse Gold Found Here
50°33′54.33″N, 121°17′59.90″W—56.2 KM

The Thompson widens and slows here, depositing the finer particles it has carried. The quantity of materials deposited over the years has created several islands.

Early prospectors, feeling that this was the perfect hiding place for gold, established placer gold workings along the riverbanks in the late 1800s and again in the 1920s and 1930s. Apparently, their work resulted in some very coarse gold, a rare commodity along this river. Unfortunately, most of the evidence of the miners' workings disappeared in major flood events.

Spatsum Flag Stop
50°33′29.52″N, 121°17′38.09″W

The Spatsum Indian Reserve borders the shore on river left. The nearby CPR siding adopted this name, derived from the Indian word *spep-sum*, "where the milkweed grows." Spatsum was a flag station along the CPR for many years.

The wife of Anglican Bishop Sillitoe describes her experience of catching the train here on August 15, 1891:

> *The west-bound train was due at Spatsum at 3 a.m. on Sunday, and the long, weary night did we spend sitting on the platform; and as if that were not enough, the train was an hour and a half late, so not till 4:30 did we get away. Spatsum is only a flag station, and about ten o'clock the man in charge brought us a lantern, telling us to wave it, and he then retired. It was 6.30 on Sunday morning before we reached Lytton.* (Gowan, *Church Work in British Columbia*, p. 181)

Quenching Highland Valley's Thirst
50°33′29.00″N, 121°17′46.62″W—55.1 KM

To process the copper ore that is extracted in the valley over the ridge to the east of here, vast quantities of water are required. The Highland Valley Copper Mine pumps water from the Thompson all the way up to the mine, which is approximately 15 kilometres to the east and 1,000 metres higher than the river. It is no wonder that this is such a huge pumphouse.

Swallows have glued their nests to the grey concrete ceiling of the overhang. Drift in close and check out their well-camouflaged nests.

Typical semi-arid desert

Coldstream Creek Terrace and Alluvial Fan
50°32′15.98″N, 121°16′58.36″W

Coldstream Creek, on river left, creates a large alluvial fan during snowmelt in the spring and after short but intense summer rainstorms.

Intermittently flowing creeks of this nature are ephemeral or short-lived. They flow down from the hills, carrying with them fine particles of sand and gravel. The water slows down when the stream reaches the flatter river terrace, and sand and gravel drop to the bottom in the shape of a fan.

The Great Rockslide and Legend
50°31′15.87″N, 121°16′27.13″W

The Great Rockslide is a distinct feature on early maps.

Colourful broken limestone and greenstone rock fragments make up the talus slope on the side of the mountain on river left, the result of constant weathering and erosion of the volcanic rock that forms the hills beyond.

Looking upstream toward the Great Rockslide

Although the upper part of the mountain is granite, the section immediately above the slide is of volcanic origin and is composed of large pieces of ejected material, which have been compacted into smaller fragments.

Indian legend records that this slope, like many other talus slopes in the area, was a burial ground. Removal of the body by anyone, including evil spirits, was impossible as soon as it was entombed in this loose broken rock. No matter how much the spirits tried to dig into the rock fragments, loose rock from above slid immediately into the excavation.

In 1978, Chess Lyons, a well-known BC naturalist and author, reminisced to me about driving up the Thompson and seeing native grave markers at the base of many talus slopes and slide areas. Markers consisted of a cedar or pine post and the deceased's favourite possessions. Because the angle of repose—the maximum slope or angle at which loose material remains stable—is constant, it is very difficult if not impossible for grave robbers to dig up the bodies that rest at the bottom of a talus slope. The grave markers have rotted away, but the graves remain.

Pukaist Village and Church
50°31′16.99″N, 121°16′42.91″W—50.9 KM

Near the base of the talus slope is an old Anglican church that dates back to about 1880. It is no longer used and sits in disrepair. A visiting Anglican bishop's wife wrote the following description of her visit here in August 1891:

> *I am writing under difficulties, with a tiny gold pencil and my paper on my knee, under the shadow of the church. We are camped out near an Indian village on a dry, dusty, and exceedingly barren flat, under a burning sun, with not a tree nearer than on the steep mountain sides which surround us. I am hardly correct in calling this a barren flat, for on it thrives a vigorous growth of cactus, and with the utmost care one cannot go many yards without getting one's shoes full of the sharp prickles. One night in rolling over in bed I got my side full of them. (Gowan, 180)*

In 1900, the *BC Mining Journal* (January edition) reported a more serious tragedy that occurred here in 1899. Seven natives drowned while crossing the Thompson in a canoe, in the dark, on their way to the Christmas Eve midnight service in the little church. Four of the natives were from one family.

At one time, there may have been as many as 800 villagers living in this extremely barren corridor. The church stands as a beacon of those past inhabitants, most of whom moved to Spences Bridge, Ashcroft, or Merritt.

Abandoned but not forgotten – the Pukaist Church

Venables Creek
50°31'11.70"N, 121°16'58.17"W—50.7 km

The creek flows through beautiful Venables Valley, emptying into the Thompson on the right. The valley and creek are named after Captain Cavendish Venables, a former captain in the 74th Highland Scottish Regiment. He secured a military land grant in the Venables Valley around 1861.

The river in all its fall glory

Cariboo Wagon Road Remnants
50°30'13.06"N, 121°17'5.15"W—48.7 KM

Until the completion of the CPR in 1885, the Cariboo Wagon Road was the main link between the coast and the interior of British Columbia. You can still see dry masonry retaining walls from the original road along this stretch; this section of the Wagon Road connected Lytton with Ashcroft and the Cariboo gold fields to the north, beginning in 1863. The remnants of the road, visible in places on river right between the CNR tracks and the highway, are monuments to the quality of this early road.

Martel Rapids (Grade 2 to 3)
50°29'58.62"N, 121°17'2.15"W—48.2 KM

The CNR calls this place Martel after Joe Martel, who ran a ranch a few kilometres downriver from here. It is only fitting that we call these rapids Martel Rapids; Joe Martel, as an old riverman, would no doubt have been pleased.

For many years, it was possible to hitch a train ride here in either direction by simply putting out a flag during the day or waving a lantern at night. The flag stop is gone, but a siding remains.

At the very beginning of the rapids, near the cliff on river right, a sly wave comes off a large rock at 45 degrees to the main flow, but only at high and medium-high water levels. More than one boatman has succumbed to this devil of a wave.

Martel Rapids at low water in October

A few years ago (long enough ago that the story may have evolved slightly), a guide for one of Kumsheen's rafting competitors decided he would run this tricky wave in his oar-powered raft. Before he could say "oops!" his raft was upside down, and he and his passengers were in the water.

First, they all floated around the corner through the medium-sized waves of the main Martel Rapids. The swim continued downriver, past their scheduled campsite at Orchard Island (also known as Fantasy Island), where another raft was already parked for the night. The guide and other swimmers called for help, but their calls went unheard. By now, some of the guests and the guide were riding the overturned raft, hanging on and hoping it would somehow end up on shore. However, it did not float calmly to shore; it headed straight downriver to Spences Bridge.

Once the raft and passengers got to Spences Bridge, almost an hour later, someone on shore spotted the overturned raft and heard the shouts for help. They called another of Kumsheen's competitors, based out of Spences Bridge. This company immediately launched a motorized raft and chased after the raft and occupants, catching them just below the highway bridge over the Thompson. No one was hurt, everyone was cold, and Joe Martel was probably laughing in his grave.

Martel Put-in
50°29'36.79"N, 121°17'36.82"W—46.9 km

It was at the Martel put-in that, in 1973, I would launch my 15-foot Avon raft for the 13-kilometre ride down to Spences Bridge. My oars were too short for the boat, and my experience was, well, limited. Armed with more enthusiasm than skill, I performed the run almost daily.

Hundreds of cars lined the river to watch me float by that summer. This was a novel scene for locals and tourists alike back then, and seldom did a car go by on the highway without at least a wave, a toot of the horn, and a smile.

Opinion in the bar of historic Spences Bridge Hotel was split down the middle. Half the spectators who went to the outside deck to watch the raft float by thought I was a lunatic. The other half, mostly locals, discussed my new rafting "business" over a few beers: "Why didn't we think of doing that?" Then they would laugh and wave to me as I floated by.

When sober again, they realized that the young, athletic, suntanned guy on the river wasn't making millions of dollars just yet, and maybe it was too soon to be green with envy.

The Pack Rat Ranch
50°29'27.03"N, 121°17'15.29"W

Up on the terrace on river left is a farmhouse that is clearly visible from the highway but not so clear from the river.

More than half a century ago, the owners came home after a lengthy absence and discovered that a family or two of pack rats had moved into the farmhouse. To evict them, the owners started a small fire in the house with the intention of smoking the rats out. Guess what? The little fire became a big fire and eventually a monster fire. The house burned to the ground.

Looking upstream toward Orchard Island

Orchard Rapids (Grade 3+) and Orchard Island
50°28'52.29"N, 121°18'0.89"W—45.5 KM

Here, the river is very wide but shallow, and most of the water flows through two narrow channels near the middle and on river right. Some water drops through a channel to the left above the island and provides access to the island's east side. Near the point where these two channels rejoin, the largest waves erupt, sometimes buckling a raft with a quick one-two-three action.

Martel Ranch

50°29′1.19″N, 121°18′8.81″W—45.3 KM

The soil and climate here are ideally suited to fruit growing. Add water and a few soil nutrients from time to time, and presto! Beautiful apples, peaches, and cherries.

Martel Ranch began operation in the 1880s by a Frenchman. Little is known of him except that his life's fortune of several thousand dollars was reportedly hidden in a tin can and buried at some undetermined spot in the great outdoors not far from here.

The ranch changed hands twice before Joe Martel (1864–1933), a small man with big ideas, took it over. Originally from Quebec, his 4.5-hectare orchard provided travellers along the Cariboo Wagon Road and Fraser Canyon Highway with fresh apples, cherries, apricots, peaches, and pears.

One of Joe's good friends was James Teit, and when Teit got the contract to retrieve silk bales from a silk train derailment on the Thompson below Spences Bridge in late December 1910, he asked Joe to assist him.

On January 3rd, 1911, when their canoe capsized and dumped them into the icy waters of the Thompson River, Teit had this to say:

> I was the first one to reach shore and as my feet touched the bottom I turned to see how my companions were doing. Joe Martel was right behind me using a downward stroke with his arms and almost bouncing over the water. Johnny Smith [another friend from Spences Bridge] was yelling, "Help, wait for me, I can't swim," although he was flailing his arms around and doing a great deal of splashing, he was making progress. (Lean, "A Year in the Life of James A. Teit–1910," *Teit Times*, 58)

As soon as Teit saw he was going to be all right, he went ashore, where Martel was already looking for material to make a fire. Martel, who had worked on river drives in Quebec and was an experienced riverman, kept matches stuck in his thick hair, and they soon had a fire going.

Later on that day when Teit and Martel were at the Morens' (Teit's in-laws and Martel's neighbours) having supper, Mrs. Morens said to Joe Martel, "But Joe, you could have been killed." Joe's reply was, "Oh, that's all right. Lots more Frenchmen in Quebec" (Teit, 58).

Joe married a widow from Yale in 1896. She already had eight children; she and Joe brought two more into the world while living at the ranch.

Pimainus Creek Hoodoos
50°27′46.16″N, 121°17′41.53″W

Geologists analyzed the sediment deposits on river left and concluded that they belong to the most recent ice age, which ended roughly 10,000 years ago. Water and wind sculpted the hoodoos—small pinnacles of weathered and unusually shaped sandstone.

Little Rapids
50°27′51.49″N, 121°17′50.03″W—43.7 KM

Caused by a slight drop in elevation, a few boils and waves skip across the surface here at higher water levels. It is quite possible to sleep through these rapids, but be sure to note the hoodoos on river left before you close your eyes.

89-Mile Stable or Morens' Ranch
50°27′20.80″N, 121°18′3.75″W

A relatively large orchard on a terrace above the river on the right was originally known as 89-Mile Stable during the days of the Cariboo Wagon Road, later as French Pete's, and still later as Morens' Ranch. It was precisely 143 kilometres north of Yale and was almost a half-day's journey (on foot or horseback) from Spences Bridge, only 10 kilometres away.

Twaal Creek and Valley
50°27′4.94″N, 121°18′22.60″W—41.9 KM

The narrow green band of water in Twaal Creek as it empties into the Thompson is all that remains after several farms, ranches, Indian reserves, and private dwellings have extracted what they need. The creek comes from a beautiful valley that is worthwhile exploring.

Mars Rock and Rapids (Grade 2+)
50°26'51.88"N, 121°18'32.81"W—39.3 KM

Just downstream and around the corner, a large, reddish volcanic rock squats in the middle of the river, affectionately called Mars Rock. It's not technically a rapid but it makes a lot of noise. One or two waves may appear as potential mountains but, as you approach, they cringe and actually shrink in size. The subdued roar is just the river grumbling about being forced over some bedrock and large boulders.

Apricot blossoms along the river mark the start of spring

Nicola River
50°25'39.84"N, 121°18'58.07"W—39.0 KM

Flowing into the Thompson on river left is the Nicola River, named after Nicolas Hwistesmetxegen (Walking Grizzly Bear), a powerful chief of the Thompson and Okanagan Nations. He was a great warrior, hunter, trader, and farmer who lived from 1785 to 1859. John Tod, the HBC trader in

Fort Kamloops, knew him well and noted in his memoirs that Nicolas was "a very great chieftain and a bold man, for he had 17 wives." He also had around 50 children whose descendents still live in southern British Columbia and Washington state.

The Nicola River is a major tributary of the Thompson and drains the Thompson Plateau, beginning 30 kilometres northwest of Kelowna and flowing in a westerly direction into Douglas Lake and then Nicola Lake. From Nicola Lake, it flows southwest for a few kilometres, then west until it meets Spius Creek, and finally north into the Thompson River after a total journey of only 70 kilometres from Nicola Lake.

The Nicola also provides a convenient put-in site for anyone rafting the Thompson. It's best to contact the Cook's Ferry Indian Band before launching your craft, as the land is Indian reserve and permission is required.

The "little forks" of the Nicola and the Thompson Rivers

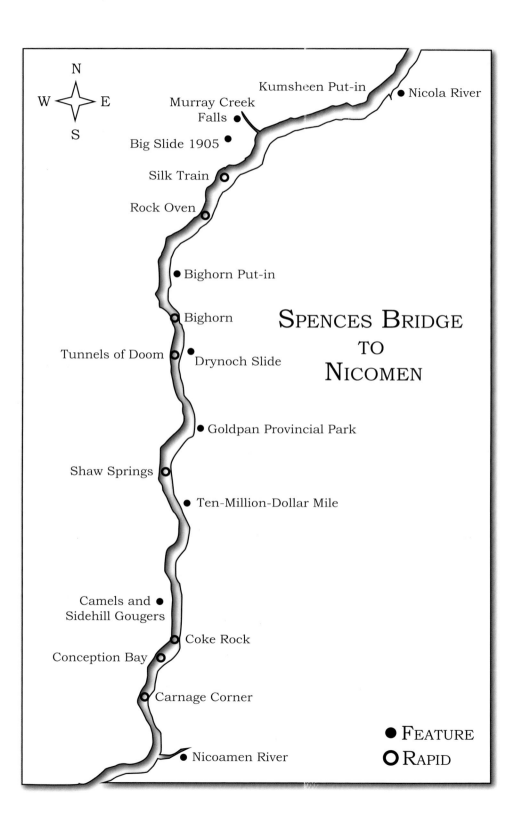

N
W   E
S

Kumsheen Put-in   ● Nicola River

Murray Creek
Falls ●

Big Slide 1905 ●

Silk Train ◯

Rock Oven ◯

● Bighorn Put-in

◯ Bighorn

Tunnels of Doom ◯ ● Drynoch Slide

SPENCES BRIDGE
TO
NICOMEN

● Goldpan Provincial Park

Shaw Springs ◯

● Ten-Million-Dollar Mile

Camels and ●
Sidehill Gougers

◯ Coke Rock

Conception Bay ◯

◯ Carnage Corner

● Nicoamen River

● FEATURE
◯ RAPID

Spences Bridge to Nicomen: *39.0 KM to 16.4 KM*

Adrenalin junkies sometimes skip the section of river from Spences Bridge to Nicomen, heading straight to the rapids of the Devil's Gorge. It's unfortunate, as they miss out on memorable rapids, great scenery, remarkable geology, and lots of mesmerizing local history.

One example of a barely credible event that happened in Spences Bridge occurred relatively recently in 1973.

Bernie's Raft Rides opened for business beside a Chevron gas station on an asphalt parking lot just south of the highway bridge over the Thompson. The business consisted of a 4 x 8 foot RAFT RIDES sign on the highway, visible from both directions; a 15-foot travel trailer that served as an office and living quarters for me and a friend; a VW shuttle van; a 15-ft Avon raft, a few lifejackets, oars, and a young man with more enthusiasm than skill.

Those early raft trips had the town talking. Back then, the only pub in town was in the old Spences Bridge Hotel, a pub that had an illegal deck overlooking the Thompson. Raft trips that began 13 kilometres upstream at Martel passed by the patrons on the viewing deck, and rumour had it that half the town was certain that I was a certified nutcase and the other half, those that drank more heavily than their neighbours, wondered, "Hey, why didn't I think of that?"

Bernie's Raft Rides became Kumsheen Raft Adventures Ltd. the following year and moved to Lytton; the gas station was demolished a few years later, and only some asphalt remains to mark the spot. Even the pub's viewing deck disappeared a few years later. It's sad.

Maiden voyage on the Thompson: June 10, 1973

The town of Spences Bridge (pop. around 125) began as a small First Nation settlement on the banks of the Thompson years before the first inflatable raft appeared on the river.

In 1861, it was Mortimer Cook and his partner Charles Kimball, both Americans, who shuttled miners and others across the river in a small wooden boat tethered to a rope strung across the river. The village was known as Cook's Ferry for three years, and still today, the local First Nations refer to themselves as the Cook's Ferry Indian Band.

Cook continued operation of the reaction ferry until Thomas Spence built a toll bridge in 1865, and the little community eventually became known as Spences Bridge.

For at least 100 years, Spences Bridge was a mecca for steelhead fishermen. Known worldwide for their large size and ferocious fighting ability, Thompson River steelhead attracted fishermen from around the globe, and Spences Bridge was the centre of the Thompson's steelhead fishing universe. Lee Straight, the *Vancouver Sun*'s outdoor editor, interviewed a well-known BC steelheader on January 27, 1948: "They're the biggest steelhead I've ever seen… I'll bet some of the fish that broke me went 40 pounds," the angler enthused. "It's the best fishing I've ever had."

Unfortunately, a few decades ago Federal Fisheries biologists made a series of fatal mistakes, beginning with the opening of a commercial chum salmon fishery at the mouth of the Fraser River just as steelhead were staging their ascent up the Fraser and Thompson Rivers. The "incidental" catch of steelhead has virtually destroyed the steelhead fishery on the Thompson. Today, only a small amount of steelhead remain, and often fishing is entirely banned because of their low numbers.

Fishing at the famous Wye pool

Spences Bridge is also famous for ethnographer James Teit and for a little Scottish schoolteacher and her new husband, all of whom arrived here in 1884. Schoolteacher Jessie Ann Smith's uncle, John Murray (who was also Teit's uncle), owner of the local store, hotel, and stables, had settled here in 1859 and established himself as a successful businessman. Murray Creek is also his legacy. The Smiths arrived here in 1884, and John Smith worked for Murray for a few years before he and Jessie established their own apple orchard.

Jessie Smith's husband died in 1905 and she took over the operation of the orchard they had established from cuttings, some originating in her father's garden in Scotland. They eventually grew 37 varieties of apples, winning international competitions and attracting the special approval of King Edward VII, who specifically requested the apples of Widow Smith of Spences Bridge, BC. She recorded her complete story in the mid-1930s with the help of her three granddaughters; her autobiography is now available as *Widow Smith of Spences Bridge* (Sonotek Publishing).

CN Wye

50°25'30.16"N, 121°19'39.11"W—37.7 KM

The area from the mouth of the Nicola down through Spences Bridge was an important First Nations dwelling, fishing, and trading area for centuries. During the construction of the Cariboo Wagon Road in 1862, an encampment at the mouth of the Nicola and perhaps near the CN Wye (wye: a track arrangement for reversing the direction of a train) was devastated by disease and death.

In 1913, the CN sliced through a farm that was located here, filled in a river channel with gravel, and diverted the river in order to construct their "Wye" siding. It still serves as a staging area for work trains and crews.

On November 13, 1953, famous fly fisherman, outdoorsman, and author Roderick Haig-Brown and his good friend Tommy Brayshaw fished for steelhead at the Wye pool, a fishing hole off the end of the railway spur. Brayshaw's diary entry is probably the first written documentation of a Thompson steelhead caught on a fly. He hooked a 12½-lb. male. After fighting the fish for 15 minutes, Haig-Brown waded downstream to a gravel bar and retrieved the fish. The Wye pool remains a popular steelhead fishing hole today.

Kumsheen Put-in

50°25'27.23"N, 121°19'46.54"W—37.6 KM

River access along the Thompson is scarce because of the two rail lines and the Trans-Canada Highway, which follow the river from Savona to Lytton. Two decades ago, Kumsheen secured access by purchasing land along the river; rafts launch here on a daily basis throughout the season.

Rigging a fleet of power rafts at the Kumsheen put-in

Old Highway Bridge

50°25'14.08"N, 121°20'35.43"W—36.6 km

This steel bridge has served Fraser Canyon Highway traffic and Spences Bridge residents since 1930. It replaced the wooden bridge that was constructed in 1896 after the flood of 1894 washed away Thomas Spence's 30-year-old bridge.

First Bridge Wooden Pylons

50°25'10.30"N, 121°20'57.41"W—36.1 km

At low water, old bridge pilings protrude from the water at this point. These pilings are all that remain of the location's three original wooden bridges.

In the spring of 1864, Thomas Spence completed his first bridge across the Thompson, which was swept away a few weeks later by the freshet. He had built the bridge too low to the water. A persistent man, he completed his second toll bridge on the same pilings in 1865 for $15,000, and eventually the village became known as Spences Bridge instead of Cook's Ferry. Bridge tolls were the following: "Indians, free; foot passengers, 25 cents; horses, 25 cents; buggies and light rigs, $1.00; stages, $1.50; freight wagons, $2.00; and all freight, 16 cents per 100 pounds" (Fandrich).

The tolls were abolished in 1872. A massive spring flood, the highest spring flood in more than 150 years, swept that bridge away in 1894.

Bernie's Raft Rides Takeout 1973
50°25'4.85"N, 121°21'11.97"W—35.8 KM

From Martel to this point for $8.00. Can you believe it? The little eddy on river left just above the highway bridge functioned as the takeout for the run that began at Martel in mid-June 1973.

Trans-Canada Highway Bridge
50°25'6.79"N, 121°21'20.03"W—35.7 KM

The Fraser Canyon Highway became the Trans-Canada Highway in the late 1950s, after extensive and expensive construction upgrades. The upgrades included new bridges like this one across the Thompson.

Like many small communities in rural BC, Spences Bridge has been in a slow decline in population and services in recent years, caused in part by the highway bypassing the village.

At some water levels, surfing waves form immediately below the bridge piers and act like a magnet for kayakers in the area.

Murray Creek and Falls
50°25'3.22"N, 121°21'41.00"W—35.3 KM

Murray Creek, named after John Murray, a prosperous Spences Bridge merchant, flows eastward from the Clear Mountain Range and ends its journey in a dazzling waterfall display. It humbly enters the Thompson River through two galvanized culverts below the railway tracks and gravel roadway.

Murray journeyed from Scotland and settled in Spences Bridge in 1859, when he founded and operated a general store. By 1880, he owned most of the flat land on the north side of the river and operated a very successful orchard that he later sold to Archie Clemes. His other interests included a greenhouse, a stable, and the Morton House Hotel. Murray established one of the first seed houses in western Canada, selling vegetable and flower seeds in little brown paper bags with his name stamped on them.

Murray Creek Falls played an important role in First Nations legends. It was believed that mysterious beings inhabited certain physical features; here, a water spirit lived in the secluded pool below the falls. Youth undergoing puberty rites drew special signs of the "water mystery" on a rock facing this pool. Unfortunately, their pictographs are no longer visible.

Murray Creek provided the water for an early irrigation system that Murray's orchard depended upon. A few remnants of the aqueduct are still visible on the side hill at the north end of the Trans-Canada Highway bridge. For many years, a pipe carried water from the top of the falls down through a turbine to generate power for the town. Currently, the creek is the domestic water source for the community.

Spences Bridge Slide as it looks today

Spences Bridge Slide and Arthur Seat Mountain
50°25'5.32"N, 121°22'13.00"W

The base of Arthur Seat Mountain has been the site of at least three major landslides in recent times. *The British Colonist* described the first landslide in August 1880: "A landslide of unusual magnitude occurred near Cook's Ferry… A huge mass of Shawnikan [Arthur Seat] Mountain was suddenly observed to be moving and…thousands of tons of earth and rock were precipitated into…the Thompson River."

The second slide, which occurred on New Year's Eve, 1900, partially dammed the river.

The largest and most catastrophic event occurred in August 1905. It was recorded by Charles W. Drysdale, an early geologist:

> *A large bluff of alluvium at the base of Arthur Seat broke away suddenly…filling the valley bottom from bank to bank…causing a mighty wave 10 to 15 feet high to sweep up the river against the current… The wave overwhelmed the Rancherie on the flat below the town of Spences Bridge, killing ten natives and injuring thirteen. Five were buried alive in the slide. A horse tied to a hitching post at the Rancherie had its tie rope broken, and was carried upstream 300 yards. It was finally thrown ashore on the northern bank of the river, where it managed to get its forefeet in the gravel bank and hold on until the waters receded.* (Fandrich, 46)

A small mound of slide material remains on river left, on the edge of the field opposite the slide.

Mud Lake
50°24'43.26"N, 121°22'18.30"W

Mud Lake, a shallow little lake with an abundance of suspended silt, lies to the northwest beyond the CN tracks. The lake is not visible from the river; only the sandy-looking bluff behind the lake can be seen.

The bluff contains material that settled out of a glacial lake from an earlier ice age about 65,000 years ago as well as sediment from the most recent ice age of about 10,000 years ago. A layer of 7,700-year-old volcanic ash, originating from Mount Mazama near Crater Lake, Oregon, is evident near the top of the bluff. It proves that volcanic eruptions like the one at Mount St. Helens in 1980 are not unique. The Mount Mazama eruption was at least 40 times more powerful than the one at Mount St. Helens.

Silk Train Rapids
50°24'17.02"N, 121°22'48.45"W—33.1 km

A CPR silk train that derailed and dumped bales of raw silk into the river near here in 1910 is the source of the rapid's name.

The river splits in two around a little island that may still have an osprey nest perched on one of the trees. Both channels contain some whitewater, but boaters usually select the right channel and enjoy the waves where the two channels merge.

1974 CPR Locomotive on Trans-Canada Highway
50°23'45.36"N, 121°23'5.72"W

Imagine driving down the highway and seeing several locomotives and freight cars bounce down a cliff and land on the highway in front of you. Well, on March 17, 1974, a CPR train hit a small rockslide and the locomotives and several cars landed on the highway, killing two crew members. It took quite a while to clean up the tangled mess.

The wreckage blocked the Trans-Canada Highway for several days

Rock Oven Rapids (Grade 3)
50°23′41.61″N, 121°23′18.36″W—31.9 km

A rock oven, built by CNR construction workers, remains on river right above the tracks, just a short distance upstream from the rapids. Quickly and easily built, rock ovens provided a ready means to bake bread and prepare meals for the construction workers. This is the only one that remains along the Thompson River.

At the rapids, the river deflects to the right because of bedrock that projects off river left, forming a series of large compression waves at high water. The largest waves erupt during extremely high water. During mid- to low water levels, standing waves make this a popular location for kayakers.

The only remaining rock oven between Savona and Lytton

Creeping Carnivorous Pine
50°23′20.84″N, 121°23′59.93″W

Most Kumsheen raft guides specialize in more than whitewater. They also entertain guests in the calm stretches of the river and regale them with tall tales, usually intertwined with threads of facts, that can baffle even the most discerning listener.

Be on your guard for the remainder of this chapter because you may also fall victim to a slight exaggeration or two. Of course, the creeping carnivorous pine tree is not one of these…or wait, you decide.

A rare nocturnal subspecies of pine grows on river right here, just above the tracks. It has a tenacious above-ground root system with tentacles like suckers that grip the tiniest cracks in the bedrock, enabling it to creep slowly and quietly over the cliffs.

The pine emits a pheromone that mammals (particularly bighorn sheep, cattle, and mule deer, and occasionally black bears) find very seductive. Unsuspecting prey is gripped by the tentacles, then captured and consumed. The capture itself remains a mystery, as hunting occurs only at night. Biologists estimate that each creeping carnivorous pine consumes on average one large mammal per month.

Calm Water
50°23′25.46″N, 121°23′49.88″W—31.1 KM

This gurgling, calm section of water is where lifejacket-clad rafters can abandon their raft and drift lazily beside it while hanging onto a bow rope. Look for a massive bald eagle's nest on river right. Hungry eagles will hover over the rafts, looking for unsuspecting swimmers who are abandoned by their crew or separated from the raft.

Bighorn Put-in
121°23′59.93″W, 121°23′55.57″W—30.0 KM

This river access is frequently used by several commercial rafting companies and by the public. It is the last unrestricted river access before Lytton.

Bighorn Rapids (Grade 2 to 3)
50°22′19.24″N, 121°23′45.86″W—28.9 KM

The rapids begin at Skoonka (pronounced "skunk-ah") Creek on river right

Surfing the standing wave at Bighorn Rapids

and continue over a rocky ledge on the left. At moderate water levels, a sharp, reversing wave forms, which is a favourite surfing wave for rafts and kayaks and a favourite photo location for Kumsheen. A back eddy on river right is large enough for motorized rafts to catch and slowly return to the head of the rapids to run them again (and again and again).

When at its finest, the surfing wave attracts Kumsheen staff after hours with their kayaks, canoes, boogie boards, and inflatable dolphins.

Barrier of Glacial Ice
50°22'19.12"N, 121°23'52.28"W—28.8 km

Skoonka Creek is the southern limit of the glacial lake silt that has bordered much of the Thompson from Savona to this point.

Geologists surmise that near the end of the last ice age, a barrier of glacial ice or glacial debris blocked the valley here and formed an upstream lake that reached past Kamloops. Then, about 9,500 years ago, the barrier suddenly released and a massive wall of water—20 cubic kilometres—roared down to the Fraser, gouging a path that changed both the Fraser and Thompson Rivers. The energy of this much moving water is impossible to comprehend.

This is where the ice dam broke free 9,500 years ago

The deluge changed the Thompson's direction of flow, so it became a feeder stream of the Fraser rather than flowing north into the Peace River, or west and south into the Columbia River drainage, or into another unnamed river that flowed north a million years ago. Geologically speaking, the Fraser pirated the water of the Thompson.

Tunnels of Doom Rapids (Grade 2 to 3+)
50°21′43.51″N, 121°23′48.07″W—27.8 km

A suspension bridge crosses the river here for the CN employees and bighorn sheep who find themselves trapped between the tunnels: both cross the bridge to get out.

The Drynoch Slide on river left causes a great deal of water to funnel through this constricted area. During spring runoff, the river growls and howls and opens its gaping mouth in whirlpools, boils, waves, and powerful eddies. As the water level drops, however, the rapid moves upstream, and at very low water there is an almost continuous rapid between Bighorn and the top of this rapid.

During a commercial raft trip with his girlfriend in August 1992, former

Kumsheen raft guide caught an eddy here. He stripped off his lifejacket and raingear, revealing a tuxedo underneath, and got down on one knee to propose to the happy woman. The marriage only lasted a year or two, however, and today the rapids are also known as the Tunnels of Doom.

Colourful Tunnels of Doom

Drynoch Slide a.k.a. Mud Slide
50°21′36.16″N, 121°23′21.80″W

Unlike the other landslides along the Thompson, the Drynoch Slide on the left is a long, narrow slide that has been contributing material to the Thompson for at least 3,000 years. A small slide area that is visible from the river suffers continuous river erosion. At some locations farther up the slide, movement as much as three metres per year occurs.

Identified and referenced in literature since 1871, Drynoch intrigued many people. Matthew Begbie, Chief Justice of British Columbia—the "Hanging Judge"—presented a paper to the Royal Geographic Society in 1871 in which he makes reference to this slide looking a lot like an "earthen glacier."

A survey completed for the CPR in 1877 described the slide, originally known as Mud Slide, as the worst feature of the proposed railway bed between Spences Bridge and Lytton. It was moving at about 2.5 metres per year.

Drynoch Slide has created problems for the Cariboo Wagon Road, the Trans-Canada Highway, and the CPR. A major stabilization program in the early 1960s attempted to slow the slide's movement, but, as can be seen from the river, it has not stopped moving yet.

The construction of the Trans-Canada Highway through the Drynoch Slide in the late 1950s exposed some very unusual artefacts buried beneath 20 metres of accumulated slide debris. An assortment of 7,500-year-old cultural material including knife and flake tools, plus elk, deer, and fish bones (upsetting the theory that there was no fishing during that era) made this a very important archaeological site. The First Nations people that camped here shortly after the last glacial period may have been the ancestors of the present-day Interior Salish.

It is unlikely that the Drynoch Slide will ever break away and dam the entire Thompson. However, it has pushed the river westward, causing it to carve a channel into the solid rock of the west bank, and forcing the CNR to construct a series of tunnels and blast out a bench on which to lay the track.

Wine from the Vine
50°21′26.62″N, 121°23′50.30″W

Kumsheen legend says that the purple colour in the rocks just above the CN tracks is the result of early First Nations people using these rocks to crush grapes. The resulting wine, collected at the bottom of the slope and stored in cedar bark containers, took six weeks or so to ferment and clarify. Ask your river guide for details.

River Gauging Station
50°21′16.80″N, 121°23′37.12″W—26.9 km

Environment Canada established this station in 1951 to measure the Thompson's water flow. In the past, readings were done manually; now a continuous automatic recorder notes instantaneous maximum and minimum volumes of discharge and water temperature. In addition, it records daily and monthly maximum, minimum, and average volumes. Rafters and kayakers use these readings as references when running the river.

Goldpan Provincial Campsite
50°20′53.73″N, 121°23′26.14″W—26.1 KM

Chess Lyons worked for BC Parks in the 1950s, and one of his jobs was to name newly created provincial parks. He named Goldpan in 1956 because of all the gold-panning activity that carried on in the area, beginning in the 1860s. The last "gold rush" was during the 1930s Depression years, when more than 600 men tried their luck between Spences Bridge and Lytton. A handful met their expenses but few fortunes officially resulted.

The park is a rare riverside campground with 14 vehicle-accessible campsites.

Drynoch Siding
50°20′43.32″N, 121°23′20.53″W

During construction of the CPR in the early 1880s, a construction camp, flag stop, and post office existed just south of the Drynoch slide on river left. H.A.F. McLeod, a construction engineer, was in charge of the camp and was the postmaster. He chose Drynoch, the Scottish seat of the McLeod Clan, for the camp's name.

From here down to Lytton, the river gradient changes from one to three metres per kilometre, resulting in more and bigger rapids.

Shaw Springs and Rattlesnake Crossing
50°20′30.38″N, 121°23′49.51″W—25.2 KM

Mr. W. H. Shaw applied for water rights on a spring on river right quite a long time ago, probably in 1930, and named that spring after himself. As you will note, it is quite green in the draw near the spring. The lush vegetation is a good indicator of just how readily plants take hold once water is available in this semi-arid desert. (Note the poplar trees, grasses, diverse shrubs, and poison ivy.)

The two black vacuum-powered pipes suspended above the river have several functions. The first and the most important one is to protect the threatened rattlesnake population on river right: the snakes cross via the upstream line to access the thriving rodent population on river left, and they use the downstream line to return with rodent lumps under their skin to their dens on river right. A second function is to provide Shaw Springs' alfalfa fields with irrigation water. It is rumoured that the water is turned off at night, allowing the nocturnal rattlesnakes access to the hoses.

Shaw Springs Rapids (Grade 2 to 3)
50°20'11.00"N, 121°24'0.01"W—24.6 km

These rapids begin at a slight constriction of the river and continue until just below a large rock outcrop on river left. There is nothing spectacular about them, but rafts have been known to bump the rocky island that divides the river in two at low water.

Army Truck Corner
50°19'59.10"N, 121°24'0.32"W—24.3 km

In the 1980s, a military convoy was returning to the Canadian Forces Base in Chilliwack from training exercises in the Chilcotin region when the driver of one of the large trucks fell asleep and drove into the Thompson at this corner. Two young men lost their lives, and for weeks the army attempted to retrieve the truck and bodies using huge drag cables, heavy equipment, scuba divers, and a barge anchored in the ten-metre-deep river.

At one point, the barge broke free; Kumsheen was contacted in a panic to try to perform a retrieval. Johnny-on-the-spot (me) launched a 14-foot Zodiac with a 35-hp outboard and waited at the junction of the Thompson and Fraser for the huge barge to arrive.

With ropes and cables dangling everywhere, it appeared under the highway bridge. I motored up and nudged the barge, hoping to push it ashore; however, nothing happened. The thing was colossal, and with the cables functioning as sea anchors, my little boat could not even budge it. I gave up and went ashore, and the barge nonchalantly continued downriver. It floated all the way to Boston Bar, where a tugboat was working for BC Forest Products, retrieving log booms from the river. The powerful tug pushed the barge ashore and a special ramp system hauled it from the river to the sawmill, as if it were the log booms for which the ramp was designed.

The truck apparently still lies on the river bottom, and the bodies of the two young men were later recovered.

Ten-Million-Dollar Mile
50°19'40.76"N, 121°23'45.95"W—23.6 KM

With the construction of the CPR in the 1880s, sections of the Cariboo Wagon Road disappeared. By the time of the Trans-Canada Highway almost 75 years later, the railway had claimed whatever land it wanted. In places, there was not a suitable grade left for a highway.

At this location, they constructed an erosion-resistant steel retaining wall, filled the gap behind the wall with coarse material, and built the road bed on top. In 1959, this little section cost one million dollars to construct.

Over time, the road salt corroded the steel that formed the retaining wall. In 2007, construction for an upgrade from steel to concrete cost ten million dollars.

Seddall Homestead and Million-Dollar Rapids (Grade 2+)
50°19'30.78"N, 121°23'39.14"W—23.2 KM

Dr. John Vernon Seddall was the first surgeon with the Royal Engineers to arrive in the Colony of BC in 1859. The railway siding on the right was named in his honour.

The CNR had a station house and flag stop at Seddall that served the early residents who farmed the benches. The station house was demolished in 1970.

For many years, a farm directly above the tracks at Seddall produced fruit and vegetables for the surrounding area. A rough wagon trail provided access from Spences Bridge to the farm, and water came from a diverted creek to the south via an above-ground irrigation ditch. The farm was long abandoned when the 100-year-old log home succumbed to a wildfire in 2005.

At high water, there is some turbulence along the Million-Dollar Mile, but at low water the rapids move downriver a few hundred metres and become a great ride.

Camels and Sidehill Gougers
50°18'21.25"N, 121°23'54.87"W

What you see see on the hillside on the right is evidence of the renowned Sidehill Gouger. Scraped out of the hillside, horizontal trails spiral all the way to the top. Sidehill Gougers are reclusive and camera-shy, so the trails they leave behind are the most concrete evidence of their presence.

One of the notorious camels

Here is the story. In 1862, 23 camels were imported from San Francisco to work as beasts of burden along the Cariboo Wagon Road (more on this in Chapter 10). This plan was a failure, so releasing the critters in the wilds of the dry Interior seemed like the best solution. Camels may be big, hairy, and smelly, but one full moon in November they tagged in with a band of bighorn sheep and just as the moon came over the mountain, animal instincts took over. It was a messy night full of grunting and banging of hooves under the rutting moon.

The new offspring the next spring surprised everyone. It was a uniquely adapted animal, unusual in some ways but with interesting features. In fact, this surprise mutation was perfectly suited for life in the semi-arid, mountainous Interior. It had long, hairy camel-like legs on one side and short, muscular bighorn sheep legs on the other, as well as the warm-blooded, spirited disposition of both parents. By nature and physical characteristics, the Gouger was a winner.

Once weaned, the offspring quickly discovered they could walk along easily, quietly feeding on the sweet grasses of the steep slopes and always walking on level ground. However, upon reaching the summit, they had to turn around quickly and immediately head downhill at the risk of falling over.

Although very reclusive, they have occasionally been spotted (usually by a bleary-eyed Kumsheen raft guide) so it is worth keeping a sharp eye on the slopes. The young are easiest to spot, as they have not yet developed their perfect camelflage.

Sackum Creek
50°18'37.54"N, 121°23'48.95"W

Sackum Creek enters from river left, coming from a miniature Bryce Canyon in the mountain above the highway. (You may have to use your imagination here.) The volcanic rocks of the canyon shimmer in magnificent pink and mauve in the sunlight. The wind and rain have created interesting hoodoos or pinnacles and, if seen from the right angle, a rooster's head appears as if sculptured from the basalt. Oh, come on, use your imagination…

Skhrowtz Creek
50°18'28.63"N, 121°23'48.76"W

Skhrowtz Creek on river right is just one of many creeks between Spences Bridge and Lytton that begin with the letter "S": Skoonka, Squianny, Sleetsis, Seddall, Sackum, Skhrowtz, Shoskpost, Shushen, and Skihist. As you might expect, these are mostly English transliterations of the local First Nations names.

Water from Skhrowtz Creek flowed north along an irrigation ditch to the Seddall homestead to irrigate the fruit and vegetables grown there. The path of the original irrigation ditch is still visible.

Coke Rock Rapids, a.k.a. Jack's Rock (Grade 2 to 3+)

50°17′47.85″N, 121°23′43.37″W—19.9 km

It's a beautiful river—can you find the eagle?

This rapid is a short one caused by a gigantic piece of volcanic rock that squats in the middle of the river. At high water the rapid disappears, at medium water it forms a smooth reversal, and at low water the rapid is around the corner and has nothing to do with Jack's Rock. But who was Jack?

Jack was one of Kumsheen's earliest raft guides. On one memorable day, he had a full boat of customers at the put-in site when his girlfriend unexpectedly appeared in her rafting clothes. He could not very well refuse her, so to make room on the raft, he took off his spare motor and left it in the truck.

He wanted to impress his girlfriend with his guiding skills, of course, and when Jack got to Coke Rock Rapids, he saw his opportunity. The volcanic boulder creates a great wave; Jack hit it at full throttle. Unfortunately, the water was lower than he judged, and the entire motor tore away from the transom of his boat.

Poor Jack had to struggle the raft to shore using the extra paddles, hike all the way up the bank, hitchhike back to the base, pick up the engine he had left behind, drive it back, carefully carry it down the steep hill, and then continue down the river. When Jack and his disgruntled passengers arrived at the takeout, I was waiting there to have a conversation with him.

Jack left Kumsheen with his river experience judiciously listed on his résumé and became a captain on the BC Ferries fleet. To this day, he ferries passengers among the islands between the mainland and Vancouver Island.

Huge Gravel Bars
50°17'16.01"N, 121°24'21.93"W—98.4 KM

In contrast to the silt that lines the river between Savona and Skoonka

Huge gravel deposits left by the glacier 10,000 years ago

Creek, it is gravel that borders the river here. The large predecessor of the Thompson River deposited it more than 25,000 years ago, before the last major glacial ice advance. As the Thompson down cut its channel, steep gravel banks remained; they continuously drop gravel onto the highway and railway beds. An enormous gravel slope projects over the railway on river right.

Conception Bay and Rapids (Grade 2 to 4+)
Rapids 50°17′18.02″N, 121°24′11.97″W—18.4 KM

Numerous stories surround the naming of these rapids. Was it a fisherman's fantasy that steelhead trout multiplied so prolifically he could catch ten-pounders forever? Alternatively, is Harvey's story correct that a rafting company owner (no names provided) sampled the powers of the bay and sired a son here to inherit the business?

Conception Bay or Indictment Hole, same big ride at high water

Whatever the origin of the name, these rapids do have powers. At very high water, two automobile-sized rocks create enormous waves that are occasionally too huge to run full-on. Building to five metres, they can curl back and unload tons of green water onto your lap. Most boaters catch the edge of the waves, giving an exciting but not suicidal ride. These rapids change dramatically at low water; they move upstream and are considerably longer, made of a series of easy waves one to two metres high.

The early name that the CPR assigned to this location isn't nearly as romantic. They called it Indictment Hole, a name associated with the risks and dangers of railway construction in the early 1880s. In short, anyone building a railway or bridge here should be indicted. It was often suicidal work; for example, to drill holes for explosives in the chasm walls, Chinese labourers often hung from ropes like spiders. Accidents and death occurred frequently.

Carnage Corner Rapids (Grade 2 to 3+)
50°16'49.76"N, 121°24'28.61"W—17.8 km

The river, compressed by volcanic outcroppings and railway beds on both banks and at all water levels, jumps into action here.

The corner on the highway on river left is as interesting as the rapids. Affectionately called Carnage Corner by Kumsheen guides and staff, it is a trucker's nemesis. Trucks loaded with goods as diverse as designer soaps, vintage clothing, electronic equipment, and dimensional lumber have careened off the highway here, spilling their loads onto the tracks and down the riverbank.

On one such occasion, Kumsheen staff played dress-up with the vintage clothing for weeks. Even normally macho guides looked like gangsters in their 1930s suits or like beauty queens in their colourful best.

So many accidents have occurred at this corner—with complete semi units ending on the railway tracks—that the CP railway has installed signal lights to warn approaching trains if debris or a vehicle has tripped the signals and is now lying on the tracks.

Railway Maintenance
50°16'31.68"N, 121°24'25.42"W

The Thompson canyon created a tremendous construction challenge for both railways, and it is still a challenge to keep the tracks free of rocks and landslide material today. From this section downstream to Lytton, various methods of dealing with the instability are evident. On river right, electric wires strung between poles above the tracks connect to signal lights. If anything contacts the wires, the signal lights activate. Trains slow down or stop until it is determined what set the trigger.

The wires have an unintended benefit for the bighorn sheep that wander over the steep cliffs above the wires. Occasionally, one loses its footing and careens down toward the tracks. When it hits the wires, it catapults back up as if shot from a slingshot, landing in the same spot on the trail from which it fell.

Retaining Walls
50°16′26.47″N, 121°24′11.82″W—17.0 km

A rock outcropping on the left deflects the river to the right, creating a powerful back eddy immediately downstream at high water. The higher the water, the more powerful the eddy and the greater the potential for undercutting the CP tracks.

Five generations of erosion defences are visible just above the water. The oldest are dry stonewalls with no masonry, built in 1863 to hold up the Cariboo Wagon Road that snaked along just above the river. The fact that the wall still stands attests to the workmanship of the day. The CPR later built more masonry stonewalls, then masonry-cut stonewalls, then poured concrete, and most recently galvanized metal.

Nicomen
50°16′7.40″N, 121°24′7.16″W—16.4 km

The Nicoamen River (the spelling of the river and falls includes an "a," while that of the site does not) is a tributary of the Thompson and is a landmark. Much history has unfolded here, including the discovery of a gold nugget that proved to be the catalyst for the Fraser and Thompson River Gold Rush.

Today, this is where Kumsheen's day trips stop for lunch, where rafts begin the afternoon Devil's Gorge Run, and where the best rapids on the Thompson begin. On day trips, Kumsheen guests walk from the river to a flat above for lunch in a restored building whose façade resembles that of the 1860s Globe Hotel in Lytton. A large deck overlooking the Nicoamen River also provides a glimpse of the impressive falls.

NICOMEN TO LYTTON

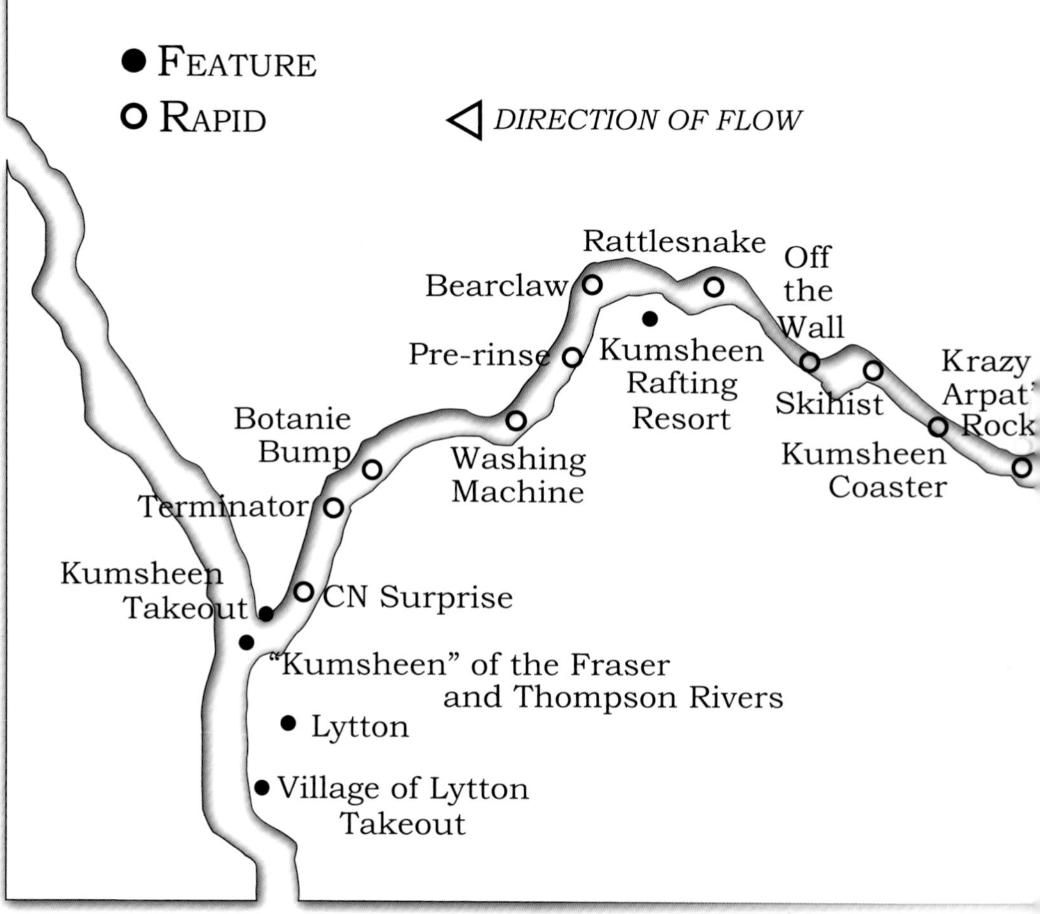

- ● FEATURE
- ○ RAPID   ◁ *DIRECTION OF FLOW*

Rattlesnake

Off
the
Wall

Bearclaw

Pre-rinse

Kumsheen
Rafting
Resort

Skihist

Krazy
Arpat'
Rock

Botanie
Bump

Washing
Machine

Kumsheen
Coaster

Terminator

Kumsheen
Takeout

CN Surprise

"Kumsheen" of the Fraser
          and Thompson Rivers

Lytton

Village of Lytton
          Takeout

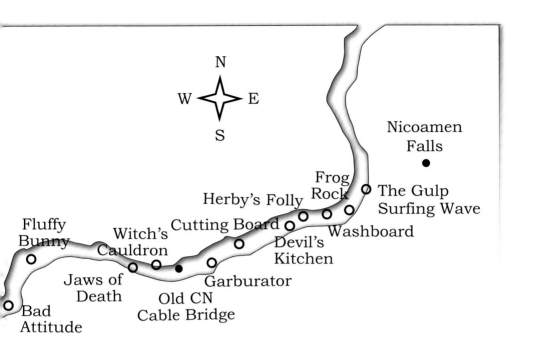

Frog Rock

Herby's Folly

Cutting Board

Witch's Cauldron

Fluffy Bunny

Bad Attitude

Jaws of Death

Old CN Cable Bridge

Garburator

Devil's Kitchen

Washboard

The Gulp Surfing Wave

Nicoamen Falls

Nicomen to Lytton: *16.4 km to 0.0 km*

The Falls at Nicomen
50°16′3.87″N 121°23′38.16″W

Without question, the most exciting, dangerous, challenging, and spectacular 18 rapids along the Thompson begin at Nicomen and continue downstream to Lytton. But there is more to the Thompson than rapids.

Almost as exciting as the rapids is a First Nations legend of a four-headed cannibal that lived in the area of the falls. Let me paraphrase this very complex, disjointed, confusing, and somewhat grotesque legend.

Opia'skay'uuxw (let's call him the Cannibal for short) turned Ndjimkaa (let's call him Rocky Jim) into a big, colourful granite slab above Nicomen falls. He's still there. Then the Cannibal stole Jim's wife and forced her to crack open the bones of anyone who ventured anywhere near the falls. His great delight was sucking the marrow from their bones, which he then cached in the pool below the falls. The falls, the river, and even the Devil's Gorge were dangerous places to frequent; like Dracula's need for blood, the Cannibal's need for human bone marrow was insatiable.

One day Rocky Jim—although as immobile as a cliff face—received a boy visitor. Let's call him the Hero. This boy had just returned from the moon (nothing in the legend describes the mode of travel) and when he discovered what had happened to Rocky Jim, he started a great battle with the Cannibal at the top of the falls.

Nicoamen River Falls and Kumsheen's Nicomen House

Early in the battle, the Cannibal somehow got his long, pointed, evil fingers on a whip. Like a magician, he struck the Hero with it and kicked him over the edge, into the pool at the bottom of the falls, the one with all the cracked human bones.

Luckily, the boy was no mere mortal. Instead of drowning in the pool, he disguised himself as a beautiful white swan and flew back up the falls to continue the fight. Eventually, the Hero connected with one of the Cannibal's heads and severed it cleanly. The cannibal was momentarily stunned and confused, so the Hero quickly cut off two more of his heads. Then he said, "Now, I'm going to be ahead of you." (Pun intended.) "Can you defeat me now?"

Eventually, with his fourth head gone, the Cannibal died. The Hero cut him into many pieces, which he scattered around the world. One piece landed in Honolulu, another in Mexico, and wherever the pieces landed, a volcano erupted. Moreover, according to legend, those places are "going to have a volcano the rest of their lives."

Rocky Jim remains firmly anchored near the top of the falls as a reminder of the great battle that resulted in the demise of the Cannibal and the creation of volcanoes.

Today, Nicoamen Falls is a landmark for river runners and highway travellers and marks the start of 18 consecutive rapids. And no longer does anyone need to worry about being eaten by the Cannibal.

Kumsheen River Access and Log Retaining Wall
50°16'5.73"N, 121°24'7.98"W—16.4 KM

Kumsheen Rafting Resort, the company that began as Bernie's Raft Rides back in the '70s, purchased the Nicomen property in 2006 in order to guarantee access to the Thompson, to provide convenient luncheon amenities for its guests in the spectacular setting of Nicoamen Falls, and to ensure that the Cannibal was truly out of the area.

Although challenging to construct because of the steep gradient and the Department of Fisheries' concerns about changes to fish habitat, the resultant ramp provides the only river access between Big Horn and Lytton.

The log retaining wall at the mouth of the Nicoamen River provided erosion protection for the Fraser Canyon Highway (built in 1923), the predecessor to the Trans-Canada Highway, for more than 30 years.

It consists of logs with stringers that go under the roadbed to hold it in place and of hand-forged iron rods that connect the stringers and outside logs. In 2009, the Ministry of Transportation and Highways contracted the backfill against the bottom third of the retaining wall with large riprap. The fill replaced the logs that had rotted and crumbled.

Tadpole Rapids (Grade 2 to 3+)
50°16′6.32″N, 121°24′10.20″W

Tadpole Rapids are the lead-up to the Frog, the first of eighteen exceptional rapids between here and Lytton. At high water, there is significant turbulence (boils & whirlpools) caused by the outcropping of bedrock on river left that compresses the river. At low water, the rapids move upstream and consist of a few waves caused by gigantic submerged boulders.

Big ride at the Frog in a large power raft

The Frog Rapids (Grade 3 to 4+)
50°15′51.82″N, 121°24′22.85″W—16.0 KM

This is where the "good stuff" starts. The sequence of whitewater between here and the Jaws of Death Rapids, I named the "The Devil's Gorge."

The Frog is a large rock in the middle of the river that, when viewed from the highway at most water levels, resembles a giant bullfrog about to leap out of the water. At high water, it is totally submerged, which creates turbulence over the Frog's head; at low water, it is an imposing bedrock island in the middle of the river.

For many years, every Kumsheen raft pulled into the eddy on river left above Frog Rock, and the guides walked along the shoulder of the highway to scout the rapids. There were several reasons for stopping.

In 1974, scouting the Frog was a ritual on every trip down the river

First, guides discussed a route through the rapids, whether to run river left or right around Frog Rock, whether the river was pushing hard to the right, whether "the Gulp" wave was a safe run.

Second, it got the guides' adrenalin flowing.

Third, it heightened the excitement and anticipation of the guests and got their adrenalin flowing.

Fourth, it allowed guides an opportunity to check equipment, snug down guests' lifejackets, and stow and secure any onboard gear and ropes.

Fifth, it allowed the guides a chance to sneak behind a large rock or sagebrush bush for some quick bladder relief.

These days, scouting missions seldom take place. The guides will tell you that it's because they are much better trained and are more experienced than in the "old days." They might be right. On the other hand, rafts can and have flipped here with incredible ease, so there was and still is good reason to be cautious. The river gradient is noticeably steeper from here to Lytton. During low water, the elevation drop from beginning to end of most rapids is evident.

Kayaker playing in the Gulp surfing wave

The Gulp Surfing Wave
50°15'53.22"N, 121°24'20.07"W—16.0 KM

One of the immense waves on the Thompson happens to be immediately above Frog Rock at mid-water levels on river left.

The river slides over a small bedrock shelf and creates a gigantic, curling, green monster wave. It is a popular surfing wave for experienced kayakers, and rafts get huge hits when the monster is visiting.

Kumsheen guides often head up to the Gulp after work on hot days in late July and August to play in the wave with their kayaks.

Washboard Rapids (Grade 3+)
50°15′49.47″N, 121°24′37.22″W—15.6 KM

The river does an abrupt right turn immediately below the Frog and begins to flow west. Here, Washboard Rapid consists of a few hundred metres of straightforward large roller-coaster waves, with the biggest waves appearing at the bottom of the run. Good at mid- to low water levels, the ride near 28,000 cubic feet per second (cfs) or 800 cubic metres per second (m³/s) is optimal.

Herby's Folly (Grade 1 to 4+)
50°15′46.57″N, 121°25′5.62″W—15.0 KM

At low water, the river is sleepy, slow moving, deep, and smooth here. However, high water summons the lurking demons waiting in the depth of this foaming maelstrom and they surface menacingly. Just ask Herby, the owner of a now defunct rafting company.

It was quite a few years ago that Herby was on a commercial trip with a European couple. Much to my chagrin, he usually ran single raft trips. This was no exception. It was very high water (probably over 100,000 cfs or 2,830 m³/s) and Herby was in the middle of Green Holes Rapids, where he had been at least a thousand times before. However, this time, the demon attacked his 22-foot motorized raft, violently flipping it upside down. As the raft was in mid-air, the outboard tiller arm pinned itself tightly under his lifejacket, and Herby found himself trapped upside down in the turmoil, held fast by the tiller extension.

Even Herby considered this a serious situation; for the longest time, he could not pry himself free. He confessed to me later that he thought he was off to the great river in the sky on this one. Just before that happened, the demons stopped holding him under, he broke free from the tiller arm's grip and popped to the surface and…air!

Looking around, he realized that one of his customers was already on top of the overturned raft. Her husband was somewhere ahead of the raft, swimming through the rapids of the Devil's Gorge.

Meanwhile, my wife Lorna was returning from Spences Bridge on the highway after dropping off some Kumsheen customers for their trip down the river. As she drove under the underpass near the Jaws of Death

Rapids, she saw a man in yellow raingear, frantically waving his lifejacket. "This is strange," she thought, and stopped to offer assistance, which was immediately accepted.

It turned out that he had just crawled up the huge, steep bank of the river. His wife, meanwhile, was still floating down with Herby. (It is impossible to right one of these rafts even on shore; it requires many helpers.) The man was taken to the Kumsheen Resort and given a warm drink and dry clothes; a Kumsheen raft guide quickly rigged a raft to take to the Fraser takeout to intercept Herby, his guest, and his overturned raft.

Well, Herby did float by. The Kumsheen guide chased Herby's raft down the Fraser and eventually pushed him ashore. Herby and his shivering guest were taken off the raft and the woman was joyfully reunited with her husband. Not long afterward, Herby moved to Mexico.

CPR Train Derailment, April 1913
50°15'43.90"N, 121°25'13.66"W—14.9 KM

Horses, cables, and pulley systems were all you needed to pull railcars out of the Thompson above Devil's Kitchen Rapids. A multi-car derailment occurred here in 1913.

Train derailments are a common occurrence along the Thompson and have been since the beginning of the railway. Some things just do not change. Except now, heavy equipment and huge cranes instead of horses pull the cars from river.

Devil's Kitchen Rapids (Grade 3 to 4)
50°15'43.18"N, 121°25'15.43"W—14.8 KM

This is another of the great rapids of the Thompson. It is a thriller at every water level but is definitely an archetype at mid- to low levels. In fact, in the middle of the winter, when the river is flowing at only 7,000 cfs (200 m³/s), these rapids are still remarkable. Try it sometime in February when the water temperature is 2°C. Be sure to wear a dry suit and mentally prepare for a cold swim, and then savour the adrenalin rush.

At medium water levels (about 65,000 cfs or 1,840 m³/s) a massive, runnable hole and wave (aptly christened King Kong) appear on river left next to the concrete wall. Scout it out first, but run King Kong if he is clean to run.

Also at medium levels, a powerful, curling, white-tipped wave erupts on river right at the head of the rapid. Dubbed the Devil's Toenail, this wave is a beauty. Watch for her but be careful of her moods.

At a very specific lower level near the toe of the rapid, where the river takes an abrupt left turn as it deflects off the bedrock on river right, an enormous whirlpool opens that flips little rafts with uncanny ease. One morning on Labour Day a few years ago, I witnessed (and photographed) two dozen private and commercial rafts in this whirlpool. Six of them flipped or dumped their paddlers into the river. The next day, none flipped: the river had dropped just a few hundred cubic feet per second and the whirlpool disappeared.

Be careful because just downstream are the Cutting Board Rapids, the ride side of which can be extremely dangerous for swimmers at low water.

Always a thriller—Devil's Kitchen Rapids

The Devil's Gorge—the best whitewater on the river

Cutting Board Rapids (Grade 3 to 6)
50°15'35.75"N, 121°25'44.05"W—14.1 KM

Immediately below Devil's Kitchen are rapids that have a schizophrenic split at low water, a mega wave at huge water, and a terrible souse hole at medium-high water. They are simply grand rapids for most of the year.

Be careful here, and be sure to scout the rapids at low water. Very experienced kayakers occasionally run river right at very low water, but it is a major drop. The rule is to run river left when the large, reversing, very steep waves appear on river right and the "falls" begin to take shape.

At medium-high water, the huge rock that sits submerged in the middle creates a mammoth souse hole. Around 60,000 cfs (1,700 m³/s), bedrock begins to poke its head through the water and either side is runnable for a while.

One October many years ago, a private rafter with his 11-year-old son ran these rapids, and instead of taking river left as is customary at low water, he ran river right. The waterfall that appears here at low water flipped them into the river, where a huge souse hole held them both, rotating them in the eddy line. Eventually they both washed through, but not before the boy received a blow to the head from the raft frame or oar. He was unconscious by the time he washed free.

Downriver at the Jaws of Death, a group of kayakers with an inflatable were on shore having lunch. They saw a lifejacket floating by, quickly paddled out, and immediately began CPR on the boy.

A RCMP officer who had received a report of the incident from someone on the highway contacted me. The local doctor and I immediately launched my 14-foot inflatable at the confluence of the Thompson and Fraser and motored upstream to intercept the group of paddlers, who were working on the boy as they drifted downriver. Unfortunately, the boy did not revive and the doctor pronounced him dead.

Garburator Rapids (Grade 1 to 4+)
50°15′31.22″N, 121°26′0.75″W—13.8 KM

Rotating at full speed at high water, the whirlpools, eddy lines, and bottomless pits of the Garburator command the respect of even the most experienced river guides. Solid bedrock far below the surface constricts the river and you get the sense that too much water is trying to push through too narrow an opening. Because of the hydraulics, this requires one of the most technical lines in a paddleboat in high water. Power rafts have a much easier time thanks to the added flotation and power of the outboards.

At low water, you look up at the sheer walls on both sides from a flat, gurgling river that is swirling gently. You will swear that this is not the same river that turned your hair grey at high water.

Witch's Cauldron Rapids (Grade 3 to 4+)
50°15′23.08″N, 121°26′26.05″W—13.2 KM

Immediately below the foot bridge that still clings to the bedrock on river right, the Witch brews her boiling pot. There is something intriguing going on at all water levels, so be on your guard. At high water, side-to-side boils and whirlpools are the challenge. They can be huge and there is no way to avoid them. At low water, a large piece of bedrock splits the river in two and creates great waves and delightful action. The boils and whirlpools are mostly gone and the Witch is napping.

At around 80,000 cfs (2,265 m³/s), a monstrous green whirlpool sometimes opens unexpectedly near the bottom left of the rapids. Watch for it if you're rafting as it can wreak havoc very quickly. I can attest to that.

Great ride in Witch's Cauldron

In 1982, I was guiding a snakelike 33-foot power raft with 22 excited guests on board. As we approached Witch's Cauldron, I watched intently for the quick-forming whirlpool in order to avoid it. I was almost through when suddenly it opened directly under me. The rear of the raft dropped into its vortex, and a few seconds later I was underwater as the whirlpool slammed shut. I clung to my boatman line with a white-knuckled grip as the violent water did its best to wash me off the back of the raft.

When I surfaced, I discovered that in the turmoil my leg had somehow got jammed between the pontoon and the floorboard. I couldn't move. I hollered for two guests to come to the back of the raft, jam themselves between the two tubes, and push hard on the tube that wedged me in. It worked. I was able to pull out my bruised and bleeding leg and gain control of the raft just as we approached the next rapid, the Jaws of Death. Then, as I watched in disbelief, the raft ahead of me went end-for-end in the Jaws of Death rapid..

Old Cable Footbridge
50°15′24.03″N, 121°26′28.81″W—13.2 KM

For many years, a private CNR footbridge hung across the river here. A very high freshet in 1982 rose to the level of the bridge, threatening it and creating a hazard for rafters. Because the bridge was impeding navigation, the CNR cut it loose from the left shore, but it is still lying along river right, high above the water. The destruction of the bridge was unpopular with anglers and hunters, who had often used it to pursue their sports on the roadless side of the river.

From 1964 until 1969, I commuted between UBC in Vancouver and my parents' home in Vernon on a regular basis. During every trip through the Fraser Canyon, day or night, summer or winter, I felt a strange compulsion to stop and walk out on the swaying bridge and inspect the river. I was always mesmerized by the turbulence and awed by how close the bridge was to the river during spring runoff and how far up it was in the winter. I little dreamed that I would be rafting under that bridge a few years later.

Highway and Railway Washouts
50°15′17.84″N, 121°26′41.13″W

A once-every-200-years event occurred here in March 2007. A freak warm spell, accompanied by torrential downpours in the Nicoamen River watershed, melted most of the snowpack and instantly overfilled the Nicoamen River and the little creeks that flow into the Thompson between Nicomen and the Jaws of Death.

The Nicoamen River almost undermined the Kumsheen building there and removed thousands of cubic metres of material from the property. It undermined the highway bridge over the Nicoamen and dislodged gigantic boulders that protected the piers of the CPR bridge over the river.

Just downstream from where the Nicoamen flows into the Thompson, a mudslide completely buried the Trans-Canada Highway for 100 metres. Then, a flash flood in a creek farther downstream undermined the railway, leaving the tracks—with a train stopped on them—dangling above a deep gorge that was created. The same creek then tore at the Trans-Canada Highway and excavated a wide ravine.

The railway closed for a week, and Canada's national highway closed for two weeks as crews hauled in material to fill the washouts and restore the railway and roadbeds.

Highway and railway washing out during torrential rains and snowmelt in 2007

Jaws of Death Rapids (Grade 3 to 5)
50°15'24.12"N, 121°27'0.64"W—12.6 km

If the rapids in the Devil's Gorge are legendary, then the Jaws of Death rapid is the King of Legends.

The name (although coined by Shakespeare in 1601) originated with the CPR. Many Chinese labourers lost their lives during railway construction at Jaws of Death Canyon, just downstream of the rapid; in 1984 the area became known as the Jaws of Death.

The Jaws instill awe, respect, and fear into the heart even today. Grown rafters tremble as they approach.

These are exciting rapids at every level. Large, powerful, Fraser River-like waves, at times almost six metres from trough to crest, erupt at high water. Dangerous, exploding compression waves and a souse hole are the challenge at mid-water levels; a massive hole on river right affectionately called "Bus Eater" appears at low water (20,000 cfs or 570 m³/s); a series of ten haystack waves emerges at around 10,000 cfs (285 m³/s). Raft guides sometimes refer to these rapids as the "Gums of Life," but only after they have made it through them.

The Jaws of Death Rapids are the only ones that have flipped a Kumsheen power raft on the Thompson. It was July 11, 1982, the river was flowing at 83,000 cfs (2,350 m³/s) and a flotilla of thirteen rafts was heading down the river. I was guiding 33-foot raft #13, running sweep, as they say, and had just had a crazy experience in the Witch's Cauldron Rapids. I had just enough time to set up for the Jaws of Death.

As I gained control of my raft, the raft immediately ahead was already into the first wave. It was a monster. However, the second wave was even larger than the first, and as I watched, the third wave grew and grew. The raft ahead entered the third wave, and in slow motion the 22-foot motorized raft flipped end over end like a tossed coin.

The emergency drills we had rehearsed the previous week were immediately implemented, although now we were pulling out people instead of empty lifejackets. Within minutes, most swimmers were out of the water and being reassured on other rafts. It took longer than we would have liked to entice a teenaged girl from under the overturned raft, and it wasn't until we cut the splashboard in the front of the boat and the guide went under the raft with her that she was brought out, scared but safe.

Jaws of Death Canyon Rapids (Grade 1 to 4)
50°15'32.53"N, 121°27'33.87"W—11.8 KM

Just when you think you are safely out of the Jaws of Death, you enter Jaws of Death Canyon. Steep and high canyon walls confine the river, and it bellows its disapproval. At extreme high water, the bedrock near the bottom of the canyon creates an enormous wall-to-wall constriction with a formidable wave that stretches across the river. Only on a few occasions has the river been high enough to create this wave; we add outriggers to the big motorized J-rigs for additional stability and safety.

During very low water, the gorge itself is quiet. The lull lets you marvel at the CPR arch bridge high on the cliff on river left.

Jaws of Death Canyon stone arch bridge

Jaws of Death Canyon Stone Bridge
50°15′31.06″N, 121°27′39.76″W—11.7 km

Scottish stonemasons built this masonry arch bridge more than a century ago. It is a unique structure: the stones are held together without mortar. Each stone, weighing up to a ton, has a half circle carved in the centre of the horizontal sides. A cannon ball is inserted into this half circle. The adjoining stones fit together perfectly, with cannon balls between them.

The stonemasons' skills are proven by the fact that this historic bridge never closes for repairs, although billions of tons of freight move over it every year.

Technically, "The Jaws of Death" refers to this section of the railway. It was difficult and often deadly to chisel and blast the rail bed out of the steep cliff here.

A train that derailed from this bridge in the 1890s apparently still lies on the bottom of the river.

Fluffy Bunny Rapids (Grade 3+)
50°15′25.53″N, 121°28′35.37″W—10.6 km

Many of the Thompson's rapids have intimidating names, so Kumsheen guides named a fluffy white wave on river right (at high water) Fluffy Bunny. Cute. At low water, a big rolling wave in the middle of the river goes by the name of Green Monster. See, there we go again…"Monster." However, this huge wave deserves its name, being much like a monstrous ocean swell at its peak. It is a very popular surfing wave for kayakers.

Pitquah CN Section Gang Camp
50°15′23.35″N, 121°28′41.07″W—10.4 km

On the upper bench on river right are the remains of a CN section gang camp. A section gang was a work crew whose responsibility it was to maintain a section of the railway. The Pitquah gang of four men looked after 12 kilometres of track from here upriver to Seddall.

To reach the highway and access civilization, they had to either cross the river here in a cable-car basket and walk up a trail to the highway or ride a sidecar upriver to the footbridge that is immediately above Witch's Cauldron.

A former Lytton Indian band chief lived here with his family in the 1960s. His father (also a former chief of Lytton First Nations) was the section foreman and took his son upriver every morning in a sidecar. From there, he would walk across the rickety footbridge to catch a school bus on the highway side of the river. After school, a bus dropped him off at the bridge, and he usually walked home the 2.6 kilometres on a trail beside the tracks. The main concern was rattlesnakes.

This story was related to me: "I was walking along the trail with my dad after school and at one spot I had to step from large stone to large stone. I was about to take a step when my dad called to me sharply to stop. I could tell from his voice that a snake was somewhere close by. He quickly found a stick and approached me, and there, coiled between the rocks and my feet, was a large rattler. Dad took the stick and flicked he snake from between my legs and off the trail. After my heart started beating again, we continued our walk home."

After the gang deserted their camp around 1965, the cable for the cable-car basket was left crossing the river. It was even possible to go for a joy ride in a dilapidated basket. Then, in 1983, a helicopter searching for a drowning victim at the Frog clipped the unmarked cable, forcing an emergency landing on the rocks at river's edge. A competent pilot averted tragedy but the cable was cut down soon after. It still hangs on the bank on river left at the bottom of the rapids.

Although the shanty buildings provided by the railway have collapsed, a few lilac shrubs and iris flowers have survived 50 years of drought, and prickly pear cactus is flourishing in this desert.

Looking down on Bad Attitude Rapids and a CN tunnel

Bad Attitude Rapids (Grade 2 to 3+)
50°15'5.13"N, 121°28'46.04"W—9.8 km

Gladwin Creek enters from river left, and that is where the waves begin. The rapids are best during low levels, as they wash out at high water. They consist primarily of easy waves, but near the bottom the river caves in and a twisting green wave called Sneaky Pete pushes the bow of your raft straight into the air. Off to the left is a shallow rock shelf that misguided boaters occasionally attempt to navigate.

Preparing for a trip down the Nicola River in 1974: Krazy Arpat facing the camera

Krazy Arpat Rock and Rapids
50°14′59.60″N, 121°29′32.85″W—8.9 KM

One of the highest water levels recorded on the Thompson was in 1972. The river flooded the Trans-Canada Highway at the Frog, closing one lane of traffic. Looking up over the retaining wall from the highway and seeing a river whose height was above the roadbed was an eerie experience.

The following year, I launched the first raft (a 15-foot Avon Professional River Runner) on the Thompson at Spences Bridge and pioneered the rafting industry on the Thompson.

In 1974, the river again flooded and almost reached the level of 1972. This was the first season that Kumsheen offered trips through the Devil's Gorge, continuing down to Lytton; I purchased two *huge* 18-foot Canova rafts (German army surplus) for the big water of the Gorge.

The high water in June was a surprise to me, and the 18-foot rafts proved tiny for this massive river. Therefore, to increase the safety margin, I lashed the two rafts together and placed a guide on each outside oar, and I did a run through the Gorge to Lytton to test the technique. It worked well, and although some mobility was lost, the additional lateral stability they provided when lashed together more than made up for it.

Three days later, ten guests signed up for the trip from Spences Bridge to Lytton. A friend from Cape Breton was along for the ride and Paul (my first employee) and Krazy Arpat were the guides, and I drove shuttle.

The trip had a problem at the outset. While being unloaded from the trailer, one of the rafts received a long gash that instantly deflated that chamber. A patch was hastily prepared and applied, and the trip launched.

Things were going well except for two problems: first, one guest kept complaining that the trip was too "boring" (he'd never seen a raft or been on a river in his life), and second, the patch wasn't holding air very well. My friend Stephen had to continuously pump air into that chamber. When asked why he had to keep pumping up the raft, he answered, "The water is cold so the air in the tubes contracts and the raft softens." The answer was technically correct, but in this case not the cause of the deflation.

As the rafts approached the rapids here, Arpat remembered a huge wave that we had run a few days earlier. It was created by an enormous rock at river left. Hoping to make the trip more exciting for the complainer, he headed toward the wave.

What Arpat hadn't calculated was that the water level had dropped since our earlier run, and the gigantic wave was now a gigantic hydraulic. (Also known as a *stopper* or *souse hole*, a hydraulic is formed when water pours down over the top of a submerged object, causing the surface water to flow back upstream toward the object.) Souse holes are very dangerous and are normally avoided like the plague on a river.

At the last moment, Arpat realized that the wave was now a dangerous place to be, but it was too late. The coupled rafts went over the rock and into the hydraulic; they were stuck there for a few moments (which felt like at least ten minutes), filled with water, and finally, after half the guests were washed overboard, they began to drift downstream.

Stephen quickly grabbed a stern line, threw it to each of the five swimmers, and pulled them back into the boat. One of the swimmers was Mr. Complainer's wife, waterlogged but all right.

The complainer no longer begged for a bigger ride. The instructions that he bellowed on behalf of his wife were now, "Miss that rapid…miss that rapid…miss that rapid."

Kumsheen Coaster (Grade 2+)
50°15'3.28"N, 121°29'46.67"W—8.6 km

These gentle waves can be run sideways, backward, forward, or even in a lifejacket while beside the raft. If you do not want to get wet, here is a chance for a quick nap, a short story, or some wildlife viewing. Watch for bighorn sheep on the slope.

Skihist Provincial Park
50°15'14.98"N, 121°30'40.75"W

Skihist Provincial Park is on the highway high above the water on river left.

Author and former parks employee Chess Lyons told me that in 1955 it was his pleasant job to name several parks in the area. From Skihist, a beautiful mountain peak is visible to the west; Chess thought he would name the park after the peak, but when he checked his topographical map, he discovered Mount Roach. "Not a good name for a park," he reasoned. Behind Mt. Roach and barely visible is Skihist Mountain. "Interesting name with a nice ring to it," he said. The rest is history.

The Skihist picnic area has a great view of White Canyon and the Thompson River. A well-preserved section of the Cariboo Wagon Road runs through the park, and a hiking trail, which heads up the mountain from the top campsites, generates great views of the surrounding area.

Skihist Rapids, a.k.a. Mother-in-Law (Grade 2 to 3+)
50°15'27.23"N, 121°30'39.75"W—7.3 km

This mother-in-law is short and sweet, but sometimes she can be really nasty. Occasionally she cooperates and lets you catch an eddy on river left to run these straightforward rapids more than once. Sometimes she does not.

Off- the-Wall Rapids (Grade 3)
50°15′25.83″N, 121°30′58.48″W—6.9 KM

Medium to low water offers the most sporting ride through these rapids, with continuous waves for 100 metres or more. The ride at mid-water is choppy, and high water throws its normal barrage of whirlpools, eddies, and boils.

The hole in the centre of the river at mid- to low water is known as the Dolphin Eater. An inexperienced boater and his inflatable dolphin took a thrashing here when they dropped into the big reversal. Eyewitnesses say the only thing visible was the dolphin's nose.

Japanese bonsai tree silhouetted against White Canyon

Japanese Bonsai Trees
50°15′44.36″N, 121°31′10.44″W

Check out the stunted bonsai trees on the barren rocks high up on river right. Planted by Japanese immigrants at the turn of the century, these little green ornamentals are at least a century old and are kept as miniatures by a little gardener who hikes through the canyon twice a year to prune the branches.

Or maybe poor soil conditions and lack of water stunt the growth of these trees.

Old Gold Mine
50°15′42.98″N, 121°31′26.63″W—6.1 km

Keep a lookout on river left for an old gold mine *adit* (a hole in the cliff where mining took place). Gold miners tend to be solitary, reclusive characters who don't divulge secrets unless it's to their benefit, and in this case nobody seems to know who created the adit or why. There seems to be a mineral vein that the miners followed; the pick and shovel work probably happened in the 1920s when a "gold walk" (as opposed to a "gold rush") occurred along the Thompson.

The skeleton of a forlorn miner—Bone Man—sometimes guards the entrance to the mine shaft. He's harmless but lonely, so keep a lookout.

Ecological Reserve
50°15′40.62″N, 121°31′30.69″W

On the bench on river left, the BC government established a 36-hectare ecological reserve to protect the relatively undisturbed forest and grassland ecosystem. The reserve also contains a registered archaeological site that consists of six pit house depressions ("kekuli holes") and numerous cache pits.

CN Rock Sheds
50°15′50.22″N, 121°31′31.07″W—5.9 km

White Canyon is the railway's nemesis. Constant erosion caused by wind, rain, and snowmelt has forced the railway to build rock sheds and tunnels to keep falling rock and debris off the tracks.

According to Kumsheen guides, these rock sheds were part of Lytton's bid for the 1924 Winter Olympics' ski jumping championship. The CNR found another use for them with the rejection of Lytton's bid.

Dramatic White Canyon across from the Kumsheen Resort

White Canyon
50°16′1.92″N, 121°31′32.39″W

Without a doubt, White Canyon is the most stunning feature along the Thompson and representative of the most spectacular geology along the river. It has been the subject of photographs for 150 years and was featured on calendars across Canada during the last century.

Here's how a geologist would describe the canyon: metamorphic granite and gneiss, through which the Thompson has down cut. Light-coloured quartz veins and dark-coloured amphibolites and gabbroic dykes are shot throughout the rock, which is highly fractured, causing continuous erosion and resulting in the rugged, sculptured appearance of the north bank (Fandrich, 69).

Old Mining Camp
50°15′46.15″N, 121°31′40.87″W

Since 1858, many mineral claims have existed in this area. The last one expired in 1976. Some serious placer mining happened here at one time, and a small mining camp squatted close to the river on the left.

Rattlesnake Rapids (Grade 2 to 5)
50°15′47.53″N, 121°31′45.09″W—5.6 km

The same high water of 1974 that gave Krazy Arpat a rough ride over his now notorious rock turned these rapids into a whirlpool monster. As I approached the rapids during high water that spring, I saw gigantic whirlpools opening and closing around my 18-foot raft and had no alternative but to run them. They were incredibly large and powerful, but, with a bit of skill and a lot of luck, I managed to keep the raft right side up. Once through the rapids, I relaxed for a moment and told my four white-faced guests that these were the biggest whirlpools I had ever seen on the Thompson.

A moment later, I realized that a powerful back current was pulling at us. This eddy headed back upriver and collided with the downstream current that created the frightening whirlpools.

I rowed furiously, trying to break the eddy's grip, but just could not get into the main downriver current. I told my guests to get low in the raft and hang on tight because we were going whirlpooling again.

I rowed furiously for a second time, still trying to break the eddy's grip, but in a few moments was back up against the cliff, bouncing to the head of the rapids again. At one stage, I relaxed to catch my breath and looked down into the water. Some debris had gathered and I saw a rattlesnake in the middle of it, its head resting on some floating wood chips. It had fallen off the cliff and the cold water must have numbed its body.

My saga continued for four or five more runs through the rapids before I finally broke free (I think the river got tired of me and spat me out) and was able to head downriver again. I was exhausted and very glad to say goodbye to the rattlesnake and nasty whirlpools.

Kumsheen Rafting Resort
50°15'37.11"N,121°32'11.73"W

On the bench above the river is the Kumsheen Rafting Resort (www.kumsheen.com). The teepees are visible from the river. On a staff river trip, one of our First Nations employees (with a good sense of humour) pointed at them and said, "Oh look, there's the Kumsheen Indian Reservation."

Teepees surrounded by balsomroot at Kumsheen Rafting Resort

Train Derailment 2008
50°15'52.98"N, 121°32'19.19"W—5.0 KM

On July 1, 2008, a sudden and record deluge (with an average year's rainfall in just a few hours) caused water, mud, and rocks to rush down the gulley here, pushing four chemical-laden cars off the tracks. Two landed in the river, and ethylene glycol, a chemical used in antifreeze, was mixed with the waters of the Thompson.

Ironically, fewer than 50 metres from the derailment, CN was busily constructing a new rock shed at a location identified by engineers as the location where slides were most likely to occur.

Bearclaw Rapids (Grade 2 to 3+)
50°15'35.51"N, 121°32'41.60"W—3.8 KM

Bearclaw is a strange name for rapids. It has a story.

Back in the mid-1970s, I saw a large black mass floating in the middle of these rapids. The river was quite high.

The mass was moving toward river left. As we got closer, I realized that it was a black bear swimming the rapid. My guests and I watched and marvelled as the bear struggled to shore and crawled out, dripping like a wet rag doll; then it stood on the rocks at the shore, hanging its head as if it were catching his breath.

Bearclaw. A good name for the bear and for his rapids.

Pre-Rinse Rapids (Grade 2+)
50°15'23.46"N, 121°32'51.83"W—3.4 KM

This 200-metre stretch of waves is strictly preparatory to the wash around the corner. At mid-water level, a wave on river right can be fun to run. Be careful, though, as it is caused by a large, smooth boulder.

Washing Machine Rapids (Grade 3+)
50°15'8.05"N, 121°33'15.59"W—3.1 KM

One of the Thompson's most memorable rapids, Washing Machine is a real winner at mid-water levels and has been compared with "riding a cork in a washing machine." High water washes out the waves and at low water, it loses some of the continuous wave action, becoming pockmarked with boulders and sporadic rapids.

Over the years, Kumsheen has assisted the RCMP with a wide assortment of river-related problems. In 1985, we received a request to go upriver with the police and the local coroner to confirm a report of a body on the riverbank near these rapids. An angler had noticed a bad odour, investigated, discovered what he believed to be the partial remains of a human body, and reported it to the RCMP.

Sure enough, at the high-water mark at Washing Machine Rapids, there it was. It had no legs, no arms, and no head—only a torso. After being examined, photographed, and carefully manoeuvred into a body bag for the trip to the local morgue, Torso Tom took his first and last rafting trip.

A month or two later, a complete human leg appeared in a log boom near the town of Hope. The leg had a scar. The scar belonged to a missing person from Surrey. Needless to say, forensics concluded that the leg was a perfect match to one that Torso Tom was missing.

Tom must have been caught doing something he shouldn't have been doing. Someone took Tom for a car ride, chain-sawed off various body parts, and threw them off the bridge over the Thompson River at Spences Bridge. The perpetrators obviously did not expect Torso Tom or his scarred leg to surface, but in the end, the RCMP got their men.

Washing Machine Rapids and the stunning Coast mountains

Botanie Creek
50°15'10.93"N, 121°33'26.35"W—2.8 km

Although you might have been distracted by the rapids and not noticed, a small creek enters the Thompson partway through Washing Machine. It enters on river right via a tunnel that was drilled through solid bedrock under the railway track. Botanie Creek drains into a beautiful valley to the north, a valley that has a rich First Nations heritage.

Uranium Mine Shaft
50°15′6.95″N, 121°33′36.94″W

Just downstream of the Washing Machine on river left is another mine adit. This 12-metre shaft did not chase a gold vein into the side of the mountain; it was chasing uranium. Yes, uranium.

According to rumour, a local old-timer regularly worked his way down the cliffs to the adit and sat in the entrance of the mine. He believed it might cure his arthritis.

In 1955, the mine's assayed ore samples did not show enough uranium content to justify further mine development, and no report is available on uranium as a cure for arthritis.

CN Train Derailment
50°15′10.78″N, 121°33′53.51″W—2.4 km

In the early morning of January 4, 2007, a CN train collided with a rockslide on river right, knocking both engines and several cars off the track. The lead engine, containing the engineer and brakeman, bounced down a steep cliff for 60 metres and skidded to a halt on the rocks just a metre or two from the river. Neither man was hurt, but both spent a terrifying night next to the river. The engineer described it as "a ride from hell." Lytton Search and Rescue lowered blankets and food to them, but it wasn't until daylight that a specially trained rescue team arrived from Agassiz and brought the frightened men back up the steep embankment.

Number 17 Rapids
50°14′55.30″N, 121°34′14.99″W—1.8 km

Wedged between two cliffs, the river turns on itself here when too much water is forced through the narrow granite walls. In high water, rafts can be bent in half by walls of water that unexpectedly erupt. During mid- and low water, the rapids move upstream and are friendlier and less aggressive, providing a pleasant ride over dozens of metre-high waves.

Terminator Rapids (Grade 3 to 4+)
50°14'41.75"N, 121°34'30.17"W—1.3 KM

For a number of years, we referred to this rapid—the last of 18 between the Frog and Lytton—as Number 18. Someone pointed out that it was a boring name and suggested that Kumsheen have a contest to rename it. Therefore, we did.

At the time, *The Terminator* movie was playing at theatres across North America. Some people still consider the popular action thriller to be one of the best movies of all time. Many do not.

One of Kumsheen's guests won the contest with the name Terminator Rapids, an appropriate name for the last thriller on the river. The prize was a free weekend raft trip for two and passes to watch *The Terminator*.

CNR Surprise Rapids, a.k.a. Last Dance (Grade 1 to 3)
50°14'12.55"N, 121°34'49.42"W—0.3 KM

These "sometimes" rapids only develop when the Fraser water level has dropped relative to the flow of the Thompson. The Fraser on average carries three times the volume of the Thompson, but occasionally the balance shifts and the suddenly powerful Thompson pushes out into the middle of the Fraser. When this occurs, rapids form under the CN Bridge and it is a pleasant surprise ending to the river trip.

CP Bridge Derailment
50°14'12.38"N, 121°34'50.74"W—0.3 KM

At 11 p.m. on July 31, 2006, a CP unit train loaded with coal derailed on the bridge over the Thompson, spilling 800 tons of coal into the river. Twenty cars derailed; eight remained on the bridge, and twelve ended up in the river.

Kumsheen had to suspend rafting operations for a few peak-season days while work crews removed the derailed cars from the bridge.

Takeout
50°13'40.56"N, 121°35'3.73"W—0.0 KM

The road that meets the river here originally led to a ferry that crossed the river at the mouth of the Thompson. Kumsheen Rafting Resort has an exclusive agreement with the Lytton First Nation to use this location as its rafting takeout.

Confluence of the Thompson and Fraser Rivers
50°14'7.26"N, 121°35'2.45"W —0.0 KM

For the local First Nations people, the phenomenon of these two great rivers mingling and joining was called *kumsheen* (hence our name).

The relatively clean, azure Thompson contrasts starkly with the brown, muddy, silt-laden Fraser. Sometimes the Thompson retains its distinctness for a kilometre or more downriver, but the Fraser always swallows it in the end. The spectacle is most apparent when viewed from the highway bridge over the river. The kumsheen of the Thompson and Fraser Rivers marks the end of our voyage down the Thompson.

Want to keep going? That brown, muddy-looking monster is known as the mighty Fraser. But that's a story for another day.

The kumsheen or "great forks" of the Thompson and Fraser Rivers

Balsamroot heralds the arrival of spring

Plants along the River

This list of BC Interior plants found along the Thompson is by no means an exhaustive one. Only 14 common plants have been selected, primarily because some anecdotal information makes them more interesting than others. These are plants found growing in the Thompson Valley and along the banks of the river.

Balsamroot

Balsamroot (a.k.a. sunflowers) turns the dry flats and hillsides along the Thompson River a golden yellow. They are a sure sign of spring.

Each plant has a cluster of large yellow flowers that emerges once the snow is gone and the frost has left the ground. If the soil is very dry because of a low snow pack or lack of rain, the blossoms last for only a few days. However, if it is a cool, wet spring with a snowpack that has melted and percolated into the ground, the blossoms may last several weeks or more.

The silver-grey leaves, which emerge from the base of a clump of stems, have tiny felt-like hairs. The leaves dry out in summer and turn brittle.

Balsamroot was one of the most important food sources for the Interior Salish people; every part of the plant is edible. They peeled and ate the tender inner portion of the immature flower stems in the spring. After the blossoms disappeared, dried seeds appeared. They were eaten raw or mixed with deer fat and boiled to tenderness using hot rocks and baskets.

The roots are generally very tough and pulpy. To tenderize them and make them more palatable, the Thompson women would bake them in a fire pit with round river rocks for several days.

Both the leaves and roots have medicinal value. The large, coarse leaves served as a poultice for burns. Once boiled, the root solution also served as a poultice for wounds, cuts, and bruises. A tea brewed from the roots was medicine for tuberculosis, rheumatism, headaches, whooping cough, and even venereal disease.

Apparently (always be on your guard when you read the word apparently), bull snakes have discovered how to use dry balsamroot leaves as a defence mechanism. These non-poisonous snakes live in the same habitat as the Pacific rattlesnake; when threatened, bull snakes will sometimes hide in a clump of balsamroot and rattle the dry leaves with their tail, emitting a sound much like a rattlesnake's rattle.

Bearberry or Kinnikinnick

Kinnikinnick is a slow-growing, low-to-the-ground evergreen plant with tough, glossy leaves, tiny pink flowers in the spring, and edible (but not great-tasting) red berries in the fall.

Bearberry has many medicinal properties

It is a common plant in the semi-arid Interior, thriving in sandy, dry soil or in rocky areas, where it pokes its roots down between the rocks. Often, kinnikinnick is the only green shrub in an otherwise brown landscape.

The shrub is also known as bearberry because bears enjoy eating the berries. Mind you, there is very little a bear won't eat.

Kinnikinnick has been used in many regions as a medicinal plant (Marco Polo reported in the 13th century that the Chinese were using it to treat kidney and urinary problems); the North American First Nations peoples have used it for centuries. In addition to urinary tract infections and kidney stones, they used it as a treatment for bladder infections, back sprains, venereal disease, obesity, stomach disorders, and chronic diarrhea. Leaves are also dried, powdered, and applied to sores and sore muscles.

Dried kinnikinnick leaves were commonly smoked and known as frontier tobacco. When mixed with regular tobacco in First Nations religious ceremonies, it conveyed the smoker's prayers to the Great Spirit in the sky.

Herbalists today sell dried kinnikinnick leaves loose or in capsule form to treat a host of ailments, much like the ones listed above.

Big Sagebrush

Whenever I am in sagebrush country, I grab a handful of the leaves and squeeze them until they emit their distinctive odour. I always associate the aroma with the banks of the Thompson River and the dry Interior.

This gnarled, grey-green shrub is normally about a metre tall but can grow to twice the size if conditions are right. It grows exceptionally well when the soil is overgrazed or otherwise impoverished.

Two features readily identify sagebrush: thin, triple-notched leaves and twisted, loose bark. Between July and October, sagebrush has clusters of tiny blossoms; later, they turn into edible little seeds.

The seeds taste bitter when eaten raw, so the Thompson natives usually ground them into flour, which they cooked in stews and soups. They made tea from the leaves to relieve stomach aches, coughing, and bleeding, and to expel intestinal parasites. The tea also treated colds, fevers, and pneumonia. A poultice made from wet leaves cured a variety of infections and provided relief for sore eyes.

The gnarly wood was used for fuel, and the pungent smoke served as an aromatic smudge to cleanse participants of evil spirits and impurities. The whole plant had a purpose: leafy branches were tied together and used as brooms and as switches in sweat baths; the bark was stripped and woven into bags, mats, and clothing; the aromatic oils were used in hair tonics and shampoos and as a flea repellent.

Big sagebrush grows well in impoverished soil

Bluebunch Wheatgrass

The term *bunchgrass* refers to types of grasses that are characterized by their growth in bunches utilizing a single root system. As the stems grow up and outward from a narrow base, the stems form an "umbrella," protecting the base and root system from sunshine and evaporation. In the same manner, the stems act as a funnel to channel moisture into the centre and down into the root system. Because of these characteristics, bunchgrasses are particularly well adapted to the very dry conditions found in the Interior.

This was the most common grass found everywhere in the Interior by Europeans at first contact. First Nations peoples used it to line their pit houses and summer dwellings, and medicinally as a cure for arthritis.

Bluebunch wheatgrass is found throughout BC's Interior

Canada Thistle

Common in the Interior, this is Canada's only thistle. Plants are either male or female, the male flowers being showier than the female flowers. Not sure why this is necessary, but it seems to work well for the thistle.

An aggressive, creeping perennial weed, it infests crops, pastures, rangeland, roadsides and non-crop areas. Generally, infestations start on disturbed ground, including ditch banks, overgrazed pastures, tilled fields, or abandoned sites. Cattle don't like it and won't graze near infestations.

Several species of birds and over 20 different moths and butterflies use the thistle as food.

Butterfly pollinates a Canada thistle flower

The name *thistle* comes from the Anglo-Saxon thistle or *pistel*, which comes from an Indo-European word that means "to prick." Ancient Greeks used thistles to help reduce the size of swollen veins, and the Interior First Nations peoples discovered that the root is edible, although it has a tendency to induce gassiness after the meal.

Death camas is one of the most poisonous plants in BC

Death Camas

In 1988, when our three children were quite young, it was common for them to play in the field in front of our house a few kilometres south of Lytton.

We lived in the mountains, and in the spring, tsewe´ta grew prolifically a few metres from our home. Local natives regularly came to the field to pick the plant; it is a traditional food source for them.

One day Murphy Shewchuk, well-known BC author and naturalist, stopped in for a visit with his wife Katharine. Seeing our three children sitting among some plants in the field, Katharine asked what they were eating; we told her that it was tsewe´ta or wild celery.

She went over to investigate and a few moments later came back and told us that, yes, the children were eating tsewe´ta leaves. Then she added, quite aghast, "Did you know that there is death camas growing all around them, in among the tsewe´ta, and all through that field?"

The obvious question was "What is death camas?" A tutorial followed. After Katharine and Murphy's lesson, I was always able to identify the plant—as could our children.

What I remember most is the fear they instilled. They told us death camas is one of the most poisonous plants in western Canada (second only to hemlock: remember Socrates?). All parts of the plant, but especially the bulb and leaves, contain an alkaloid or poison that can be fatal if enough of the plant is eaten.

It does not take much to kill a human; ingesting just two of the bulbs induces vomiting, diminishes muscle control, and creates breathing problems. Eat any more, and you foam at the mouth, slip into a coma, and die.

They said that death camas could even kill big mammals like cattle and horses. It follows that it could also kill elk and a few deer, although deer are usually browsers and not grazers.

I am not so sure about bears, because those critters eat garbage bags, paint cans, and diapers, and they drink solvents just for the fun of it. Sheep are the most vulnerable mammal; there is one instance of 500 sheep dying when an unusually wet, early spring brought death camas to the surface before the other normal plants. Because it was the most plentiful food available, the sheep ate it, and they all died.

Every spring, the field in front of our house still produces death camas. I fear for the elk that come looking for fresh shoots of grass and often graze the poisonous leaves in the spring. The herd has diminished from 300 elk in 1982 to fewer than 30 in 2012; no doubt, death camas has played a role in the decline, but predators, poaching, loss of habitat, and collision with vehicles also account for their low numbers.

Death camas is a member of the lily family and the bulb resembles an edible wild onion. It has several long, grasslike leaves with an unmistakable groove on the bottom side, and a main-stem flower spike that produces small (about one centimetre in diameter) creamy-coloured blossoms. Not long after blooming, the plant shrivels and dries to almost nothing; however, the poisonous bulb remains in the ground.

Livestock are very susceptible to toxins in larkspur

Larkspur or Delphinium

Many years ago, while on a three-day rafting expedition from Savona to Lytton, we pulled into shore to establish an overnight camp not far below and across from McAbee Station.

I went ashore to ensure that there was nothing unusual around that had to be dealt with before we hauled all the camping and personal gear off the rafts. Rattlesnakes were always foremost in my mind.

I was only 30 metres from shore when I spotted something unusual: a young dead horse. It had died very recently and wasn't yet bloated. I pieced together its struggle in the grass and could see where it had fallen several times, gotten up, and fallen again. My first thought was that it had succumbed to a rattlesnake bite.

The other possible culprit was a plant that flourishes in the area. Called larkspur or delphinium, it has purple or bluish flowers in the spring. Young plants are the most toxic, and the seeds are the most poisonous part of the plant. All livestock are very susceptible to the toxins in the plant.

I never learned whether a rattlesnake, the poisonous larkspur, or something entirely different had killed the foal. However, seeing evidence of its obvious agony created in me a new respect for both larkspur and rattlesnakes.

Poison Ivy

Common along the river, this toxic plant is often the only bright green plant growing profusely among the rocks. That is the first clue that you've met with poison ivy. The second is its relatively large, wavy-edged leaves grouped in clumps of three. The third clue is the whitish berries that hang in loose clusters from midway up the main stem during the months of August to November. Flowering occurs from May to July.

Poison ivy grows prolifically along the banks of the Thompson

Every part of the plant—the leaves, berries, and stem—contains oil that has poisonous properties; contact with the oil causes severe skin rashes, especially to anyone with sensitive skin.

The most common way to come in contact with the tiny droplets is through second-hand exposure from shoes or pants that have touched the plant. Burning the plant releases resin droplets in the smoke, and this too can create a rash. Directly touching any part of the plant guarantees a nasty reaction in most people.

Multiple washings with soap and water are the best way to remove the oil from the skin. Once a rash develops, calamine lotion is the most practical way to soothe the itching.

A word of caution: never use the plant leaves as toilet paper, no matter how soft and enticing they look. The toxic oil truly loves mucous membranes and knows how to inflict intense suffering.

Young and old ponderosa pine cones

Ponderosa Pine

Ponderosa pine trees are prolific throughout the semi-arid Interior of BC. Unfortunately, they are not nearly as common now as they were before the mountain and western pine beetle attacks during the first decade of this century.

133

Well adapted to a hot and dry climate condition in the summer and to cold in the winter, the ponderosa establishes a long taproot to siphon water. The root also stabilizes the tree. The tree grows relatively quickly to a height of 45 metres and can live to be 600 years old. Unfortunately, the pine beetles attacked the oldest trees first and destroyed thousands of hectares of old pine forests.

Indigenous peoples used the needles, bark, gum, cones, seeds, pollen, and roots for a wide variety of applications, from underarm deodorants to medicine for cough and fevers. Most of the plant—pitch, seeds, cones, bark, buds, and cambium—is edible.

The pitch works as an ointment for sores and scabby skin, backaches, rheumatism, earaches, inflamed eyes, and as a sleeping aid for infants. The boughs cure muscle pain when used in sweat lodges, and when boiled the potion stops internal hemorrhaging.

Ponderosa pines were the tree of choice for the roof of the Interior Salish subterranean winter home, as the high pitch concentration reduces the rate of rot.

Countless birds are dependent on pine seeds as a diet staple and use the trees as roosting and nesting sites. Blue and spruce grouse line their nests with the needles. Chipmunks and squirrels rely on the seeds, and ungulates like deer crawl under the tree branches for shelter and shade.

Prickly Pear Cactus

This little plant grows throughout the semi-arid Interior and beyond. In the spring, it comes to life with beautiful blossoms. After the blossoms disappear, the cacti blend into their surroundings and it is common for them to lodge themselves into any shoe, pant leg, or other appendage that accidently comes in contact with them.

Here are some thoughts about the cactus, written in 1880 by Mrs. Sillitoe, Bishop Sillitoe's wife: "I am hardly correct in calling this a barren flat, for on it thrives a vigorous growth of cactus, and with the utmost care one cannot go many yards without getting one's shoes full of the sharp prickles. One night in rolling over in bed I got my side full of them" (Gowen, *Pioneer Church Work in British Columbia*, 180).

Prickly pear is an edible plant, but the challenge is to remove the spines without having them get the better of you. First Nations peoples burned them off or swept sagebrush over the fruit to remove them. They ate the pulpy interior raw, boiled, or dried, but usually added it to stews and soups.

Prickly pear cactus provided a meal of last resort

Early settlers boiled the complete plant to remove the spines, and then fried the pulpy interior. When cooked, there is a hint of a cucumber or pear (an active imagination will help you make the connection).

In fact, prickly pear traditionally was a "meal" of last resort. In desperate times, the settlers would burn off the spines and feed the plant to their livestock rather than eat it.

Medicinally, this plant acted as a diuretic and treated diarrhea, skin sores, infections, and backaches.

Rabbit Bush

Common rabbit bush is smaller than sagebrush but looks similar, unless you zero in on the details. An impressive, artsy photo I took of rabbit bush hung for years in the Kumsheen office, wrongly identified as sagebrush. It took many years for me to notice the difference between the two plants.

Adapted to a variety of climates, rabbit bush is one of the first late summer/early fall shrubs to bloom in the semi-arid Interior, and for me, the blossoms mark the end of summer.

It has small yellow flowers (but bigger and brighter than sagebrush flowers) that are not particularly aromatic, but look lovely. It is fascinating how the blossoms suddenly appear after a long hot summer or drought.

Rabbit bush blooms in the fall

Bees visit the blossoms; the resultant honey is dark, strong, and usually left in the hive for the bees' winter food. Yes, bees eat honey to survive the winter.

The Interior's native women manufactured sanitary napkins from rabbit bush leaves. Tea made from the leaves relieved sore throats. Some indigenous peoples pulverized the wood and bark and made chewing gum. Branches provided stretcher material for tanning hides.

Deer and mountain sheep graze the plants, and small critters and rabbits use the low branches for security and protection.

Farmers who ran cattle in ranges that contained rabbit bush realized that none of the cattle grazed on it until they were very hungry. Therefore, government range inspectors equated poor range management with heavily grazed rabbit bush.

Saskatoon Bush

This attractive, ubiquitous shrub sometimes grows into a tree that is seven metres tall or more. It is hardy and has beautiful white blossoms in the spring and edible berries in early summer.

Both trees and shrubs grow at the Kumsheen Resort. The branches of a particularly large tree overhang the giant outdoor chessboard and decorate it with purple berries every summer.

Saskatoon berries - a food staple for the natives and a food item today

To the indigenous peoples along the Thompson, saskatoon berries acted as a food staple. Because they could be eaten fresh, dried like raisins, or mashed and dried and applied to soups and stews, their usefulness was unsurpassed by that of other foods. Berries mixed with meat and fat made pemmican, the indispensable sustenance of natives and early voyageurs.

Although saskatoon berries are still considered an essential food item today, the method of preservation has changed from drying to freezing. Instead of pemmican, today's uses include pies, jam, muffins, syrups, and wine.

Saskatoon blossoms typically emerge in mid-April (give or take a week or so), and the berries are usually edible by the end of June or the first week in July.

In the past, the Thompson natives followed the ripening of the berries into higher elevations, especially in Botanie Valley, which guaranteed them a continual harvest that lasted most of the summer.

Medicinally, the juice relieved an upset stomach, boiled berries made excellent ear drops, and green or dried berries acted as eye drops. The inner bark and twigs also had medicinal uses.

Men made arrows and spears from the saskatoon's straight, hard branches. The strong, flexible wood fibre became basket rims and canoe cross-braces.

Deer, elk, moose, and cattle browse the saskatoon shrub. They prefer the young shoots and small branches. Bears devour the berries as only bears can, by roaming from plant to plant, standing on their hind legs, reaching up, and bending over a branch or two. The critters then mouth and strip the berries and most of the leaves from the branches.

Even coyotes like ripe saskatoon berries. They crawl under a plant, reach up with their snouts, and pick the low fruit before lying down for their afternoon nap.

Tsewe´ta (lomantium nudicaule)

This plant (also called Indian celery or Indian consumption plant) is a member of the carrot family and grows profusely in the field in my front yard a few kilometres south of Lytton. Every spring, I pick and dry the leaves; in the summer, my wife, Lorna, harvests seeds, just like the Thompson native peoples did for centuries.

The celery-flavoured leaves are eaten raw, steamed, or used in soups and stews. I simply steam them like spinach when they are green. I also add dried leaves to both soups and stews to bring a unique flavour to the pot. Lorna picks the dried seeds and steeps them to make tea.

Tsewe'ta seeds, leaves, stems, and flowers are all edible

For the Thompson peoples, the leaves and young stalks served as an important spring vegetable. Seeds, leaves, stems, and flowers are all used as flavouring for teas, meat stews, and tobacco. Tsewe'ta tea is a good tonic for colds and sore throats.

The plant normally grows in the dry Interior, and our field is almost its southern limit. Several local native families traditionally harvest tsewe'ta leaves in our field. They come every spring, sit among the plants, and gather bags of the leaves and young stems.

Tumbleweed

Imagine a Wild West movie: the villain ties his horse to a railing, the street is deserted and dusty, and a tumbleweed rolls down the street, driven by the wind. Then the "good guy" appears, and the protagonist and antagonist glare at each other through the dust.

They should be glaring at the tumbleweed, that symbol of the Wild West deserts. In fact, as the plant rolls down the street, it is dispersing seeds: a quarter million of them. No wonder the tumbleweed, also known as Russian thistle, is the scourge of the barren earth.

Almost everyone recognizes a tumbleweed plant. Whether they are as small as volleyball or as large as a Volkswagen beetle, in the fall, they are a-rollin' in the wind.

Most people, however, wouldn't recognize the seedling and juvenile plant's bright green, succulent, grasslike shoots, which are usually red or purple striped. Inconspicuous green flowers grow where a leaf branches off the stem.

Mice, bighorn sheep, and pronghorn antelope eat the young, tender shoots. In former times of drought, farmers had no choice but to make livestock silage using young tumbleweeds.

As far as I know, nobody except movie producers has invented a use for the plant once it is dry and a-rollin' down the highway.

Tumbleweed is the scourge of the barren earth

Wild Asparagus

Asparagus, cultivated for at least 2,000 years, grows wild along the Thompson. The plant is more a garden-variety asparagus that escaped the confines of the garden and has found the right conditions to self-sow than a true wild plant.

Asparagus likes a lot of water, sandy soil, and direct sunshine, exactly the conditions that are found along the river. In fact, it grows all along the Thompson, and local people, both native and non-native, treasure their favourite gathering sites.

In the late 1970s, usually in the spring, Kumsheen offered ethnobotany workshops in conjunction with the Continuing Education Department at the University of British Columbia. Camp was on Asparagus Island (see Chapter 3, 63.4 км), and the dinner vegetable was traditionally wild asparagus, picked there that evening.

Another popular natural asparagus garden is at the Kumsheen put-in at Spences Bridge. The conditions are ideal: sandy soil, an abundance of water, direct sunlight.

The young, fleshy shoots are sweetest just as they emerge from the ground. As the plant ages, it branches, becomes fernlike, and is not edible. Once mature, it looks nothing like the fleshy, sweet, edible shoots of spring.

Wild asparagus is a springtime delicacy in the Interior

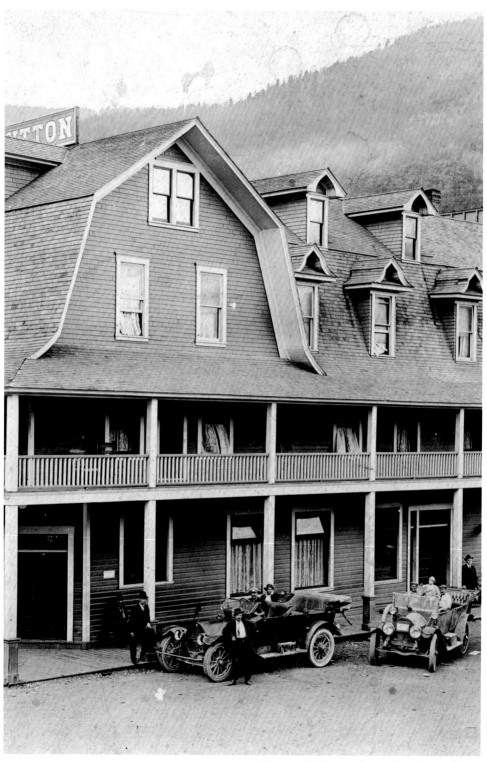

The stately 60-room Lytton Hotel around 1912

7

Old Lytton

The Village at the Great Forks

Throughout history, the First Nations village at the junction of the Fraser and Thompson has been referred to by many names both in literature and on maps. Camchin, the Great Forks, Shilkumcheen, Thlikumcheen, Tl´cumjane, Clicumchin, and Lkamtci´n are some of Lytton's former names.

The explanation for this array of titles is simple. The Thompson people had no written language, so interpreting the sounds of their language into English phonetics wasn't an exact science.

For example, in 1808, Simon Fraser called the village Camchin. How did he arrive at Camchin? Fraser relied on others to edit his journals and it's probable that his Camchin was how Fraser or an editor interpreted Fraser's articulation of the Salish word for the Great Forks.

Twenty years later, in 1828, Hudson's Bay Company governor George Simpson and his travelling companion, Archibald McDonald, navigated the Thompson in the river's first recorded descent. They referred to most tributary rivers that emptied into the Thompson and Fraser as "forks." For example, they referred to the junction of the Nicola and Thompson Rivers at Spences Bridge as Coutamine Forks.

Other rivers in their records were Little Forks, Small Forks, Lower Forks, Upper Forks, and so on. In their diaries, the village at the junction of the Thompson and Fraser was the Great Forks, Grand Forks, or simply The Forks.

A.C. Anderson, the HBC surveyor who came to The Forks in 1847, called the village Shilkumcheen. An 1859 map compiled from his earlier surveys refers to it as Thlikumcheen or Great Fork. Both Shilkumcheen and Thlikumcheen are transcriptions of First Nations' pronunciation of the Great Forks, and are almost identical in their pronunciation.

An Arrowsmith map from 1858 refers to the village as Tl´cumjane. Arthur Bushby, Judge Matthew Begbie's clerk, referred to it as Clicumchin in his journal in March 1859.

Ethnographer James Teit lists at least four different names for the indigenous people of Lytton (people of Lkamtci´n), each one slightly different from the others, and all are tongue twisters. "They are sometimes simply called Nlak´a´pamux. I shall call them the Lytton band" (Teit, *The Thompson Indians of British Columbia*, 170).

Teit studied and was fluent in the Thompson language. His spellings probably most accurately reflect the English transcription of the Thompson language pronunciation for these words, yet he couldn't settle on just one name.

The common denominator of the different spellings and pronunciations is probably *kumcheen* or *kumsheen*.

HBC Fort Dallas

In 1857, James Douglas, governor of Vancouver Island and chief factor of the HBC, was anticipating an influx of miners into the Interior and wanted to ensure that mining supplies were available to them.

Although only First Nations paths and the HBC Fur Brigade Trail existed in lower sections of the Fraser Canyon in 1857, Douglas decided to establish an HBC transport corps whose purpose was to outfit the miners and to trade with the local population.

The junction of the Thompson and Fraser Rivers was the new depot's location. He called it Fort Dallas, naming it after his son-in-law, Alexander Grant Dallas.

The fort, built under contract about three miles downstream from the junction of the two rivers, cost $3,500 to build. But the buildings, although completed on budget and on time, were never used as a miners' supply depot by the HBC.

Getting building supplies to the job site was a challenge. Several trips were made during low water on the Fraser River between Yale and Lytton from late fall of 1857 to very early spring 1858. A heavy, flat-bottomed boat called a *bateau* was loaded with supplies in Yale, poled or rowed (often with the aid of sails) upriver to Lytton, and drifted back down empty to Yale. Moving supplies along the river was simpler but much riskier than carrying them up the rugged canyon along almost nonexistent trails.

With the establishment of the Crown Colony of British Columbia in August 1858, the Fort Dallas project was abandoned, and Governor Douglas requested the transfer of most of the building components to Oswald Travaillot, the local government gold commissioner.

Travaillot, instructed to erect a log building for the government's service, used the window sashes, glass, hinges, and door locks from the Fort Dallas buildings. The new government building cost less than the HBC post to build ($2,158) and was located within the present townsite of Lytton.

Lytton Sports Day pole vault (with a hard landing) on Main Street in 1910

Lord Lytton

In 1858, James Douglas, the governor of the Crown Colony of British Columbia, decided that as a sign of respect he would name the settlement at the Great Forks in honour of Baron Edward Bulwer-Lytton, the British secretary of state for the Colonies. Bulwer-Lytton had sponsored the act that created the Colony of British Columbia.

Lord Lytton wasn't exactly the finest secretary of state that the British Empire ever produced, according to some. One historian at the time remarked that not all secretaries of state were incompetent; only Lord Bulwer-Lytton deserved that reputation.

Although somewhat undistinguished as a statesman, Lytton was a prolific and popular author whose writing was theatrical and melodramatic. He wrote 29 novels, three books of prose, and three plays.

He coined several phrases that are still widely used today, such as *the pen is mightier than the sword*, *pursuit of the almighty dollar*, and *the great unwashed*.

Perhaps regrettably, Lord Lytton is best remembered today by a popular literary contest for the worst opening for a work of fiction. His novel *Paul Clifford* opens with a competitive example:

> *It was a dark and stormy night; the rain fell in torrents—except at occasional intervals, when it was checked by a violent gust of wind which swept up the streets (for it is in London that our scene lies), rattling along the housetops, and fiercely agitating the scanty flame of the lamps that struggled against the darkness.*

The tongue-in-cheek Bulwer-Lytton Fiction Contest, sponsored by the English Department of San Jose State University in California, attracted only three entrants in 1982, its first year. After drawing international media attention, it elicited over 10,000 entrants the following year. It continues to be a popular contest, attracting aspiring bad writers from throughout the world.

In 2008, the great debate over whether that opening line is truly a literary tragedy was brought to the Lytton River Festival, an annual Labour Day event that I founded in 2004 and have coordinated ever since. The live argument between the great-great grandson of Lord Lytton and the founder of the tongue-in-cheek contest was widely reported in various media, including *The Globe and Mail*, *The New York Times*, and *The Guardian*. Mr. Lytton-Cobbold easily won the crowd's vote.

Lytton's First Jail

Built in October 1859, Lytton's first jail was simply a log cabin that was converted into a kitchen and three jail cells: two cells for prisoners, and one to use as a storage room for seized property and to store the personal belongings of the jail keeper.

The jail got a fair amount of use, mostly when the one-man constable picked up "drunk and disorderly" miners and needed to hold them until they sobered up and appeared before the justice of the peace, H.M. Ball, the next day.

In 1859 fines varied from $2.00 to $10.00, with an average fine of $5.00. Charges of "assaulting a police officer" resulted in a fine of $25.

Lytton's first jail, complete with broken glass on top of the outside wall

Stealing $30, a pair of blankets, two pairs of trousers, and two shirts from the cabin of a miner on the Fraser River netted imprisonment for a period of four months with hard labour.

Lytton's Constable Boyd caught the local blacksmith shoeing a horse on Sunday and charged him with "illegally working on the Lord's Day." More serious than shoeing a horse on Sunday was selling spirits to the local natives. Two Lytton residents, Alexander McWha and Patric Kilroy, pleaded guilty before Justice Ball, who levied a fine of $50 ($1,300 in 2013) to each of the men. These were huge fines in 1861 and reflected the seriousness of the offence. Both McWha and Kilroy found the fines excessive and appealed to the Supreme Court.

On July 13, 1861, Christian Homan was charged with "feloniously stealing a tin pot with beans in it of the value 10 cents, the property of Henry Buirley of Kanaka Bar. Prisoner pleaded guilty and was sentenced to

2 months imprisonment with hard labor in Lytton Gaol" (Lytton Museum and Archives Newsletter, Nov. 2004, pp. 3–4). Homan obviously already had a reputation in town to be levied such a severe sentence.

The following year, not long after getting out of jail, the same Christian Homan burned down a "dwelling house" of Eugene Comber & Co. at Kanaka Bar and was charged with "maliciously and feloniously setting fire to the dwelling."

While awaiting trial, Homan escaped from the Lytton jail by cutting away the lower sill of one wall in his cell and loosening the upper board, apparently with a hatchet. Then he removed some of the boards between his cell and the storeroom, broke a window in the kitchen, and escaped.

As he was leaving the jail, Homan stole three sacks of gold dust, a watch, a pistol, two pairs of boots, one pair of pants, one cap, one knife, and a carpet sack. These items all belonged to the jail keeper, who offered a personal reward of $500 for Homan's capture. Surprisingly, Homan didn't burn down the jail as he was leaving.

It took two months to find and apprehend Homan. His court appearance was short and the sentence severe: ten years in jail with hard labour.

There is no record of whether the jail keeper's stolen property was returned to him or whether three sacks of gold dust remain hidden at the base of a pine tree somewhere in Lytton.

The Capital of British Columbia?

On October 13, 1866, *The British Colonist* waded in on a debate about whether Lytton should become the capital of British Columbia. To understand how this came about, a brief history lesson is in order.

In 1849, the Crown Colony of Vancouver Island was formed to bolster British claims to the Island and adjacent Gulf Islands, and to provide a port for the Royal British Navy at Fort Victoria. The remainder of what is present-day British Columbia was an unorganized territory under the control of the Hudson's Bay Company.

On August 2, 1858, the Crown Colony of British Columbia was created by the British Columbia Act. This act marked the transition from a Hudson's Bay Company fur kingdom to a gold colony for much of the province. The next year, New Westminster was officially designated the capital of the new Crown colony by its governor, James Douglas.

The new Crown colony excluded all the land on Vancouver Island and the Gulf Islands, which, of course, was its own official colony. It also excluded much of the northern part of the province, regions east of the Rocky Mountains, and all of the other coastal islands.

Governor James Douglas administrated both the Crown Colony of British Columbia and the Crown Colony of Vancouver Island with an iron fist from Victoria, the capital of the Crown Colony of Vancouver Island. He cared little for New Westminster.

In 1864, when Douglas stepped down, Frederick Seymour became governor. The two colonies were officially united two years later (1866) and Victoria was designated the capital.

The decision wasn't made without antics in the House of Assembly. On the day of the vote on whether the capital should be in New Westminster or Victoria, one member of the assembly, a Victoria supporter, did his best to foil an opponent's speech. He shuffled the pages of the speech, so the speaker lost his place and read the first paragraph three times. Then, the lenses suspiciously popped out of the speaker's glasses, so the poor New Westminster supporter could see nothing at all of his shuffled speech. After a recess to settle the resulting uproar and allow the member a chance to sort out his speaking notes and his spectacles, the speaker of the assembly (also a Victoria supporter) refused to allow him a second chance to speak. The subsequent vote was 13 to 8 against New Westminster.

Lytton in 1865, a year before a petition asking that it become the capital of the colonies

For three years from 1866 to 1869, Frederick Seymour acted as governor of the amalgamated colonies that were unofficially known as the United Colonies of Vancouver Island and British Columbia.

Although Victoria was the official capital, a debate raged about the location of the capital of the united colonies. Some politicians and residents were convinced it was best served near the population centres of New Westminster or Victoria, but others wanted it located in the Interior. A petition urging the government to make Lytton the capital stirred the boiling pot for a while.

The British Colonist newspaper commented on the idea of making Lytton the capital of the United Colonies of British Columbia on October 13, 1866:

Lytton City as the Capital of the United Colonies

A petition is being circulated for signature in the interior of British Columbia, praying Her Majesty's Government to establish the capital of the united Colonies at the town of Lytton, which is situated at the confluence of the Thompson with the Fraser River. Report states that the document was being Numerously signed; but we cannot believe that, outside of the district intended to be most benefited by the removal of the seat of Government to that locality, a dozen men will be found willing to affix their names to a paper that prefers such an unreasonable request. The only argument that can be advanced in favor of Lytton as the capital, is that its location is central. In every other respect, there is not a hamlet on the Lower Fraser that does not possess advantages superior to those it has to offer. For nearly four months of the year the town is almost unapproachable from the lower country, and until a railroad has taken the place of the wagon road, and the iron horse has superseded the patient pack animal, it is folly to imagine that the prayer has any chance of success.

Besides, supposing that Lytton be an excellent location for the capital, there are no Government Buildings for the accommodation of the officials, and the financial state of the country is such that it cannot allow to erect the necessary buildings. What Lytton may become ten or twelve years hence, is another matter; but it certainly offers small inducements at present for the establishment of the capital there; and any man who holds it out as a bait to the Lyttonites has too much sense to believe that it will be carried out—at least, during his time.

Of course, Lytton never became the capital of BC. But, what if the CPR had replaced the Cariboo Wagon Road in, say, 1868? Or what if it stopped snowing in the Fraser Canyon in the winter? Imagine if you can, Lytton, not Victoria, as the capital of British Columbia.

Chinese Joss House

A vacant lot at the south end of Main Street in Lytton was once the location of a Chinese joss temple.

A story about the temple appeared in *The Sunday Province* a long time ago (circa 1920). George M. Murray, a journalist with the *Province* and later a newspaperman and publisher in his own right, wrote the article. Murray lived in China for several years, and perhaps the following article reflected his concern with and interest in the plight of the Chinese in BC.

Murray also served as a BC Liberal MLA for many years (beginning in 1933) and as a federal member of Parliament. He and his famous outspoken wife, "Ma Murray," co-founded the *Bridge River-Lillooet News* in 1934. Ma Murray is a Lillooet legend.

Here is the intriguing story that was provided to me by Joe Chute of Lytton; unfortunately, the precise date that it was written could not be determined.

Gods in a Lytton Woodshed
by George M. Murray

The Chinese Republic had made protests to Great Britain and to Ottawa about it; but the Chinese joss house at Lytton has passed legally into the hands of Signor Guiseppe Taverna, native son of Italy and as reliable a track patrolman as the Canadian Pacific Railway employs.

It took twenty-one long years to win the joss house. And now the Chinese gods and goddesses, tenants there since 1881, rest in Taverna's woodshed. Every son of Han in interior British Columbia is angry about it. The Chinese consul at Vancouver has written strong words about it to home government at Nanking, and Nanking has written the British and Canadian authorities about it. But Taverna, a man with an iron will, has won out. He now owns the joss house. And to prove that a devout Christian respects even the idols of old China, the Lytton deities are now snugly housed by Taverna free of cost.

The story of the Chinese joss house at Lytton is officially recorded in the land office at Kamloops. There is a file of letters there, some inches thick, which give in detail the various steps in the struggle of Guiseppe Taverna to obtain the land and building so sacred to the Chinese of the district. Taverna was next door to the joss house. He had a small lot. His family was growing. He looked across the fence and dreamed of the day when he would be able to extend his boundaries and annex the joss house properties.

What was a joss house more or less? Taverna thought to himself. The Chinese pay little attention to it. Some days they come, bring a fat pig or chicken or imitation money and place it before one of the idols there. They light a taper, burn some incense and go away. Then the tramps come from the main line freight trains, smell the cooked pork or chicken, enter stealthily, and then help the spirits hovering about the gods and goddesses to consume the sacrificial offerings.

This went on year after year. The fruit trees in Taverna's yard spread their branches over the fence above the ground of the Chinese joss house. The Taverna grapevine was as anxious as its owner to get possession of the adjoining land.

In 1901 Guiseppe Taverna addressed a letter to the Dominion land agent at Kamloops "Re: Lot 2, Block 13, Town of Lytton." Upon which was a certain house owned by Chinese, the house being a frame building, 18 by 27, on a lot of 50 feet by 33. In this letter he stated the lot and building was Dominion property, since the Chinese had no deed to the land.

At once the Dominion land agent looked into the matter. He consulted with the late Tom Earl, the rancher, one of Lytton's oldest residents, who had planted the first orchard in that part of the country. The late Mr. Earl informed the government agent that the Chinese had taken over the property there previous to 1881. There had been an epidemic among Chinese on C.P.R. construction and among Chinese miners along the Fraser and in the Cariboo. The late Mr. Earl said that the leader had decided that the ancient gods were merely expressing anger because British Columbia Chinese had forsaken the gods of their ancestors.

In the records it was found that the first entry covering the land and joss house was made in 1901, when the following Chinese had made application to purchase Lot 2, Block 13, Lytton: Hong Wo, Wo Pin, Foo Sang, Lee Seen, and Lou Alaak.

Taverna continued to apply to the land office for purchase of the lot. He, or his agents, wrote letter after letter. Taverna alleged that the lot was an eyesore. The building, he said (in 1911) would soon fall down of its own weight. The furnishings—which included Kwan Yen, goddess of mercy; Shen Nung, god of cereals and the god of medicine—were said of Taverna to be of no value whatsoever.

Kwan Yen, goddess of mercy, gives courage to her worshippers. She is the taking-away-fear goddess. Her powers must have passed to Taverna, because he went ahead fearlessly to gain control of the joss house property. The god of medicine must have had a beneficent influence on Taverna's household. At any rate his family continued to increase and his need for more land continued more imperative. The god of medicine controls the six virtues—wisdom, benevolence, magnanimity, righteousness, loyalty and harmony. All these virtues Guiseppe Taverna possessed and enjoyed as he went daily to his task on the C.P.R.: but he did want that joss house.

In 1917 the Dominion Government instructed the Kamloops land office to ascertain at once the value of the joss house. This was the result of a fiery letter written by the minister of the Interior of that time by the late Mr. James Murphy, Ashcroft lawyer, brother of Mr. Justice Murphy of Vancouver. The late James Murphy had known Taverna for many years. Mr. Murphy was of Irish extraction, Taverna was a true son of Italy. Mr. Murphy had a keen sense of humour, and from the records at Kamloops entered heartily into the fight to gain the sacred edifice for his friend and client.

Adding to the correspondence from Mr. Murphy are further letters from Taverna. In 1918 there is a letter with Taverna's mark alleging "it is a fire trap. Tramps go there to sleep and eat. They throw matches and cigarettes about. If it burns, my own house will burn as well and maybe all of Lytton. There will be loss of life."

Mr. Murphy pointed out in 1918 that "Forty years ago hundreds of Chinese washed gold in that locality. The building was of value to them then, but had recently been more or less forsaken." Despite all this, the Dominion Government refused to move. In 1919 the

Kamloops office was asked for a further report. The report went to Ottawa that the Chinese residents then in Lytton believed that while the joss house was not much use, that if it was destroyed the Chinese believed that they might all get sick again as they or their people did in 1881. The government of Sir Robert Borden apparently felt that it was no time, with the war being on, to arouse the anger of the Chinese gods in British Columbia. They left the Lytton joss house alone.

Chinese joss house is above the word "Lytton" in this photo from the early 1900's

Time passed, and in 1927, Taverna, having learned to read and write since he first began to apply for the lot, wrote in a bold script to Ottawa a letter, in which he said: "Children play in the joss house. Tramps sleep there. I offer $35 for the property."

Then J.W. Benzie, homestead inspector, was ordered to report on the matter. He did so, declaring that the joss house itself was but 18 by 27 feet of frame. It would make a good chicken house. He suggested a valuation of $50.

The joss house was put for sale in 1928 at 2 pm, at the Globe Hotel, Lytton. The sum of $42 was bid by Taverna. H.J. Parker, Dominion land agent at Kamloops, duly reported the holding of

the sale to Ottawa.

Taverna also wrote to Ottawa asking what he should do with the building in that year.

No sooner had the sale been held than Chinese began to appear from all parts of the West to visit the joss house, to offer sacrifices before the idols which continued as tenants.

Mr. Chenhow H. Pao, then consul-general for the Republic of China at Vancouver, addressed a letter to the Government of Canada, alleging that the contents of the joss house were valued at $3,000 and that the building and contents belonged to the Chinese Benevolent Association.

Then Mr. Parker reported again to Ottawa that "the building was very old and dilapidated, and it would not pay to have the building demolished." A patent was duly issued to Taverna in 1928.

The Chinese consul-general then replied, "It is true the building was very old and dilapidated, but has been repaired by the Chinese occasionally from time to time. It is unreasonably unfair to state the building has not been in use for twenty years. It is well decorated and the furniture is worth $1,000."

The records further show that Chenhow H. Pao then reported the whole matter to Nanking to the government of President Sun Yat Sen.

Meanwhile, [the] Chinese warned Taverna personally not to move the gods or goddesses. Taverna did remove the gods and goddesses to his own woodshed. He then took over the Chinese joss house and converted it into a fine chicken house. Where the God of cereals, Shen Nung, once sat and received offerings, Taverna now throws scratch feed to his numerous fowls. A rooster crows where the god of anger once leered and winked. On land where Chinese of other days brought offerings of imitation money for the gods, Taverna now, by his energy and thrift, derives an income of real money. Tramps can no longer plunder the premises because the doors are well locked.

But over the entire property still hovers the spirit of evicted gods and goddesses. They rest under that cover of the Italian's roof. But Taverna fears to destroy them and also dislikes the idea of continuing to board them. He might sell them, but he is not sure that he owns them. He came by them lawfully enough, he feels. But then, a god or goddess is not anyone's property. Such deities are of the other world, the Chinese believe. They are not real estate and they surely are not holdings and they cannot be classed as furniture.

The latest development in this strange case is that the Chinese continue to claim ownership of all that pertains to this certain joss house at Lytton. They are not unduly loud in their protests about it. They are not going to court about it. But officially the matter is not yet disposed of as between the consul-general's office at Vancouver and the land office at Kamloops.

Chinese point to the unemployment menace which affects the Chinese community of British Columbia so severely, and declare that neglect of their gods is not unconnected with the present plight of Chinese labourers. There is not a wholesale dying off as in the eighties, when the building of the Lytton joss house helped to stay the hand of the Grim Reaper. But who can say what the future has in store. Taverna has not come under any blight as a result of disturbing the peace of the gods and goddesses. He and his family have flourished to the full. True, the death of Mr. James Murphy, the talented Ashcroft lawyer, who helped Taverna win the house, was under tragic circumstances. Many of the employees of the Dominion land office lost their positions at Kamloops when the railway belt, in which the joss house stood, came under provincial jurisdiction. But that may or may not be connected with the affair.

The provincial god of the lot, Shen Nung, became a deity 2,825 years before Christ. The god of the six virtues has ruled over happy families in China for more than 5,000 years.

Nicomen's popular roadhouse in 1870

8 Towns along the River

Lytton, Spences Bridge, Ashcroft, and Savona have remained as towns with distinctive personalities in the Thompson River corridor. Nicomen never blossomed into a full-fledged village although it is historically very significant, and Walhachin has seen sporadic development in the past decade but its heyday was 100 years ago.

Nicomen

In a way, the stimulus for the eventual creation of British Columbia belongs to the First Nations village at Nicomen.

Although the first discovery of gold in what is now British Columbia occurred in 1833, at a stream that emptied into Okanagan Lake, the news never reached the masses and no gold rush ensued.

However, in 1856 a major gold discovery took place on the Thompson River, a few hundred metres below the mouth of the Nicoamen River. Discovered by members of the Nicomen Indian Band, fine and coarse gold, including a gold nugget, were catalysts for the great Fraser Canyon Gold Rush of 1858.

The Hudson's Bay Company sent 800 ounces of gold by ship from the Thompson and other sources to San Francisco for assaying. It arrived in February 1858. The great California Gold Rush had recently petered out and thousands of men were idle, looking for something to do and somewhere to do it. Word about the gold's arrival spread like wildfire.

Within a few months, more than 30,000 miners converged on the almost uninhabited wilderness of what is now British Columbia, changing it forever.

Nicomen too changed, almost overnight. A roadhouse for travellers was built. Miners staked the area, and a mining community sprang up around the many mining claims and workings that dotted the landscape. For a while, the area was even known as Nicomen Mines.

The roadhouse's claim to fame was a visit from Governor Douglas in 1860. He apparently enjoyed a hearty breakfast before moving on down the horse trail to Lytton. A gristmill near the mouth of the Nicoamen River ground wheat for the many residents, and visitors and BX had a horse stable and rest area here a few years later. (Barnard's Express, later known as the British Columbia Express Company or BX, was a pioneer transportation company from 1861 until 1921. You'll read more about it in Chapter 10.)

During the construction of the Lytton to Spences Bridge section of the Cariboo Wagon Road in 1863, the contractor Walter Moberly stationed a construction crew here.

When the CPR arrived almost 20 years later, Nicomen became Thompson Siding and a colourful couple, the Clements, operated the roadhouse. Mrs. Clement was a strong woman who took no nonsense from anyone, particularly boisterous men.

Nicomen increased in importance and grew to be a small village when railway construction began. In 1882, it boasted two hotels, the one near the mouth of the river owned by Arthur Clemes, a Spences Bridge resident. Clemes also ran the BX stables located a few kilometres north of Nicomen.

While at Nicomen, Clemes raised pigs as a side business, probably selling them to the Chinese railway workers, who considered them a great delicacy. His employer at the Express office did not want employees moonlighting so Clemes moved to Spences Bridge, where he took over the management of a hotel.

More recently, construction crews for upgrades to the Fraser Canyon Highway camped at Nicomen. Long-time Lyttonite Lloyd Dodge worked for the BC Public Works Department as a cook's helper in 1942. One of his jobs was to retrieve the butter and meat from a cooler that was anchored in the river under the bridge.

Another long-time Lytton resident, Francis Van Dyke, purchased the Nicomen property in the 1960s and lived here until his house burned to the ground a decade later. He discovered a skull and some bones on a corner of the property in the 1970s; an archaeological dig ensued that identified 22 graves. Evidence uncovered at the Van Dyke site indicates that a trade link existed between the Nicomen and Kootenay people more than 300 years ago. These were mobile peoples.

Chinese workers stayed in a tent camp at Nicomen during the CPR construction in the 1880's.
Courtesy Public Archives Canada Photo #C

Chinese railway construction camp at Nicomen in 1884

Recently, Kumsheen Rafting Resort purchased the Nicomen property to provide a scenic and historic luncheon stop for rafting guests. Rafters walk up from the river to the old Van Dyke building that has received a radical facelift. The Globe Hotel, which presided over downtown Lytton in 1858, was the inspiration behind the reconstruction.

Today, no more mining occurs here, nobody pans for gold, and the closest thing to a roadhouse is the Old Globe Hotel replica and the RV Park.

Spences Bridge

Prior to the Fraser Canyon Gold Rush that began in 1858, Spences Bridge was inhabited only by First Nations and sporadically by the fur traders.

In 1858, everything changed. Almost overnight, the "Little Forks," as Spences Bridge was referred to in HBC journals and early maps, became an important junction of two paths used by miners and by cattlemen who drove their large herds of cattle from points south through Spences Bridge to the Cariboo.

Crossing the Thompson prior to 1859 was not a simple task, and foot travellers had to rely on local natives who willingly assisted with their canoes.

In 1859, two Americans, Mortimer Cook and Charles Kimball, built and operated a reaction ferry using a rope strung across the river to which they tethered their craft. Cook also opened a store, and with Kimball's departure the following year, the growing community became known as Cook's Ferry, a name that stuck for almost 25 years. The completion of the Cariboo Wagon Road in 1863 from Lytton to Spences Bridge meant a bridge across the Thompson needed to be built. Entrepreneur Thomas Spence and his friend, Arthur Stevenson (later the government road superintendent), constructed the first bridge across the Thompson as a private initiative, charging a toll to cross.

The community grew and prospered and by 1882, a vibrant hamlet existed. The 1882–1883 British Columbia Directory listed 44 names on page 291 under Spences Bridge District and described the community as follows:

> *At Cook's Ferry, on the left bank of the River, there is a post office and telegraph station; also a good Inn with excellent accommodation, and close by it is a blacksmith's establishment of great repute; also two stores for general merchandise, notably that of Mr. Mno. Murray's on the north side. On the flat overlooking this cluster of dwellings and places of business, the Railway Company have their buildings. The road to Nicola Valley turns off at Cook's Ferry, and crossing the Nicola bridge follows a fair wagon road. The Thompson is at least 300 feet wide at Spence's Bridge, a beautiful structure which rests on a number of piers with cut water fronts, and is capable of resisting an enormous water pressure. Quite a little settlement at this point exists. Morton's Hotel might grace a city, the garden adjoining is filled with every variety of annual flowers, and produces all kinds of fruit and vegetables, and will yield this year some hundreds of pounds of grapes of finest quality. There is also a tinsmith's store on this side, and excellent stables for horses attached to the Inn.* (www.vpl.ca/bccd/index.php/browse/title/1882-1883/British_Columbia_Directory)

By 1883, CPR construction crews arrived in town and local merchants benefitted from the increased activity brought about by the hundreds of workers needed to build the railway.

Arthur Clemes, a prominent Spences Bridge personage at the time, began a business venture a few miles downstream at Nicomen before moving to Spences Bridge.

Gradually he acquired numerous properties and businesses including a new hotel, a general store, orchards, and management of the post office. After purchasing the Murray property and orchards in 1890, he experimented with new apple varieties and even won prizes for his apple displays in international exhibitions.

His expansive new hotel in 1892, at the site of the current Spences Bridge Hotel, had a strong Mexican flavour with a motif that was suitable for the dry, brown grass and sagebrush-covered hills of Spences Bridge. He later added a pool room and dance hall to the centrepiece of the community.

Spences Bridge riverside hotel in 1887

Prior to moving into the Interior, Clemes had purchased property in Vancouver, then just worthless undeveloped land. Before the turn of the century, however, his property in Vancouver was under development. This included prime real estate at the corner of Georgia and Hamilton streets. He also owned hotels, theatres, and other buildings in Vancouver and New Westminster.

In 1898, Clemes travelled to Europe and attended the World Automotive Exposition in Paris. He spotted a new horseless carriage that was under development in Europe, and one caught his eye—a 1904 two-seater, single-cylinder, 6HP Wolseley. He immediately ordered the car for shipment to Spences Bridge.

It took a few years, but his car and Clemes travelled by steamer to BC, then by rail to Spences Bridge. The tiny car did not have the power to climb steep, rough grades and often had to be pushed to get anywhere. Roads, of course, were in poor shape and simply didn't exist in a lot of places.

The car made the people of Spences Bridge proud, and although it was impractical because of its limitations, Clemes drove it in May Day and other parades for years. The vintage car remained in the Clemes family for generations, and then became focal point of the Kamloops Museum's heritage automotive display.

Clemes was largely responsible for establishing the Spences Bridge Light and Power Company. This utility company constructed a turbine just west of town at Murray Creek Falls, diverted water through a pipe at the top of the falls, and ran it through the turbine, generating electricity for the community. The little utility company was taken over by BC Electric (later BC Hydro) in 1953.

Clemes died in 1922 at age 70. His obituary labelled him "Owner of Spences Bridge."

Ashcroft

Few people know that "Saint Cloud" was the original name for the cluster of farms that later became Ashcroft. Probably named after one of the wealthiest towns in France, St. Cloud was also where Napoleon Bonaparte led a coup d'état in 1799. The Bonaparte River just upstream from Ashcroft was named to honour Napoleon, and perhaps local wealthy farmers, to flaunt the significance of their diminutive locale, in 1868 chose the name St. Cloud.

In fact, no town as such existed at its present location until 1884, the year that the CPR construction crews arrived. For 20 years before that, Ashcroft referred to the Cornwall brothers' ranch and roadhouse on the main Cariboo Road far above the river and to the west of town.

The early history of Ashcroft is closely linked to an American from Kentucky, John Christopher Barnes. He moved north from the California Gold Rush in 1858 and prospected for gold along the Fraser River, then worked as a road builder and later as a packer on the Cariboo Wagon Road and as a surveyor for the CPR. He took up farming along the Thompson River in 1868 with an American friend, F.W. Brink.

Several large ranches were already established in the vicinity of the Bonaparte River, near Hat Creek, upstream along the Thompson and to the west of present-day Ashcroft. Bunchgrass flourished and was perfect for raising beef cattle and feeding horses and mules used on the Cariboo Wagon Road. Cattle ranchers had a ready market for their beef, especially during the Cariboo Gold Rush.

The Barnes and Brink ranch included the future townsite of Ashcroft and extended a few miles along the river and toward the Highland Valley to the east. Their ranch diversified and prospered by selling fruit, vegetables, cattle, horses, and hay to neighbouring towns and ranches.

In 1883, a government-run ferry operated on the Thompson, connecting the east and west sides of the river at the Barnes ranch. It was still unknown exactly where the CPR would be located, but Barnes was an entrepreneur and he worked on a CPR survey crew so he had a better idea than most where the track would be laid. He and his friend Oliver Evans (Brinks died unexpectedly in 1879) constructed the Thompson River Hotel, where the ferry tied up on the east side, hoping to take advantage of the anticipated railway boom.

Evans and his wife became the hotel proprietors in January 1884. That summer, railway construction reached St. Cloud, and Barnes and Evans watched as the CPR built a log bunkhouse and a station. Much to their chagrin, it was built on the flat above the river away from their new hotel. Wanting to be adjacent to the railway, they simply jacked up the hotel, put it on skids, hooked a large team of horses to the structure, and dragged it to its new home next to the railway station. They christened it with a new name—the Ashcroft Hotel.

Meanwhile, Evans surveyed lots on his farmland that quickly sold to people and businesses wanting to settle in the area. Government surveyors arrived to decide the location for the future bridge across the Thompson, thus cementing Ashcroft's importance as a future railhead for the Cariboo. Bridge construction quickly followed as did a connecting road from town to the Cariboo Wagon Road to the west.

In 1885, the Ashcroft post office relocated from the Cornwall ranch down into St. Cloud, and with that move, the present town of Ashcroft originated. Apparently no tears were shed but it's fun to speculate whether St. Cloud would have followed in the footsteps of its French counterpart and emerged as the wealthiest town of the Interior. Move over, Kelowna…

Cariboo freight team stuck in the mud in Ashcroft

With the arrival of the CPR, the town became the railhead for the Cariboo and points north. Barnard's Express (BX) assessed the business opportunity and relocated its head office from Yale to Ashcroft in 1886. BX bought 500 horses and mules from the Harper Ranch in the Chilcotin (present-day Gang Ranch) for its stagecoaches and freight wagons, and from then on, Ashcroft—the hub of the Interior—was mile zero on the Cariboo Wagon Road.

The following year, heavy freight wagons pulled by oxen and mules crossed the bridge and plodded up the long, steep hill out of Ashcroft, headed for the wagon road a few miles to the west. On Mondays, Wednesdays, and Fridays, the fast passenger carriages pulled out of town, drawn by adrenalin-charged horses headed for Barkerville, a three-day trip.

In no time at all Ashcroft was flourishing. There were warehouses, blacksmith shops, saloons, general merchandise stores, and four Chinese businesses. After it was overhauled and a new floor, door, desks, and windows were installed, a school was created out of the old bunkhouse originally built for the CPR construction workers in 1884.

Several hotels sprang up and competed with the Ashcroft Hotel, including one that was dismantled in Yale and reassembled in Ashcroft. Shortly after assembly, it blew over onto its side during the first big freak windstorm. No problem—it was pulled upright again, and when anchored to solid footings it fared much better.

By the turn of the century, Ashcroft was in its heyday with more than 600 residents. It boasted eight Chinese businesses, three churches, a bank, a county court, and its own Water, Electric, and Improvement Company. A plant located on the Bonaparte River generated electricity that serviced most houses. The BC Electric Company took over the plant in 1953. Many small BC towns weren't serviced by electricity until the 1940s or '50s.

Water pumped from the Thompson River into two 50,000-gallon tanks 250 feet above the town supplied residents with fresh, clean, gravity-fed domestic water. Five mining companies were active in the area including one that mined coal in the Hat Creek valley and supplied residents with energy for their stoves, fireplaces, and furnaces.

A key to Ashcroft's growing economy was the bridge across the Thompson. The first one was built in 1884, replacing the reaction ferry service established around 1860. The first bridge was swept away in the flood of 1894, the highest water level ever recorded on the Thompson River. The same flood also tore the Savona and Spences Bridge structures from their foundations and inflicted serious damage to the Lytton Bridge. (Its decking float away but its piers remained, albeit badly damaged.)

For a few months, it was impossible to get the cable across the river to revive the reaction ferry because of the extremely high water conditions. A rowboat served as a ferry in the interim. Until the completion of the new bridge in 1895, all the freight unloaded from the CPR that was heading north was loaded onto the reaction ferry and floated across the river for BX freight wagons. The 1895 bridge lasted 12 years. In 1907, a new bridge was built that in turn was replaced by the 1931 steel bridge. The current structure was built in 1985.

The collapse of the Cariboo mining boom, World War I, and the construction of the Pacific Great Northern Railway and the Grand Trunk Pacific Railway were the main catalysts for Ashcroft's gradual economic decline. The railway tore the heart out of BX's core business—the moving of freight. No longer was there as much freight to move north to the gold fields, and what was there was now shared with the very competitive railway.

A disastrous fire in 1916 razed most main street businesses, and following the fire the soul was torn out of the previously booming community. But all was not lost, and the community rallied after the fire. BX converted their freight shed into a tomato cannery, and a new industry developed in Ashcroft. The community became known for its tomatoes, potatoes, and pumpkins. Additionally, disease-free potatoes and alfalfa seeds were exported widely.

Epsom salt plant was built to the west soon after, and a few decades later Bethlehem Copper opened a mine to the east of town. Mining has been the backbone of the community ever since.

Then BX lost the mail contract to another business that did not use Ashcroft as its central depot. The bankruptcy of the British Columbia Express Company in 1921 was the nail in Ashcroft's coffin.

Ashcroft's fortunes have risen and fallen many times, but the town has survived. It has a deeply entrenched personality that is reflected in the town's heritage buildings and the people who proudly flaunt its history.

Car in front of the Ashcroft Hotel in the early 1900s

Walhachin

In 1907, Charles Barnes, an American land surveyor living in Ashcroft, had a vision: he dreamed of starting a special high-end community and converting a desert into an oasis.

His idea was to entice well-bred, wealthy Englishmen and women to fulfill his dream and pad his bank account. The plan was to sell the estates to settler families, specifically upper-class and upper-middle-class English families, the second son of whom often was encouraged to make his own way in the world.

State-of-the-art farm machinery plowed the fields

Barnes travelled to Victoria and met with the B.C. Development Association—a company controlled by upper-crust British businessmen—that owned development properties in various parts of the province. They bought into Barnes' idea and formed two subsidiary companies, one to build and manage the townsite, and the other to build and manage the irrigation system and croplands. Barnes took charge of the cropland development.

In 1908, a survey of the future town was completed. The company purchased 4,500 acres of land on both sides of the Thompson. The townsite was on the south side, and most of the growing land was on the benches on the north.

The land purchase included ranch property owned by Charles Pennie, a rancher with a very small orchard and a large cattle ranch with mostly undeveloped land. According to *The Ashcroft Journal*, Pennie was paid a premium for his ranch, almost 200 times more than the going rate.

The development company paid for the construction cost of the town that eventually included four-room houses, a hotel, three laundries, a bakery, general store, barber, butcher shop, dairy, livery stable, women's store, two insurance offices, a post office, and a packing house. Imported state-of-the-art tractors ploughed and prepared the soil for 35,000 seedling fruit trees.

Through an elaborate series of flumes, aqueducts, and ditches, water from the upper Deadman River flowed 22 miles to the farms and into

First-class dining room of the Walhachin hotel

town. The water system proved to be the Achilles' heel of the project.

As a name for the town, the developers chose *Walhachin*, a native word that the promotional brochure interpreted as "abundance of the earth." In fact, it more properly meant "land of the round rock."

By 1910, 56 settlers lived in Walhachin, with at least as many workers living in the surrounding area.

Initially, filler crops of potatoes, tomatoes, corn, and onions grew between the trees as they matured. Record vegetable crops developed.

Crops like barley and even tobacco flourished. Other specialty operations like poultry farms kept residents supplied with fresh fowl and produce.

Meanwhile, as the fruit and vegetables grew, the upper-class English settlers enjoyed the life of the aristocracy. They formed a golf club, a cricket club, a hunting club (chasing coyotes instead of the English fox), a tennis club, a hockey club, and a football (soccer) club. Fancy balls and dances and music recitals in the community hall, which claimed to have the springiest floor in BC, occurred regularly.

The highest-ranking English nobleman, Lord Anglesey, who was still only in his twenties, built an elaborate house with 12-foot ceilings, French doors, and indoor plumbing.

While the wealthy landowners played, the Chinese, First Nations, and local workers performed hard manual labour and often provided the only fruit and vegetable farming expertise. Most of the estate owners relied on money from home, and only one in six performed any labour on their farm. The remainder learned little about the land they owned and were often helpless in a crisis.

By 1913, the first fruit was ready to ship to market. However, the dream was slowly unravelling. Difficulty in getting the fruit and produce to market before it rotted and competition with lower American prices made many of the estates unprofitable. Higher than anticipated maintenance costs to the water system compounded the problem.

Then, an early cold winter rolled in. Frosts and strong winds killed many of the trees. Some apple varieties were not suitable for the climate, and all the soft fruits were a veritable writeoff because of the cold wind and temperatures. In addition, the soil was not particularly rich in nutrients, and the early filler crops planted between the rows of trees robbed the soil of essential nutrients needed by the young fruit trees.

However, the irrigation system caused the biggest problems. The foundations of the flumes were poorly built, and the troughs were built using multiple-length, poor-grade lumber. Washouts that should have created minor repairs instead caused the destruction of huge sections of the flumes. They leaked everywhere, and maintenance was nonstop and expensive.

By 1914, seven years after the birth of the idea, 150 settlers inhabited the new community, including 40 women. The same number of workers and Chinese domestics also resided within a daily commute.

Suddenly, a nightmare occurred: World War I broke out in Europe. Dedicated to King and country, 97 of the eligible 107 young men hurried home to England, anticipating a short, victorious war.

The few old men left behind to care and manage the estates lacked the experience, skill, and finances to accomplish their complicated tasks. To make matters worse, a relatively small landslide wiped out a mile of the water flumes because of the defective design and construction.

With no water, no crops grew. With no crops to sell, no income to pay for rising expenses existed. No income, no upper-crust friends—no reason to remain in Walhachin.

According to Kamloops historian Joan Weir, and contrary to local legend, most of the upper-crust young men survived the war and returned to Walhachin after the war. To their utter dismay, they discovered an inoperable irrigation system and non-producing orchards.

To complicate matters, the Marquis of Anglesey became the new majority owner of Walhachin, and his appointment of an affable but incompetent new manager demoralized returning settlers. They quickly lost faith in the manager, and when the quote for the repairs to the irrigation system came in at $250,000, they packed their bags and headed back to England.

By 1922, Walhachin was deserted.

Savona

Savona began as a First Nations wintering village at the west end of Kamloops Lake. Using dugout canoes made from cottonwood trees, the natives were at home on the lake and occasionally ventured down the Thompson River.

The HBC journals referred to these people as the Boute du Lac Indians (literally translated as end-of-the-lake Indians). The fur traders had little reason to cross the Thompson at this location, and when they did, the friendly natives lent them their canoes.

A drowning occurred here in 1841. A disgruntled native boy from the Shuswap tribe had murdered HBC chief factor Samuel Black, the chief administrator in charge of Fort Kamloops at the time. After many missions by the HBC to find the murderer, he was finally apprehended with the help of one of his own people. Travelling back to the fort with their prisoner, the group had to cross at Boute du Lac in native canoes.

While crossing the Thompson, the fugitive saw more of his own people lined up on the opposite shore, waiting to take him to the Hudson's Bay post, and ultimately to his death. He overturned the canoe and floated along with the current, singing his death song, and was shot by someone on shore.

The gold rush in 1858 brought close to 30,000 miners into the Interior of BC, many of them coming overland through the Okanagan and north to Kamloops following the Fur Brigade Trail. Boute du Lac became an important crossing point for the miners who were on their way to the lower Thompson and Fraser Rivers.

The need for a crossing device was obvious to François Saveneux, the Savona entrepreneur mentioned in Chapter 2. Although little is known of his early life or career, one story elevated him to being an Italian from a beautiful township in Genoa, Italy, named Savona. He more likely was French Canadian.

Savona with the HBC post and reaction ferry cable in 1871

The spelling of his name depended on the whims of the HBC clerk or the newspaper recording it. Spellings included Savannah, Savonah, Savenner, Saveneux, and Savona. The name Savona (pronounced Sa-va-na) stuck. Although the spelling of his name varied, he was almost always referred to as a Frenchman.

Savona began his ferry service in 1858 in conjunction with an HBC wharf and warehouse on the north shore. His original boat could be described as a very small barge, substantial enough for one or two men and their horses, but not large enough to ferry cattle. Livestock swam across the river. His business grew and prospered.

He married a very practical and hard-working local young lady who quickly joined him as a ferry operator. Their ferry business grew, and in the fall of 1861, when Savona's health was failing, he hired an assistant operator. In 1862, the Savona's Ferry post office opened, and the name stuck for many years.

His premature death, reported in *The British Colonist* in Victoria on Christmas Day 1862, did not provide an exact date or cause of his passing. His widow continued to operate and manage the ferry after his death.

In 1866, the Royal Engineers completed a wagon road from Cache Creek to Savona's Ferry, and a new, larger ferry capable of carrying wagons and freight was put into service. By 1870, the provincial government had taken over the ferry operation.

High water was a particularly dangerous time to operate the ferry, and it broke free in 1875, 1878, and 1879. The last time was tragic—it resulted in the death of a retired HBC employee riding the ferry as it broke free from the cable.

Requests for a bridge were repeatedly made, but not until the CPR construction gangs arrived in 1883 was anything done. The bridge was completed in 1884 at a cost of $15,250.

High water four years later almost washed the bridge away, but the monstrous flood of 1894 tore it from its footings and floated the entire structure down the river. It wasn't rebuilt until 1906. In the meantime, another reaction ferry, with a new cable and new scow, was summoned back into service.

With the arrival of the railway crews in 1883, a village was laid out on the south bank. Additionally, a Chinese camp of up to 1,000 men was clustered around the railway. The population of villagers on the north shore of the lake also increased.

In 1883, a large hotel called Lakeview House opened in old Savona. It did exceptionally well during the construction period of the CPR and with the opening of the first bridge across the Thompson. A few years later, it was advertised as a fishing resort, and business was brisk enough to require an addition to be added. It became a popular, short-holiday destination for

Kamloops businessmen. They regularly bragged in the Kamloops *Sentinel* newspaper about the size and quantity of fish they caught in the Thompson River and in Kamloops Lake.

The growing village and CPR station on the south shore was christened Port Van Horne in honour of Sir William C. Van Horne, a general manager of the CPR. He apparently considered it an insult rather than a compliment for such a small settlement to carry his name. However, the name stuck until 1910, when the CPR changed the station's name to Savona.

Obviously, most of the action was close to the CPR so eventually most of the little north shore village relocated itself to the south bank. Legend has it that many buildings were simply skidded across the frozen lake during the winter. Other structures were dismantled and barged across, piece by piece.

Locals continued to call the community Savona's Ferry until at least the mid-1920s, and in 1927, the name Savona for the post office and train station was officially adopted by the BC government.

The 1906 bridge lasted only two years and had to be replaced. In 1929, a steel structure replaced the 1908 bridge, and a new bridge in 1956 replaced the previous one.

I remember driving across the '56 bridge because the deck was constructed of sectional steel grates and the vehicle tires made a strange humming, buzzing noise when crossing. The present bridge was built in 1993. I miss that old bridge.

A gold dredge floats by as natives mine for gold

9 Events along the River

Discovery of Gold

Although not the first location where gold was discovered, the Thompson River was pivotal in creating the Fraser Canyon Gold Rush of 1858.

The first discovery of gold in what is now British Columbia occurred in 1833, at a stream that flows into Okanagan Lake (probably Mission Creek). This finding predates the epochal discoveries in California (1848) and Australia (1851), but news of this find did not spread to the outside world.

David Douglas, an eminent biologist (the Douglas fir tree is named in his honour) who discovered this Okanagan gold, died tragically the following year in Hawaii by falling into a deep, camouflaged pit used to trap wild cattle. They kicked him to death. News of his gold discovery seems to have died with him.

It was almost two decades before the next discovery (1850), this time by indigenous peoples in the Queen Charlotte Islands. The find so excited them that they slipped the gold into a canoe, paddled south to the Hudson's Bay Company fort on Vancouver Island, and started bartering with the chief trader. HBC traded supplies for the gold and encouraged the natives to continue the search for more.

Early the next year, a native woman unearthed a nugget on the beach at Moresby Island, also in the Queen Charlottes. It was a huge nugget and so interested HBC that it immediately sent a ship to look into the discovery. The *Huron* returned with just a sampling of gold quartz, but that was enough to send more ships to investigate and to mine some of the ore.

The word spread quickly, and two American ships from Puget Sound and six from San Francisco sailed north to investigate the quartz vein. The vein (seven inches wide and traceable for 80 feet) was blasted and the ore removed. Unfortunately, this was contrary to the wishes of the local First Nations people who had made the original discovery, and tension ensued.

The next location of importance in the search for gold was the BC Interior. Gold extracted by natives from the Similkameen River and from the Deadman River arrived at Fort Kamloops in 1852.

Years later, a *Victoria Daily Times* article confirmed the early discovery with a story on August 21, 1919, entitled "Gold shipped from here as early as 1853." It related a first-hand account of a Victoria resident who visited a gold-bearing ship in 1853. On board the *Norman Morrison*, the young girl was shown a secret keg full of gold that was on its way to the Hudson's Bay Company office in London, England.

A First Nations group placer mines using sluice boxes at Lytton

A few years after the 1853 secret shipment to England, the Nicomen natives found gold and carried it to chief trader Donald McLean in Kamloops. McLean then rode his horse down to Nicomen, inspected the gold-rich ground near the Nicomen find, and was suitably impressed with the potential for finding more of the precious metal. This probably occurred in 1855.

McLean wrote to Roderick Finlayson, chief factor at Fort Victoria, describing the extraction of the gold: "They pick it out with knives, or…use their fingers for that purpose." McLean requested that "iron spoons [were] to be used by the Indians for the purpose of extricating the nuggets from the crevices in the rocky beds of the creeks" (Rickard, *British Columbia Historical Quarterly*, [1938], 11).

The spoons served as pry bars and tiny shovels, making the natives more efficient in their mining efforts. When the spoons arrived, McLean further encouraged the Nicomen natives to search for gold and exchange his commodities for any gold they found.

The next milestone in the history of gold was the discovery of a huge gold nugget on the Thompson River, just downriver from the mouth of the Nicoamen River. Most historians surmise that this took place in 1856; however, the exact year of the nugget's discovery is difficult to verify. The same 1938 *British Columbia Historical Quarterly* article by T.A. Rickard quoted above dates the discovery as "probably in 1852" (Rickard, 9). Some historians have dated it as late as 1857.

Historians also link the Nicomen discovery with a gold find near the Hudson's Bay fort at Colville, Washington, just south of the Canadian border. Writing in 1889, George Dawson, a distinguished Canadian geologist, explained his understanding of the Colville connection:

> *It seems certain that the epoch-making discovery of gold in British Columbia was the direct result of the Colville excitement. Indians from Thompson River, visiting a woman of their tribe who was married to a French Canadian at Walla Walla, spread the report that gold, like that found at Colville, occurred also in their country, and in the summer or autumn of 1857, four or five Canadians and half-breeds crossed over to the Thompson, and succeeded in finding workable placers at Nicomen, on that river, nine miles above its mouth. On the return of these prospectors the news of the discovery of gold spread rapidly.* (Rickard, 4).

The Thompson First Nations people who went to Walla Walla in 1855 or 1856 were probably from the Nicomen Band. It is difficult to say whether they were referring to the Thompson River gold found near the mouth of Deadman River in 1852 or to that found near Nicomen.

Regardless, after the Walla Walla visit by Thompson natives, a small group of people came directly from there to Nicomen to search for more gold.

Not long after his request for iron spoons, chief trader McLean reported that the "Indian tribes…having tasted the sweets of gold finding, are devoting much of their time and attention to that pursuit" (Rickard, 11). Apparently, not every gold collection and shipment from HBC forts was reported. Thanks in part to the diligent Thompson natives, however, an official shipment of almost 300 ounces of gold left Fort Kamloops in October 1857.

Governor Douglas considered the discovery of nuggets on the Thompson below the Nicoamen significant enough to mention it four years after the event took place. In his private papers of 1860, he wrote, "Gold was first found on Thompson's River by an Indian ¼ of a mile below Nicomen. He is since dead. The Indian was taking a drink out of the river. Having no vessel he was quaffing from the stream when he perceived a shining pebble which he picked up and it proved to be gold. The whole tribe forthwith began to collect the glittering metal" (Rickard, 9).

When Douglas's gold stockpile, no doubt coming from a variety of sources, reached 800 ounces in late 1857, he shipped it to San Francisco, where it arrived in February 1858. Shipments of gold would normally have gone straight to England, but the timing and destination of this particular shipment were calculated.

Douglas knew that the California Gold Rush was over and that the idle men who remained there were easy bait for another gold discovery. He anticipated that the news of the precious metal's arrival in San Francisco would provoke significant interest and encourage the arrival of miners in BC. These miners would head to the Fraser and Thompson Rivers and establish settlements in the Interior, which in turn would justify the British claim to the land.

But instead of a reasonable trickle of miners heading north, suddenly the biggest human flood in the history of the new Crown Colony of British Columbia began.

Accounts differ of the number of miners who headed north that year because no precise figures were recorded. Historian Alexander Begg made an educated guess in 1894 in his often-quoted *History of British Columbia*. He estimated that by July 1858, only five months after the 800 ounces of gold arrived in San Francisco, 30,000 miners had arrived in the Crown colony.

Normally the men would have come overland, following fur brigade trails; however, the US Army was currently waging an indiscriminate war against the natives in the interior of Washington state, and it was extremely dangerous to be anywhere near the area. Therefore, about 23,000 men travelled by sea, while just 7,000 men worked their way overland.

Begg estimates that by January 1859, all but 3,000 of this first influx were back in the US. Many returned north the following spring, accompanying a second flood of newcomers.

The Crown Colony of British Columbia was never the same again.

Fly Fishermen on the Thompson

While reading an 1859 journal of Arthur Thomas Bushby, the personal clerk and registrar of the famous "Hanging Judge" Matthew Baillie Begbie, I discovered a very significant reference. Most people would not consider the find earth-shattering, but as a fly fisherman, I was quite excited.

Bushby, while in Lytton, recorded in his journal on Sunday, April 3, 1859: "I went out with Begbie and he tried the Thompson with a fly but with no success—while I lounged on the sand in the sun a cigar *en bouche* and the Chinook vocabulary *en main*!!" (Smith, *British Columbia Historical Quarterly*, Vol. 21 [1957–58], 154).

This is the first written record of fly fishing on the Thompson, and probably even the first written record of fly fishing on a stream in BC.

Anglers occasionally exaggerate the size of their catch, tell stories about how many fish they caught, and, if the fishing is exceptional, they may even be guilty of an understatement or two. A couple of years after Begbie fished the Thompson, Dr. Walter Cheadle, a young man who chose to travel across the country "just for pleasure," arrived at Lytton. (His journal is fascinating and worth reading in full.)

Dr. Cheadle added a rather interesting notation in his diary on Tuesday, September 15, 1863. "At Lytton we found Captain Ball the magistrate, a very jolly fellow indeed; flies in his hat; told us good fishing in streams about Yale & Hope; none to be killed in Fraser or Thompson" (Cheadle, *Cheadle's Journal of Trip across Canada 1862–1863*, 230).

Now, why would Magistrate Ball be wearing a hat that was displaying his favourite fishing flies if the closest fish was a two- or three-day ride away on horseback? Evidently it was a tongue-in-cheek comment, and what Ball really meant was that the fishing in the Thompson was beyond description.

In fact, the morning before, Cheadle had feasted on delicious white salmon at Cook's Ferry (Spences Bridge): "Breakfast at [ferry operator] Mr Cook's; excellent white salmon, fish rather resembling the bass" (Cheadle, 230).

Almost 50 years later, in 1907, Dr. T.W. Lambert published a book in London entitled *Fishing in British Columbia*. It has a great section about fishing the Thompson and is an interesting read, especially for anyone who has fished this majestic river.

Dr. Lambert was a surgeon for the CPR for 12 years and was obviously an avid angler and a keen observer. He accurately describes and classifies steelhead trout, but at the time, conventional wisdom declared that no steelhead could swim past Hell's Gate on the Fraser River, so he simply referred to the large fish as "rainbow trout." In *Fishing in British Columbia*, he describes the Thompson River:

> On the whole there is probably no fishing river in British Columbia to beat this one for the size and quality of the fish, though it does not afford the large bags that can be obtained on the Kootenay. It is a very sporting river, owing to the strength of the current, for a big fish is hard to hold if it once gets out into the main current, away from the side eddies.
>
> . . .
>
> I once was shown at Spence's Bridge three supposed salmon in the winter which had been speared and sold by the Indians for two shillings [less than ten cents] apiece. I noticed their perfect condition and bright red side stripe, and, on examining them more carefully, pointed out to an experienced fisherman who was present, and to the proprietor of the hotel and others, that these fish were large rainbow trout. The largest weighed 15 lb., the two others 12 lb. apiece. This incident happened at Spence's Bridge, on the Lower Thompson. (Lambert, 14–16)

Now, it is up to you whether you believe Magistrate Ball's claim that there are no fish in the Thompson.

British Fisherman Decides the Canada-US Border

Deciding where the Canada–US border should be located was not a simple matter. The early history of the Crown Colony of BC is rife with stories and explanations of why Britain abandoned the Columbia River in favour of the 49th parallel.

Here is one of the more creative explanations, and who knows, perhaps more than a thread of truth underlies the decision.

Reverend George Grant was an Anglican minister who travelled across Canada in 1872, just a few decades after the 49th parallel became the border. For some reason, he wrote this in Lytton after viewing the confluence of the "noble Thompson and Fraser Rivers." Grant apparently had inside knowledge of the workings of the British government:

> *But in this, as in every case of disputed lines in America, US diplomatists knew the value of what they claimed, and British diplomatists did not. Every one in the Province believes that they lost the Columbia, because the salmon in it would not take a fly. At the time of the dispute, when the Secretary for War was using brave words in the House of Commons, the brother of the Prime Minister happened to be stationed on the Pacific coast, and fished in the Columbia without success, because the salmon were too uneducated to rise to a fly. He wrote home "there was no use making a fuss about the country for it wasn't worth a _____."* (Grant, *Ocean to Ocean*, 314)

The Story of Inflatable Boats

From sheep stomachs to high-quality, state-of-the-art fabrics, inflatables have held air longer than anyone can remember.

About 3,000 years ago, the king of what is now Iraq decided to launch a sneak attack on his enemy. Eventually he spotted his adversary's army on the other side of the Tigris River, but he had no boats to get across the Tigris and do battle. No problem—he improvised and created personalized watercraft for each of his men.

He spotted a flock of sheep and in no time, each of his troops had a personal inflatable—a greased sheep's skin. The skin, inflatable, stitched tightly together with sinew, and coated in animal grease, was not completely airtight, but it held air reasonably well.

The king waited until dark then launched his surprise attack. His troops paddled and kicked their way across the Tigris while balancing on their inflatable sheepskins. To stay afloat, they continually blew air into their "inflatable dingies."

Although technically not an inflatable boat, animal skins often served as flotation devices in early civilizations.

Fast-forward to 1839. An Englishman tested an inflatable boat made of cotton fabric with a rubber coating crudely vulcanized on both sides. It had a valve, held air, and could be inflated with a little pump and deflated and rolled into a convenient package very easily.

A few years later, the world's first round-nosed inflatable boat, called the Halkett India Rubber Cloth Boat, rolled off the assembly line in the England.

Immediately, the Hudson's Bay Company saw the potential in the boat and purchased several. John Rae, a well-known Canadian Arctic explorer who worked for the Hudson's Bay Company, used one of the original boats that measured 9 × 4 feet. The boat had brass valves and carried three men and some gear. Deflated, it folded neatly into a backpack and was very portable. Rae loved his boat.

During a September 1848 Arctic journey in search of the lost Franklin expedition, Rae, his men, and their supplies had to cross the Richardson River in the far North. It was so cold that his Halkett boat froze stiff and became quite brittle. No problem: he lit a fire to warm and soften the material so it regained its shape, and then he inflated the boat.

Then Rae discovered that the boat's paddles were still in his previous camp, many miles away. No problem: two tin plates improvised as paddles. For the next four hours, Rae and his men paddled their inflatable across the 300-foot stream 14 times, ferrying men and supplies back and forth.

Four years later, the search was still on for the Franklin expedition. British commander Robert McClure worked his way deep into the Arctic ice packs, and then his ship froze in for the winter. He had expected that; what he had not expected was to be frozen in the Arctic ice pack for three years.

Fortunately for McClure and his men, they had a Halkett inflatable boat along. It proved invaluable in crossing 50 feet of open water between the immobilized ship and land. By this time, the boat was ten feet long and three feet wide, weighed 25 pounds, and carried six men. McClure was very happy with his boat.

Fast-forward again, this time to the Second World War. Inflatable boats became assault craft. The quality of vulcanized rubber improved dramatically during the war and contributed to experimentation with various shapes and sizes of craft. A U-shaped boat emerged. With a wooden transom designed for an outboard motor, the military immediately wanted it so Zodiac patented it in 1943. A completely new inflatable manufacturing industry emerged.

Fast-forward to the 1950s. An entrepreneur in the United States sensed the business potential and created a whitewater rafting company using military surplus rafts to take screaming passengers on thrill rides

Assembling an army pontoon bridge in the 1950s

down the Colorado River in the Grand Canyon—just for pleasure.

A few years later, in the early 1970s, commercial rafting emerged on several Canadian rivers including the Thompson and Fraser. Most company owners simply purchased military surplus rafts and pontoons and turned them into whitewater craft, but even then the Avon Tire Company in the UK was manufacturing a few whitewater inflatables designed and built specifically for running rivers.

Gradually, an entire industry was born.

My first commercial raft on the Thompson in '73

In 1973, I purchased a 15-foot Avon Commercial River Runner raft from Mac & Mac, a wholesale general merchant in Vancouver that had imported the craft the previous year for a possible sale in BC.

Nobody was interested in this particular raft until I come along. Mac & Mac was glad to get rid of it; I was glad to buy it for $890.

My Avon inflatable and I bounced through the Thompson's rapids at least 100 times in 1973. We went down together again often in 1974, and for many years after that.

My Avon is retired now (like me), but still holds air and still gets out on the river for occasional fun (like me).

Reaction Ferries

Reaction ferries are pontoon vessels that use the current of a river or stream for propulsion. Used for more than 150 years in BC and for centuries in other parts of the world, they are a cheap and efficient means to cross a river or stream. In the old days, a simple, crudely built scow or rowboat that was tethered to a cable or rope strung across a stream, qualified as a ferry.

As early as 1863, a very simple ferry crossed the mouth of the

Thompson at Lytton and another crossed the Fraser a short distance downstream from the two rivers' confluence. At Spences Bridge, Mortimer Cook and his partner, Charles Kimball, tied a rope across the Thompson, tethered a boat to the rope, and charged for the trip across. Similar craft operated at Ashcroft, Savona, and Walhachin.

Lytton's first ferry

Along the Thompson, when a bridge washed away because of extreme spring floods, it was common practice for a reaction ferry to be brought back into service until the bridge was replaced.

The reaction ferry that operated across the mouth of the Thompson was typical of other reaction ferries in BC. This one operated under contract between 1867 and 1873, prior to the construction of the first bridge, and the proprietors charged a toll and paid an annual fee to the province for the right to provide the service.

Here are the terms of the 1867 contract according to an article in the Lytton Museum and Archives newsletter in August 2004:

1. *An annual rent of one hundred and thirty-five dollars shall be paid in quarterly instalments ($33.75)*
2. *The rates of toll shall not exceed the following:*
   Passengers with personal baggage $ .50
   Man and horse 1.00
   Cattle per head .50
   Pack trains – each animal .50
   Sheep and hogs .25
   Freight per 100 lbs .25
3. *A good and proper boat for the transport of foot passengers shall be kept and a person for working of the same shall always be in attendance, also a large boat capable of ferrying animals across not less than 6 pack horses at a time. Boats must be kept in good repair.*
4. *All government officers, government animals and government baggage to be crossed free of charge.*
5. *Rates to be posted in conspicuous place.*
6. *If a bridge is built, ferry owners shall not be entitled to claim recompense, and on completion of the bridge the ferry must cease.*
7. *Lease started Jan. 1, 1867. Conditions to be strictly adhered to. If in default all boats forfeited to the government.*
8. *The right of the ferry shall extend one mile up the Thompson River from its mouth, and one-half mile up the east bank of the Fraser River, commencing from boundary lines of Byron Earnshaw ferry on said river.*

The Lytton ferry across the Fraser originally crossed downstream of the confluence of the Thompson and Fraser. It was built and operated by an Englishman, Byron Earnshaw, who made an agreement with the constable at Lytton who represented the B.C. government. What was notable was Earnshaw's right to collect a fee from anyone crossing the Fraser on the ice in winter or by swimming or wading across. He insisted that everyone help pay his $25 annual license fee.

Earnshaw operated his ferry under contract for only three years and then sold it. The government took it over in 1894 and ten years later moved it upstream into its present location a kilometre from Lytton.

Lytton's reaction ferry is a rarity in BC today

It has had its share of breakaways, problems, protests, and tragedies. In the early 1960s, the main cable line broke at its tethering point on the west side of the river. The ferry didn't break free but swung around and ended up near the bank on the east side of the river. The three Lytton passengers and crew on board weren't hurt, but the story is that one of the native passengers turned white from fear and refused to ride the ferry for nearly five years.

A car with four locals inside rolled off the end of the ferry into the Fraser in 1967, killing all four occupants. The ferry had no radio or telephone, so the operator rode his bicycle two kilometres into town to report the incident to the RCMP. It took more than a month before the river dropped enough to retrieve the car with the bodies still inside.

The local protests accelerated after the deaths of the four residents.

Still, Phil Gaglardi, provincial highways minister at the time, refused to make changes. Petitions, visits to Victoria, and even protests in Kamloops at Gaglardi's home didn't result in any better service or a safer ferry.

Later that year, two men were shot to death on the ferry, which created quite a stir in town. One was the ferry operator who had ridden his bike into Lytton to report the drowning a few months earlier. No clues were evident and no murder suspect was arrested.

Every day, as many as 40 school children crossed the ferry to attend school in Lytton; the parents had legitimate concerns. They demanded basic safety precautions, basic operator safety training, safety equipment such as lifejackets for every passenger who boarded the ferry, and a safety boat.

In May 1979 (by then I was living in Lytton and operating Kumsheen Raft Adventures), the ferry broke free again. There was a small safety boat on board, and the two employees and the single passenger got to shore but not before several anxious moments of trying to start the stubborn outboard on the tender. The ferry, along with the passenger's car, continued downriver and was caught halfway to Boston Bar by a tugboat working there, pushing log booms to a sawmill in Boston Bar.

After the 1979 breakaway, the Ministry of Highways completed major improvements. Pontoons were extended by 12 feet, the deck enlarged, a larger inflatable safety boat purchased (even I was asked for input), cables and towers re-engineered, and generally, the ferry attained a higher standard. A lifejacket for every passenger was available. Employees even received formal operations and safety training.

Several times in the early 1980s, the highways supervisor called at dawn to tell me that the ferry was stranded in the middle of the Fraser. He asked me to launch my Zodiac and shuttle the ferrymen to their jobsite, which was now mid-river, not the usual berth for the reaction ferry.

Apparently, a former disgruntled employee, returning home late from the hotel bar in town, needed a ride across the river. The ferry was closed for the night, so he simply untied the craft on the east side, rode the ferry across to the west, jumped or staggered off, and allowed the ferry to leisurely drift back to the centre of the river, where it gently swayed in the current for the remainder of the night. A heavy chain and large lock were a simple solution to this problem.

Today, the ferry still operates full-time as a public conveyance and is a component of the British Columbia highways system. A ride across the Fraser is free and definitely worth twice or even ten times the money.

The Peerless

The *Peerless*, a paddlewheeler constructed and launched in Kamloops in November 1880, was built to capitalize on the CPR construction activity.

She was an impressive 131 feet long by 25 feet wide, drew only 18 inches of water, had 16 watertight compartments, and could move at 18 knots (about 35 KM/H). If you've rafted with Kumsheen, visualize three J-rig power rafts tied side by side. Now add five more rows of three rafts and you can get some idea of her massive size.

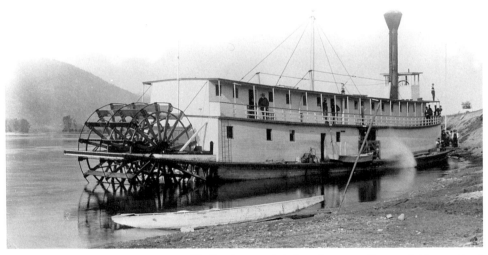

The Peerless *made it from Savona to Spences Bridge and back*

In June 1881 (it would have been high water), the *Peerless* headed down the Thompson to Harper's Grist Mill on the Bonaparte River, across from the rafting put-in above Ashcroft. Captain Irving, a highly skilled riverman, had little difficulty getting the boat back up the Thompson to her berth in Savona.

Feeling good about the first downriver run to Ashcroft, the *Peerless*'s skilled captain made a second run, this time all the way down to Spences Bridge. The paddlewheeler carried flour and other supplies for the CPR construction crews working near Spences Bridge. This was a test trip to evaluate the feasibility of regular supply runs; Irving hoped to bring fruit and other produce upriver from Spences Bridge to the construction camps and towns near Kamloops while running railway supplies downriver.

The scheme was good, but the excursion did not go according to plan. Downriver was smooth sailing. The *Peerless* made good time and arrived in Spences Bridge unaffected by the journey. She loaded fuel and supplies and headed upriver again. Although she struggled against the fast current and rapids in places, she made it to Black Canyon without major difficulty. In Black Canyon, however, the battle started.

It was June and the river was in full runoff mode. During high water in Black Canyon, the hydraulics increase exponentially as the water rises. The *Peerless* groaned and hissed against the fast currents. The huge boils, whirlpools, powerful eddies, and back eddies common during spring runoff nearly smashed her against the steep canyon walls and rocks, over and over again. She would gain a few metres only to lose them in the next big surge of water.

For days, she fought her way through the canyon's rapids and hydraulics. Captain Irving, her skipper, was the only reason that she was not smashed against the rocks and canyon walls and destroyed in Black Canyon. His river and boating skills kept the *Peerless* alive.

Finally, five days later, when the weary paddlewheeler glided back into dock at Savona, her skipper's mind was made up. She belonged on Kamloops Lake, not on the Thompson River, and Spences Bridge would never become a regular, scheduled destination.

The Skuzzy

In 1882, Andrew Onderdonk, the contractor building the CPR between Yale and Lytton, put together a rugged riverboat designed specifically for the mighty Fraser. Her purpose was to carry railway construction equipment and supplies between Boston Bar and Lytton.

The Cariboo Road was the alternative way of transporting supplies for the railway, but once construction started, the freighters (men who were the equivalent of truckers today) hiked up commodity tolls. However, Onderdonk was a shrewd businessman. He did the math and immediately commissioned the building of the *Skuzzy* in order to avoid the extravagant tolls and to improve his bottom line.

Built in Spuzzum (near Yale), she was 127 × 24.2 feet and drew only 18 inches of water. Delays in assembly meant that she was not ready for the upriver trip from Spuzzum to Lytton until the river was in spring flood. As fate would have it, the spring deluge was the highest in almost 40 years. This did not bode well for the *Skuzzy* or for Onderdonk.

Onderdonk, however, was not fazed. He simply brought in a very experienced big-river boatman from the Stikine River in northern BC, Captain Nathaniel Lane Jr., to take her upriver to Lytton. Lane came down from the north, made his way up the Fraser to Spuzzum, took one look at the flooding river in the canyon, and decided that he had no interest in the job.

The Skuzzy *heading back to Lytton from Boston Bar*

Undeterred, Onderdonk hired the most experienced riverman on the upper Fraser, Captain Ashbury Insley, to replace Lane. Insley came down, scouted the river, and decided it was a 50/50 proposition; he would at least get on board and try to run her upriver.

On May 17, 1882, he nosed the *Skuzzy* into the current and headed upstream from Spuzzum. By now, the Fraser was a raging torrent, pretty much in peak flood; every rapid in the canyon pounded the *Skuzzy* mercilessly. Nevertheless, he got her to the lower reaches of Hell's Gate.

For days, Insley tried to inch her upstream through the huge waves, whirlpools, and gigantic boils of the rugged canyon. Eventually, however, he turned around and headed back down to Spuzzum, where he tied her up, resigned. The Fraser in flood was mightier than the *Skuzzy* and he knew it.

Still not dissuaded, Onderdonk was no loser and he definitely did not want to take the *Skuzzy* apart, haul her piece by piece to Boston Bar, pay the extravagant tolls, and then reassemble her. Instead, he decided to wait until the Fraser's water level dropped before trying again.

This gave him time to find and hire a team of three highly experienced and competent rivermen from the upper Columbia in Idaho. Captain S.R. Smith, his brother, David, and their engineer, J.W. Burse, agreed to do the job for Onderdonk. This crew had been running rivers together for many years and were probably the best in the business.

On September 7, the crew waved goodbye to the send-off crowd onshore and inched the *Skuzzy* out from her moorage at Spuzzum. By now, the Fraser's water levels had dropped and the river was no longer in flood. Slowly, the Smith brothers manoeuvred her through the formidable rapids and canyons leading to the foot of Hell's Gate Canyon.

They made several runs at the rapid but each one failed. Hell's Gate, aptly named, pushed back with all its might. Meanwhile, five train cars of cheering spectators arrived daily to watch and bet on or against the *Skuzzy*. Odds fluctuated with the mood of the spectators, but at one point they were 100 to 1 against her making it up through Hell's Gate.

Onderdonk still was undaunted; besides, he had too much invested to abandon her (nobody knows how much money he bet on the *Skuzzy*), and now it was also very much a matter of pride.

After a few failed attempts, he resorted to ingenuity and ordered holes drilled into the granite walls of the canyon and ring bolts installed. Then, 125 Chinese labourers from his construction camps nearby were brought in and lined up along the river's edge.

With engines hissing at maximum steam, her steam capstan winch hooked to the ring bolts and straining under the forces, and 125 Chinese dedicated to winning their game of tug-of-war, the embattled craft inched her way up through the raging maelstrom of Hell's Gate Canyon. On shore, the crowds cheered wildly; those who had bet on her success, Onderdonk among them, cheered the loudest.

Once through Hell's Gate, the *Skuzzy* still had China Bar, Skuzzy Canyon, and several more rapids to overcome. The Smith brothers were master rivermen and Burse continued to push the boilers beyond the red line. The *Skuzzy* prevailed, one battle at a time, but in the fight, she received wounds from the canyon walls and rocks.

Days later, she pulled into Boston Bar, her sides and bottom badly bruised and her hull sporting a gaping hole. Nevertheless, she was in one piece, and Onderdonk had won his gamble.

At Boston Bar, patched, bruised, and mended, the *Skuzzy* again nosed into the current, this time heading for Lytton, 35 kilometres upstream. It took only seven more hours to arrive at her final destination at the kumsheen (confluence) of the Thompson and Fraser Rivers.

With no major rapids between Boston Bar and Lytton, the return trip to Boston Bar took only an hour and 27 minutes under full steam. By October 27, the *Skuzzy* was fully loaded with railway construction supplies and for two years, she ran back and forth, saving Onderdonk thousands of dollars in freight costs and padding his deep pockets.

At the end of her work life in 1884, the *Skuzzy* retired in a big back eddy at Keefers, between Lytton and Boston Bar on the Fraser. Then a transformation occurred: her innards were stripped and installed in another boat, and she became the *Skuzzy II*.

Eventually her hull washed away and the *Skuzzy* vanished into the bowels of the Fraser, a fitting burial for a feisty riverboat that refused to give up.

The Great Slide

On August 13, 1905, a loud thud and an earth-shattering roar suddenly broke the silence of a peaceful Sunday afternoon. Startled Spences Bridge residents looked downriver to witness a huge chunk of the mountain south of town crashing down across the Thompson and up the valley on the other side.

Just a few minutes earlier, two young girls from town had been saddling their horses for a ride down the Thompson to visit their friends at Indian Chief Lillooet's small First Nations village at the base of Arthur's Seat Mountain.

They pointed their horses downriver, but the ornery critters seemed to have minds of their own. They stopped, danced sideways, and lifted their heads high, always turning to go back upriver.

The girls did their best to turn the horses, but they were insistent. Finally, the girls gave in and galloped upriver to visit a different friend who lived in the opposite direction. The horses had saved their lives.

The impact of the slide hitting the Thompson created a great wall of water over 16 feet high. It rushed upstream and downstream like an enormous tidal wave. Chief Lillooet's village, where nearly 100 natives resided, was directly in the path of the rubble and water.

Landslides below Spences Bridge wreaked havoc on the community

Eighteen villagers instantly died from the rubble or the tidal wave. The slide buried many alive. Dozens more scrambled to safety the moment they heard and saw the slide. At least 18 more were seriously injured and almost 100 villagers were instantly homeless. The tidal wave drowned three native fishermen who were netting salmon on the banks of the Thompson.

A CPR passenger train was approaching from the south just as the mountain let go. The engineer caught sight of the slide and triggered the emergency brakes, stopping the train just short of the rocks, mud, and water that swept across the valley. The slide obliterated a section of the railway track directly in front of the train.

Men from Spences Bridge immediately ran or rode on horseback to the slide with shovels and picks and, even just using their bare hands, tried to make an outlet for the water to break through the dam. In town, residents tied their houses and outbuildings to trees with chains and ropes as the river level immediately began to rise. For more than four hours, the river rose steadily behind the rubble dam.

Finally, two rifle shots rang through the air. This was the agreed-upon signal that the water had broken through the dirt dam and resumed its downriver flow to the Fraser.

A special train arrived at 11 p.m. with a doctor from Ashcroft and another from Kamloops. Two nurses arrived with the doctors and treated the wounded day and night.

The community rallied together. The Spences Bridge Hotel became a hospital; a train transported the most seriously injured to Ashcroft. Local residents donated their medicines, ointments, clothing, and food to the wounded and the homeless.

Today, the slide still deflects the river, creating a big bend around the graves of the 18 indigenous people buried under the mass of silt and debris. A small, muddy lake nestled against the bluffs to the west marks the old riverbed, and ponderosa pine trees dot the slide like gravestones.

Silk Trains

Silk trains were single-purpose or unit trains with top priority rights on the track and specially constructed railcars. Their sole purpose was to transport bales of raw silk from Vancouver to Eastern Canada and the Eastern US as quickly as possible. They were the kings of the tracks between 1887 and 1940.

For these trains it was all about speed: silk is perishable and the priority was to get the silk to market swiftly so it could be converted into luxury items such as dresses, shirts, ties, and scarves. The wealthy needed their silk attire.

A single bale of silk was worth as much as $800 in 1925: one bale would buy three top-of-the-line Harley Davidson motorcycles. Each railcar could carry 470 bales, so a 14- or 15-car train could easily be carrying more than five million dollars in silk.

High insurance rates were another incentive for the fast delivery of the bales. The railways carried special insurance for their silk trains, and the insurance clock started ticking the minute the silk bales were loaded onto the train from the Oriental ships docked in Vancouver. Costs accumulated by the hour until the precious cargo was unloaded at its eastern destination.

The specially built silk railcars had shorter and lighter suspension and wheel systems that resembled those of passenger cars rather than boxcars. Their design accommodated higher speeds and sharp curves more safely than regular cars. Railway police and insurance agents rode shotgun on every train.

On the flat, open prairies, trains often travelled at more than 60 miles per hour. Pit stops to change crews and to switch to fully supplied new steam locomotives happened every 120 miles on average, and these took only seven minutes. Relatively few accidents occurred in spite of the trains' high speeds.

A rare derailment less than a mile below Spences Bridge occurred a few days after Christmas in 1910. The derailment never made the newspapers, so the CPR archives have no record of it.

However, James Teit, one of the best-known personalities living in Spences Bridge at the time, received the contract to retrieve the bales of silk. Teit kept a record of the experience in his diary.

December 1910

28th. Fixed canoe forenoon – ran down river after dinner to below the wreck, crossed 81 small bales of fine silk and 2 rolls of Japanese matting. ["Crossed" probably means that he carried the bales in his canoe from the roadless west side of the river to the east side, where both the railway and Cariboo Road were located.]

29th. Worked all day – crossed 2 bales silk 2nd class + 3 rolls matting. Salved 100 packages fine silk + 1 bale silk 2nd class. Brought all together foot of rapids below Indian graveyard. (Lean, "A Year in the Life of James A. Teit–1910", *Teit Times*, 36)

Keeping in mind the scant information available on the wreck, the best deduction is that the train derailed on the corner just south of the TCH bridge (at approximately 33.0 km). The silk bales were swept through the rapid and picked up and piled below it.

Teit also canoed downriver from Spences Bridge to Drynoch Siding (about 12 km), inspecting the pools and eddies and picking up a few bales of silk along the way. In total, he spent 16 days retrieving bales of silk and bales of goatskins from the same train.

On January 3, he had an accident on the icy river. In his diary, he noted:

Located 1 bale on head of bar between two rapids. In going over there had accident thru pole sticking between rocks + canoe swinging down broadside in riffle hit three rocks one after another – stove in 4 ribs + capsized, all of us swam ashore. (Lean, 36)

That evening, he related the accident to his mother-in-law, Mrs. Morens:

I was the first one to reach shore and as my feet touched the bottom I turned to see how my companions were doing. Joe Martel was right behind me using a downward stroke with his arms and almost bouncing over the water. Johnny Smith was yelling, "Help, wait for me, I can't swim"; although he was flailing his arms around and doing a great deal of splashing, he was making progress. (Lean, 58)

As soon as Teit saw he was going to be all right, he went ashore where Martel was already looking for material to make a fire. Martel, who had worked on river drives in Quebec and was an experienced riverman, kept matches stuck in his thick hair, and they soon had a fire going.

Johnny Smith quit working for Teit after the mishap and Indian Drynock Johnny replaced him. Teit and his helpers continued the salvage operation for another 11 days without serious incident.

Death at the Frog

It was February in the mid-1980s, and frigid north wind gusts blew down the Thompson canyon.

As I was passing the Frog Rapids on my way home from Kamloops, I was surprised to see a score of people standing beside the highway, leaning against the guardrail and staring at the river with blank faces. I followed their gaze and spotted a small white boat broached against a rock about 200 metres below the Frog.

As I drove by, I thought, "This is strange. What are these people doing here in the cold and wind, and why is the boat up against the rock?" I was sure it hadn't been there when I passed the spot that morning. To satisfy my curiosity, I turned around and drove back to ask if something was wrong.

On the side of the highway, I learned that a man and his teenaged son had just drowned in the river, and it was their boat up against the rock. I learned more when I got home: there was an urgent message from the RCMP, asking for one of my rafts immediately. The message was already several hours old.

The local RCMP office filled me in on the rest of the story. The father and his two teens had rowed across the river immediately above the Frog, ready for an afternoon of panning for gold on the riverbank. The new gravel bars that emerged as the water dropped in the winter would be optimal for panning.

Their boat was very small, so the man crossed the river with one son at a time. They panned for a few hours; late in the afternoon, the father took the first boy back across to the highway side of the river. Crossing with the second son, he popped an oar that landed in the current, out of his reach.

As it was impossible to manoeuvre the little boat with only one oar, the current swept it into the rapid on the right side of the Frog Rock. Huge waves instantly filled the boat with water and it capsized; as the boy on shore watched in horror, both his father and his brother slid under the bitterly cold water. Neither had been wearing a lifejacket. Neither surfaced again.

The little white boat had some buoyancy because of the air trapped under it, so it drifted downstream 100 metres or so before the current pinned it against a rock.

When the RCMP received the report, they immediately called and asked me to launch a raft and begin a search. Unable to reach me, they went to plan B: a helicopter flew over the river, looking for any sign of the two victims.

Through previous experience, I knew that an immediate search was futile. When someone drowns, the body quickly sinks to the bottom and usually lodges against a nearby obstacle or rock. Because there is little current in the very bottom of a river or stream, the body does not move until gasses form in the body cavity and positive buoyancy occurs. How long this takes depends on the temperature of the water and the body mass of the drowned person.

The father and son were from a well-known and respected First Nations family in Merritt. It became an obsession of the bereaved mother to find the bodies, especially that of her son. Volunteers from Merritt, Spences Bridge, and Lytton watched the river for weeks, waiting for a body to surface, even probing the shallows of the river with long sticks. The water was almost freezing so decomposition was happening very slowly.

Finally, a spiritual shaman from Penticton came to the river and predicted a precise date when both bodies would surface. Volunteers watched the river with increased diligence as the date approached.

Almost a month after the drowning and on the precise date predicted by the shaman, the watchers spotted a body floating by at White Canyon. It was the remains of the father. Much to the dismay of the grieving mother, her son's body was never recovered.

Cariboo Road, a mile above Martel

Events along the Trails and Roads

Paths, Trails, and Roads

When Simon Fraser descended his river in 1808, he encountered the Nlak´a´pamux First Nations—the Thompson River Salish people—a subgroup of the Interior Salish people. These natives, following their age-old trails and footpaths through the Fraser Canyon, guided him from Lytton to Yale. The trails were treacherous and included places that, in Fraser's opinion, were not suitable for a man—only for animals. But Fraser and his men slowly inched their way along the cliffs and rope ladders made from vines, and his entourage all arrived safely in Yale. A few days later, they hurriedly inched their way back upriver after encountering hostile natives and realizing they were not exploring the Columbia River.

When the 49th parallel became the Canada–US boundary in 1849, the HBC needed a new route from Fort Kamloops to the coast, as the Columbia River and Fort Vancouver, Washington, were no longer available to them. A new brigade trail was the solution; it led from Kamloops to Nicola Lake, then up the Coldwater River and west over the North Cascade mountains to just north of Spuzzum.

At Spuzzum, horses swam across the Fraser and continued down to Yale along the Douglas Portage. This was a 12.5-mile horse trail that Governor Douglas commissioned that linked Yale to Spuzzum inland to the west of the Fraser.

For the next ten years, some fur brigades travelling between Kamloops and Yale used the Kamloops–Spuzzum/Douglas Portage route, but it was very steep and often dangerous. A modified route that went from Kamloops to Hope, following the Coldwater and Coquihalla Rivers, was an easier and preferred trail and used by almost all brigades.

When the Fraser Canyon Gold Rush started in 1858, there was no road—only perilous native trails—through the Fraser Canyon or along the Thompson River.

Freight wagons arrive in downtown Lytton

It was relatively easy to get to Yale from Victoria or New Westminster because a sternwheeler could navigate to that point; getting from Yale to Lytton, on the other hand, was tough slogging. In April 1859, it took Judge Matthew Begbie five challenging days to walk from Yale to Lytton, a journey that today takes less than an hour by car. In his opinion, "The trail by which we advanced, is by this time, I should think, utterly impassable for any animal, except a man, a goat, or a dog."

There were First Nations trails along the Thompson River that were also used by some of the early fur traders. The trails along the Thompson went through easier terrain than the Fraser Canyon, yet it was steep and winding in places, and a slip could mean a fatal plunge into the Thompson's Jaws of Death or maybe a hard landing on the rocks along the river.

Construction began on the Cariboo Wagon Road in 1862 (in those days it was also spelled *Waggon*). Walter Moberly got the nod to construct most of the road between Lytton and Clinton. These sections were tough to build and very expensive, and Moberly started out with two partners who eventually bailed on him. Governor Douglas withholding funds didn't help Moberly either; that prompted most of the white men he'd hired to simply lay down their tools and go in hot pursuit of Cariboo gold.

Next, Moberly hired Chinese and First Nations workers to replace the errant miners and was very pleased with their work and dedication. He established worker camps along the route, the first one on the outskirts of Lytton, probably at what is now the Kumsheen Rafting Resort. He had another camp at Nicomen, and still another about eight miles upriver from Spences Bridge.

A well-preserved section of the wagon road near Kumsheen Rafting Resort

The wagon road along the Thompson was an extension of the road from Yale to Lytton, which had been completed the previous year. A journey that had taken Judge Begbie five days in 1859 took a stagecoach only eight or nine hours once the Cariboo Wagon Road was completed.

Stout and the Canyon War

The Canyon War (also called the Fraser River War or Boston Bar Massacre) was a violent confrontation between gold miners and Upper Thompson Salish people in the summer of 1858.

There are many theories about what started the conflict. Was it the rape of a native girl by two French miners? It is improbable that this alone was enough to spark a war. Did the natives feel threatened by the hordes of American miners who swarmed into their territory? Yes, there is no doubt about it. Were they worried that they would lose their monopoly to mine for gold? Definitely a factor.

There is no question that "the discoveries of gold on the mainland… must be credited to the Indians; it was they, and not any canny Scot or enterprising American, that first found the gold on the Thompson and Fraser Rivers, or first proceeded to gather it for purpose of trade" (Pickard, 9). It follows that the natives were possessive of their monopoly and would act aggressively toward the miners who flooded the Interior in search of gold.

The Thompson First Nations intensely disliked most Americans. The Yankees were not just a threat to the native mining monopoly; they were also disrespectful and were deeply resented for their mistreatment of not only native women but of the whole tribe. Americans would often destroy and carry away native root crops without thinking of compensation.

The erratic war that the Americans had launched against the Okanagan natives in Washington also served to deepen animosity toward Boston men, a name the natives called miners from the USA. Arthur Thomas Bushby commented on this animosity in his journal: "[It] is quite strange to see how soon the Indians detect the Boston men [Americans] & how they dislike them" (Smith, *BCHQ*, 152).

The Canyon War was the inevitable outcome of their resentment.

In 1914, Dr. W.W. Walkem, Vancouver's first European medical doctor and a writer, interviewed Yale resident Edward Stout, a participant and survivor of the Canyon War. He published Stout's remarkable story along with other stories of early BC pioneers shortly after the interview.

Stout and a group of 25 other men living in California had heard rumours about gold on the Fraser River. The California Gold Rush had recently petered out, and these men felt compelled to verify the rumours. Gold Fever consumed them.

The group left San Francisco in March 1858, travelling by schooner to Bellingham Bay and reaching the Fraser River in mid-May. They worked their way up the Fraser to the present town of Yale, encountering virtually no one along the way, and immediately began placer mining.

Stout's was one of the first mining parties to arrive in Yale that spring of 1858, though there was a small party a few miles downriver at Hill's Bar, mining one of the Fraser's richest claims. Within a week of their arrival, hundreds more men poured into Yale; Stout's group decided to make its way upriver.

Eventually, they ended up at Nicomen. They found some gold there and remained until late July. During their stay, a young woman from the Nicomen Band formed a strong attachment to the group's supervisor, Jack McLennan. Her allegiance to him, manifesting itself in the form of a warning, ultimately saved Stout's life:

> *One night—it must have been close on midnight and many of us were still sitting in front of the blazing log fire—this woman suddenly appeared, and, placing her finger on her lip as she walked to take a seat close to Jack, said in a very low and subdued voice, "Hist!" Taking her seat upon a fallen tree, she stared gloomily, if not sadly, into the fire. Cautioning silence, Jack said to us: "Boys, something serious has happened or is going to happen, which concerns us all. This woman would not have come here tonight unless she had something important to tell us."*
>
> *She kept her eyes fixed upon the blazing logs and twice made a move as though to speak. Finally, in a most intensely sad tone of voice, she said: "Before sun up you white men go. Go back in the stick, far, far, then you back to salt chuck [water]. Indian kill all white men in canyon, by-by he come kill you all. Tomorrow he come. Go now, go quick," and rising from the log she disappeared as suddenly as she had come. (Walkem, Pioneer Days in British Columbia, 32–33)*

The men understood her to say that the natives down the Fraser were killing the white men in the canyon, and they had to leave immediately. They carefully doused their fires and headed downriver with jerked venison for food, guns, ammunition, a blanket for each man, and the clothes on their backs. They stayed away from the native trails, travelling through the trees at night. During the day, they rested.

The group slowly reached Jackass Mountain ten miles south of Lytton, and as they traversed a slide, they were suddenly fired upon by warriors concealed in the bush above them. Three of the group were wounded with poisoned arrows, and all three died the next day after suffering terrible convulsions. "At death the poor fellows turned black" (Walkem, 33).

Stout's group lost a man nearly every day. At Slaughter Bar, between Jackass Mountain and what is today Boston Bar, they lost six of their group in a vicious battle. Fights continued, and by the time they got to China Bar Mountain (near Hell's Gate), they were down to five wounded men, they had no ammunition, and they were too weak to carry on down the trail.

The men expected that the following day would be their last. Still, they built a crude barricade and tried to hide behind it. The next day, no attack ensued; instead, an armed volunteer force of 100 miners rounded the bend on the trail. Stout and his companions were jubilant.

Stout later learned the sequence of events that led to his rescue:

> *In late summer the miners decided to take action against the Indians. A meeting was held at Fort Yale and a volunteer force formed. On August 18 over 100 heavily armed miners under H.M. Snider left the Fort and fought their way up the Canyon. This display of force and solidarity impressed the Indians and a week later peace treaties were signed with all the tribes between Yale and Lytton.* (Walkem, 34)

During his group's retreat from Nicomen, Stout was shot with a musket ball, fired from an old Hudson's Bay Company musket that was intended for hunting game, and hit in the groin. During the interview, he showed Dr. Walkem more than 40 scars that covered his body from all the arrow wounds he received, and a large scar in the groin from the musket ball.

The attacks killed an unknown number of miners. In Walkem's interview, Stout recollected the devastation:

> *Captain Snider and his men took out of the water at Yale ten dead whites; at Deadman's Bend on the opposite shore they took out nineteen; and the Hudson's Bay Company at Hope took out thirty-two. Of those who were murdered, all of them had their heads and arms cut off, while those who were killed otherwise were not mutilated, but simply had arrows sticking in their bodies.* (Walkem, 34)

The natives, on the other hand, suffered fewer casualties. James Teit, unquestionably the expert on the Thompson River Indians, mentions the Fraser River War in *The Thompson Indians of British Columbia* and the number of natives that were killed:

> *In 1858 some of the Lower Thompsons [natives from between Lytton and Spuzzum] carried on a desultory war for several months with the white miners. One engagement was fought near Boston Bar, in which the Indians had eight or nine men killed.* (Teit, 271)

The Fraser Canyon War has been studied and analyzed for more than 150 years. Analysis only serves to prove the complexity involved in sorting through the information and arriving at straightforward conclusions. Two things are perfectly clear, however: Edward Stout was a very lucky man, and the woman from Nicomen saved his life.

Stout became known as "Ned the boatman" on the Fraser River, running boats both upstream and downstream from Yale to Lytton for many years. He was the only boatman who did not get out of his boat to run it through Hell's Gate or the Jaws of Death, then a rapid on the lower Fraser downstream of Hell's Gate.

Ned lived a full, eventful life, dying in his 97th year in Yale.

Scourge of Smallpox

Walter Moberly, the contractor for the Cariboo Wagon Road from Lytton to Cache Creek, established a work camp at Nicomen in 1862. He related an interesting but gruesome story about smallpox.

To set the stage, it was 1862, and smallpox had already killed thousands of Coast indigenous peoples. The pandemic gradually moved into the interior of the colony, killing as it moved. In this story, Moberly's tent was on the north side of the Nicoamen River while his workers (mostly Chinese) had set up camp on the south side.

He stood at his tent and spotted an approaching native across the river who was leading a horse on which another native was seated. The man on the horse had a veil over his face. They rode past the Chinese camp and crossed the Nicoamen, obviously planning to camp near Moberly.

Suspicious that something was wrong, Moberly walked over to the two men, lifted the veil, and to his horror, saw a face covered in smallpox.

He informed them that they could not stay anywhere near his men and must immediately return to Lytton, where the government had a doctor appointed to vaccinate the natives. But they claimed they had no money or food, so Moberly went to his supply tent, filled a large sack with food, and wrote a letter to the doctor to have them properly looked after. They departed.

A few days later, Moberly was on his way to Cache Creek to choose the route for the Cariboo Wagon Road that he was building. He learned from the ferryman at Cook's Ferry (Spences Bridge) that the two natives, instead of returning to Lytton, had passed the ferryman's house and continued on to the First Nations village at the mouth of the Nicola River.

A few weeks later, Moberly returned in the dark from a survey trip farther up the road. As he approached the workers' camp that lay 7.5 miles upstream of Cook's Ferry, he heard the wailing of native women on the mountainside above his trail. He knew the wailing was a "certain indication of death having visited their community" (Robinson, *Blazing the Trail through the Rockies: The Story of Walter Moberly and His Share in the Making of Vancouver*, 47).

In Moberly's own words, here is what he soon discovered as he left his camp not far above the Wye at Spences Bridge:

> *The next day I proceeded on my way to Nicomen, and, as I rode along the mountain side, I saw several Indian horses grazing on the "bunch grass" that then grew in profusion in the valley of the Thompson River, and in the little bay below me the tents of the Indians, but I saw no indication of human life about the tents. I therefore dismounted and went to the tents, where I discovered the horrible sight of the putrefying bodies of the Indians, some in the tents and others among the rocks that lined the river bank, through which*

they had evidently tried to drag themselves to the river to assuage their burning thirst, or to plunge into the river. All the Indians in that encampment had been dead several days.

I now proceeded [down] to the ferry and went [upstream] to the Indian village at the mouth of the Nicola River, where the same melancholy and disgusting sight was met that a few hours before I had seen at the little bay on the Thompson River, for all the Indians were dead. I hurried on to my camp at Nicomin [sic], fearing that the smallpox had broken out among my men, but was greatly relieved to find that such was not the case. (Robinson, 47)

Moberly had employed a number of the Spences Bridge "Indians with their little horses" to pack supplies between his work camps, and considered them excellent workers. He was extremely distressed with these morbid discoveries.

Here Come the Camels

In 1862, three ranchers from the Interior and a businessman from Lytton put their heads and money together and purchased 23 two-humped Asian camels from a camel dealer in San Francisco. They paid $300 apiece, twice the cost of a good mule.

The plan was to use them as pack animals along the Cariboo Wagon Road. In theory, camels were faster and stronger than packhorses or mules because they were larger.

The proud owners reasoned that they could quickly recover their investment. First, because the dromedaries could carry very heavy loads; second, because they walked much faster than the competitors' mules and packhorses did; and third, camels stopped less frequently to catch their breath.

The camels were loaded onto a ship in San Francisco and arrived in Victoria on May 2, 1862. Half the town watched the parade as they were carefully herded from the steamer into a pen in downtown Victoria.

The British Colonist newspaper had a lot of fun with the event and reported that one female camel "fired through her nostrils about two gallons of dirty water" onto an ill-mannered spectator, and then fled into the wilderness with her calf.

The remaining 21 camels eventually arrived via boat and barge at the north end of Harrison Lake, where the Douglas–Lillooet Trail started, and then were marched on up the road to Lillooet.

"The Lady", the last of the camels from the wagon road

In no time at all, the Asian camels, loaded with 400-pound packs, trudged along the Wagon Road on their way to Barkerville. Their journey had barely begun when one got spooked, fell off a cliff, and died. Now there were 20 camels, and the trouble really started.

A little farther along the trail, the camel train and a pack train of mules were about to encounter each other on the road. Long before they met, the mules sniffed the camels and panicked.

A cook, riding the bell mule (she was the favourite: the other mules always followed her), had all his kitchen paraphernalia hanging around him. He was immediately bucked off, and the entire mule train stampeded into the woods in hot pursuit of the bell mule and the noisy kitchen gear.

The camel owners, discovering that their animals stank, doused their big two-humped pets with perfume to try to disguise their smell. It didn't help. All the mules and horses encountered along the trail still bolted; even well-trained stagecoach horses went crazy at the smell of a camel, whether it smelled of cheap perfume or not.

Judge Matthew Begbie also had a bad experience with the camels. His story was reported in Vancouver's *Province* newspaper: "Judge Begbie was riding his cayoosh [horse] leisurely along when the cayoosh espied the camel train and despite the most strenuous efforts on the part of the rider carried the judge into the jungle, making havoc of his unmentionables" (Ramsey, *Pioneer Days in British Columbia*, 65). Begbie became a camel-hater when the swelling of his unmentionables subsided.

Besides their smell, the camels had other problems. Their hooves, designed for sand and not rock, quickly cracked on the wagon road; some animals went lame. A shoemaker was brought in to make special protective camel booties out of rawhide. But those were just a temporary fix.

The next difficulty was their ferocious appetites. Camels would eat and chew anything and everybody within their reach. Hats, ears, noses, fingers, and even parts of other camels always were a potential meal. Special camel muzzles were built and fastened to their faces, but then the camels became even more ornery.

To show their displeasure, they spit gallons of gooey mucous through their nostrils at anything or anybody close by. The average camel was not fond of much, so they spit often.

By October, the owners were down to a dozen animals still willing to work. As winter set in they were camped near Quesnel, where winters were always harsh. The Asian camels were simply let loose to spend their first Canadian winter on the outskirts of town, shuffling around in the snow to eat whatever they could forage.

The next spring, they were rounded up and marched back to Lillooet. However, everyone, including the owners, had enough of the camels. The last straw for the owners was when the stagecoach drivers either threatened or initiated lawsuits to get the two-humped competition off the Cariboo Road.

Nevertheless, disposing of bunch of ornery camels was not something easily done. Besides, a lot of money had been invested in them so there was a reluctance to discard them. In the end, the miners had no choice: the camels had to go. Some of the critters simply had their noses pointed in the direction of the wilderness and were kicked in the butt. Neighbouring ranches adopted several others; one poor long-haired beast wandering around in the woods was mistaken for a grizzly bear and shot by a miner. After that, the miner was known as "Grizzly Morris." And that particular camel didn't go to waste. Instead, he appeared on the menu at a local hotel in the form of a dinner special called "Grizzly's Bear."

One of the camel drivers led three of the friendliest, hardest-working longhairs to his farm at Westwold to help him clear land. However, they didn't live up to expectations and soon after, 404 pounds (two animals' worth) of well-trimmed camel meat became the property of the Hudson's Bay Company in Kamloops.

The third—a cuddly, smelly female christened "the Lady"—became a family pet. All the farm boys of Westwold, and even an occasional brave farm girl, rode her. The Lady, sheared like a sheep every spring, donated her hair for pillow and mattress stuffing.

Finally, in 1905, at a ripe old age that nobody knew for sure, the gentle critter leaned against a tree, hung her head, and died of old age.

Barnard's Express (also known as the BX Company)

Growing up on a small farm north of Vernon, I lived close to the BX Ranch. As a preteen and young teenager, I often walked or ran down the bank from our acreage to the BX Valley and fished for trout in BX Creek. A few of my favourite fishing holes were on ranch property.

I remember a large white country house, a rundown barn, and an outbuilding or two; the place always seemed deserted. I learned later that the original ranch house and barn had burned to the ground in 1911, taking the life of the then-owner's wife. What I saw in the late 1950s and early '60s were the replacement structures.

I have to admit that as a youngster, I was interested in fishing and not in history. It wasn't until years later that I first read about the connection between the company called Barnard's Express and the BX Ranch.

What eventually evolved into Barnard's Express began humbly in Yale in 1860. Francis Barnard, an entrepreneur, knowing that there was no mail service for the miners who had flooded into the Interior with the Fraser Canyon Gold Rush, took it upon himself to establish one.

The first "postman" in the Fraser Canyon, Barnard walked from Yale all the way to Barkerville and back in the fall of 1860, a distance of more than 750 miles, delivering mail (at $2.00 a letter) and papers along the way. On his return in early winter, he picked up mail and papers and transported them to Yale on his back.

In 1862, Barnard upgraded his operation to include a horse that he loaded with mail and led along the wagon road and trails. His pony express carried more letters and documents and was considerably faster. The next year he won the government mail contract and operated a regular pony express service between Yale and Barkerville.

Freighters set up camp for a much-needed break

With the completion of the Cariboo Wagon Road in 1863, he expanded the operation to two horses and a wagon. Now he could carry merchandise as well. In the winter, a sleigh replaced the wagon. In 1864, he hooked four horses to a stagecoach and transported people as well as freight. Later that year he upgraded to six horses and a still larger stagecoach and was able to carry up to 15 passengers at a time.

In 1868, Barnard sent his foreman, senior driver, and eventual owner of the company, Steve Tingley, to Mexico and California; Tingley purchased 400 horses and drove them back to Barnard's BX Ranch in Vernon. These horses became the breeding stock from which Barnard drew the horses needed on the stagecoaches and freight wagons. All the horses were broken exclusively for pulling a stage, a process that took three months.

In 1878, Barnard incorporated the British Columbia Express Company, which became known as BX. In 1886, he sold the business to Tingley, who moved the head office from Yale to Spences Bridge in 1884 and then to Ashcroft two years later.

Threshing grain at the BX Ranch in Vernon

By this time, BX was the largest express company in BC and operated very efficiently. Although the head office was in Ashcroft, the company had branch offices throughout its operating area. It had stations every 18 miles along the Cariboo Wagon Road, where fresh horses replaced the team that was pulling the stagecoach.

Tingley drove teams continuously until 1897 and then sold the company to a group of Toronto lawyers. In 1910, the company expanded into sternwheelers on the Fraser and automobiles along the wagon road. The stage operations continued until the opening of the Pacific Great Eastern Railway in northern BC in 1917. Stiff competition and operational problems created by the railway forced the closure of the stagecoach runs. The company folded in 1921.

The BX Ranch in Vernon has since been sold, subdivided, and resold many times and is now part of a private tourism operation called Vernon Hill Ranch. BX Creek still flows through the valley into Swan Lake north of Vernon. The BX Valley and BX Road are present-day reminders of Francis Barnard's successful entrepreneurship that commenced more than 150 years ago.

Thomson's Road Steamers

In 1864, shortly after the completion of the Cariboo Wagon Road, the colonial government granted permission to operate massive road steamers or steam trains along the road between Yale and Barkerville. The steamer was essentially a large, steam-powered, three- or four-wheeled tractor that pulled wagons loaded with supplies or coaches loaded with people. Invented by Robert Thomson in Ireland, road steamers were popular in many countries.

The vehicles had received rave reviews in Australia, India, and the United States as a fast (22 mph) and efficient means to move supplies and people. Each steam engine weighed over five tons. Each was 8½ feet wide and 15 feet long and had tires of hard, vulcanized India rubber that was five inches thick.

Roads were optional as these machines could go wherever they wanted—at least according to the promotional literature. The BX Company believed the promotional literature put out by the Scottish manufacturer that these units would replace horses and mules on the road in no time at all.

BX ordered six of these road steamers to carry freight and people along the Cariboo Wagon Road. Each was capable of hauling five tons of freight, but if the optional coaches were hooked to the main steam engine, 65 people could be pulled along behind the belching road tractor.

Two road steamers and two operators were eventually shipped from Scotland. The tractors were wood-burners and fitted with vertical boilers instead of horizontal ones. The vertical type worked well on the flat, but as was soon discovered, they threw a convulsion on any sort of incline.

But at the outset, the owners were optimistic. To prepare for the trip up the mountainous Fraser Canyon, they contracted woodcutters to stack firewood along the road at intervals from Yale all the way to Barkerville.

Advertising the new mode of transportation on the wagon road

In April 1871, after the first steamer finally arrived in Yale, it was immediately dispatched up the Cariboo Wagon Road, bound for Barkerville. Three wagons, each loaded with five tons of freight—no passengers on the first run—were hooked to the colossal tractor.

The tractor made good progress to Spuzzum, although it stopped more often than planned. The water level in the vertical boilers sloshed back and forth on every hill, causing overheating throughout the complicated tubing system. Overheating required frequent stops to cool the fireboxes. Stopping was not a good thing, since time was money.

The wood-burners also stopped frequently for firewood. Still, the first one made it from Yale to Spuzzum the first day; not a great start, but the operators admitted wrinkles still existed that needed fixing and then things would improve.

The second day, it chugged into Boston Bar amid cheering and waving from a crowd that had never heard of or laid eyes on such mechanization.

Early the third morning, the steamer was bound for Lytton. All went well until it was confronted by the steep incline at Jackass Mountain south of Lytton. Here the steamer stalled, coughed, moved a few feet, then stalled again.

Much like a stubborn mule, the "road train" finally refused to move any farther. Its 80-horsepower engine and gearing simply was not adequate for the combination of the steep road, the weight of the steam engine, and the 15 tons of freight that it was pulling. Although proud of the hills that his machine had traversed in Scotland, the brilliant inventor Thomson had not designed them for the rugged, steep mountains of BC.

The experiment failed before it shifted out of first gear. On the Cariboo Wagon Road, horse-drawn coaches and wagons were more efficient, cheaper to operate, and climbed Jackass Mountain to the top in half a day. Besides, horses didn't chew up the wagon road and leave ruts like those caused by the steamer.

The owners returned five of the units to Scotland and sold the sixth to Vancouver pioneer logger, Jeremiah Rogers. For years, Rogers used the steamer to skid logs from the forests of Shaughnessy, Kitsilano, and Little Mountain in Vancouver.

With the road steamers gone, it was back to the tried and proven horses, mules, and oxen. For more than four decades, they continued to haul people and freight along the road. It wasn't until the 20th century that automobiles began to slowly replace horses and mules.

First Cars along the Cariboo Wagon Road

The Cariboo Wagon Road is, after all, a road. Since it had been travelled by humans, horses, oxen, mules, and camels, it was fitting that, in the 20th century, automobiles also travelled along the wagon road.

A fleet of cars was based in Lytton in 1912

As early as 1907, a few vehicles owned by private freighters shuttled people along the Cariboo Road between Ashcroft and Soda Creek, then an important settlement and road terminus located 38 kilomeetres north of Williams Lake. Three years later, the largest freighting company in British Columbia, Barnard's Express, decided to get in the business and run automobiles on the Cariboo Road in addition to its teams of horses.

The Winton Sixes lined up in Ashcroft

Two cars manufactured by the Winton Motor Carriage Company, a pioneer US automobile manufacturer, arrived from a Seattle outlet. They had a base cost of $1,500 each (about $36,000 in today's money) plus additional features such as a battery-operated horn ($50), kerosene lights ($75), and special tops (only $150). The Winton Company provided two drivers, who also acted as trained mechanics, and sent them to Ashcroft to help keep the vehicles operational.

Service stations did not occupy every corner back then, so Barnard's Express built one at Ashcroft, along with a machine shop, to service the fleet. They made an arrangement with Imperial Oil for a supply of gas and oil in drums out of Vancouver. The drums were stationed at key locations along the wagon road between Ashcroft and Soda Creek, the route assigned to the two cars, to provide fuel.

The old and the new—a freight team passing an automobile on the wagon road

Soon, the company had a fleet of eight of these popular vehicles; advertisements guaranteed departures from May to October, regardless of the weather. To keep the cars on the road, a large crew of mechanics and drivers were hired and trained.

The cars grossed the company $67,233 in 1913 (about $1.6 million today); however, expenses were also very high with tires alone costing $15,835 ($375,000), and in the end it netted only $3,337 ($77,000). Barnard's Express disbanded the red and yellow vehicles (the company colours) several years later because the risk and investment did not justify such an insignificant profit.

Rattlesnakes

The rattlesnake, BC's only poisonous snake, lives in the hot, dry grassland habitats on the Thompson River between Savona and Lytton.

Rattlesnakes are BC's only poisonous snake

Shy by nature, it avoids confrontation whenever possible, especially with humans. When threatened, its distinctive rattle activates as a warning device; it will do its best to avoid sinking its teeth and ejecting poison (unless, of course, it is hunting for food). However, when it is surprised, the natural reaction is to strike at the threatening animal or person.

The rattlesnake is part of the pit viper family and has a very sensitive heat sensor called a pit between its eye and mouth. This heat sensor enables it to hone in on prey by noting a minute change in air temperature. The snake also flicks its tongue to "taste" the air and pick up the scent of any nearby prey.

The rattlesnake hibernates in a communal den from September to April, returning to the same den each year. Dens are generally located in rocky fissures or caves on south-facing slopes or ridges, and are far enough underground to prevent them from freezing in the winter. A rattlesnake can live up to 25 years and reach a length of 1.5 meters.

Years ago, a local old-timer told me that he had found a den in White Canyon, across the Thompson from the Kumsheen Resort. Every fall, as he drove his cattle back to Botanie Valley along a cattle trail near the canyon's spires, he would encounter rattlers heading back to their winter den. The location of this den may account for the rattlesnake in the Rattlesnake Rapid story (5.6 км).

In the past, indiscriminate hunting killed rattlesnakes by the hundreds. Now, the BC Wildlife Act recognizes rattlesnakes as an endangered species and serves to protect them.

There are many records and stories of rattlesnakes biting humans, and almost as many remedies for treating the bite. Here is a first-hand account of the application of one remedy for rattlesnake bites, as related by Anglican Bishop Sillitoe in August 1891:

> *We rode about twelve miles [upriver from Spences Bridge], passing on our way an Indian lying in his tent, ill from the bite of a rattlesnake. These reptiles are said to be very numerous in these parts, but from the fact that recovery from the bite is possible if the right remedy be used in time, I imagine they are not so deadly as in other countries. I am afraid I shall shock you if I describe the remedy; but remember it is a case of life or death. The bite is usually on the foot or leg, and a tight string is at once tied above the wound to prevent as far as*

possible the circulation of the poison in the blood. After that the patient is dosed with raw spirit [usually copious amounts of whiskey or rum] until the system becomes saturated [and the patient passes out]. The poison causes intense pain, and it takes a long time for it to work its way out. As there is a strict law in force in British Columbia forbidding the sale of liquor to Indians except on an order from a clergyman, doctor, or J.P., it is no easy matter for them to obtain the required remedy in time. (Gowan 183)

Another victim of a rattlesnake bite was not as fortunate as Bishop Sillitoe's patient. On July 2, 1904, *The Ashcroft Journal* reported the death of a prominent citizen, the daughter of Judge and Mrs Cornwall of Ashcroft Manor. She was bitten at 3 p.m. on June 30 and died the following morning. Here in part is what the paper reported:

The deceased was with her husband picking flowers from the veranda and it was while her hand was stretched out and near the ground, that the fatal blow was received on the finger. Mr. Barclay at once took such means as seemed best to check the deadly effects and sent a messenger to Ashcroft for Dr. Sanson. It was nearly two hours after the incident before Dr. Sanson arrived at the house where he stayed until the end.

Mrs Barclay was beloved by her friends and neighbours and the suddenness of her death has come as a severe shock to them. The heartfelt sympathy of the entire community goes out to the sorrow stricken husband, her father and mother, and other relatives. Besides her husband four sons survive, the youngest six months and the eldest about five years. Thirty-two years of age the deceased was the eldest child of his honour Judge Cornwall and Mrs. Cornwall.

Mrs Barclay's gravestone is still visible in the family plot across the highway from the Ashcroft Manor. Today, less than one tenth of 1percent of rattlesnake bites are fatal.

In the late 1970s, Kumsheen regularly hosted a group of 20 doctors and nurses from the Abbotsford General Hospital on a two-day rafting adventure between Ashcroft and Lytton. It was an annual event and the overnight trip offered them an opportunity to unwind. True to form, these doctors and nurses always brought along a black medical bag filled with basic tools and medicines.

On one of the two-day excursions, I stopped in at their overnight camp at Murray Creek Falls in Spences Bridge for a visit. I had hardly arrived when the doctor who had organized the group came running up to tell me that a rattlesnake had bitten him during the lunch stop at Asparagus Island.

It happened like this: one of the other doctors, a city type, had found a small snake while wandering around the island, picked it up by the tail, and brought it back to show his colleagues. He wandered around the luncheon table, waving the snake in the faces of the others, who were otherwise enjoying their lunch. The organizer saw this and recognized the snake as a young rattler. As he reached up to take the snake from his colleague's hands, the distressed little reptile bit him on the finger.

By the time I arrived, his finger had doubled in size from the swelling. He said that the emergency doctors who witnessed the bite had followed normal snakebite procedures—tourniquet, lance the wound, suction out the contaminated blood—but the swelling was worsening. He asked if I had any suggestions.

By coincidence, I had recently read some literature about rattlesnake bites and learned that infection caused by the snake's fangs often compounded the problems of the snake venom. I suggested that they dig into their black medical bag again and load up the finger with penicillin.

I saw the group again the next morning and was happy to see that the penicillin, along with the other treatments had worked. The finger was again almost at normal size. The doctor, however, was a wee bit hung over. He reported that yes, penicillin was injected; he had also tried an old whiskey remedy.

A week later, a photocopy from a page of a 1901 *Home Medical Text* arrived in the mail:

> *Give the patient all the Whiskey he can drink. From a quart to a gallon should be drunk in six to eight hours. No fear need be entertained of making the patient drunk. You may fill him with Whiskey, and then let him swim in it, and it will not make him drunk, so long as the poison of the snake remains in his system… It should be drunk like water for a few hours, and continued, at short intervals, until the patient gives*

signs of intoxication, when the quantity should gradually be diminished, as the disease is now beginning to recede. (Gunn, *Gunn's Household Physician, or, Home Book of Health,* 625)

Accompanying the excerpt was a handwritten note. The doctor wrote that from personal experience, he vouched for the old whiskey remedy. He added that many of his colleagues would also vouch for it, from their own experiences, as a preventative measure rather than a cure.

The Bonaparte Murder
Version #1

There are 80 pounds of gold (that would be worth millions of dollars) lying along the Bonaparte River somewhere between Cache Creek and Ashcroft.

In the 1860s, during the early days of the Cariboo Gold Rush, a miner was riding down from Barkerville to Yale with his stash of gold. Just south of Clinton, someone attacked, robbed, and violently murdered the unsuspecting man.

A local native, who had hidden in the bush and witnessed the murder, sneaked ahead and reported it to the manager of the Bonaparte ranch, not far from Cache Creek. This chap kept an open mind but also kept his gun handy and a sharp lookout for anyone or anything suspicious.

Sure enough, the manager soon saw what he assumed to be the bandit riding the miner's horse and carrying the miner's blanket roll and gold. (Obviously, the native must have given a very detailed account of the murderer.) Just like in the movies, a gun battle ensued. The rancher was a crack shot, but muskets have a short range and he wasn't sure he'd made a hit. The last thing the rancher thought he saw was the murderer hightailing it at full gallop along the Bonaparte River trail, heading toward the Thompson River.

Three weeks later, a riderless horse mysteriously appeared across the Thompson, not far from where the Bonaparte empties into our big river. A bloodstained saddle hung upside down under its belly. Clearly, one of the manager's musket balls had wounded the murderer.

The constable at Ashcroft pieced the puzzle together. First, the saddlebags were empty, but still attached to the saddle. He reasoned that the murderer, wounded, must have emptied the saddlebags and buried the 80 pounds of gold to lighten the horse's load for the swim across the

Thompson; he then made an effort to swim his horse across in order to camp in the hills until the air cleared. He would have intended to return later and retrieve his gold. As fate would have it, in his weakened condition the murderer fell off his horse and drowned while trying to cross the river. The stolen gold remains buried.

Now, where exactly should we begin our search?

The Bonaparte Murder
Version #2

While the actual events of the Bonaparte murder may never be fully known, the next account is probably closer to the truth. This story appears in Mark Wade's *The Cariboo Road*.

In 1863, Thomas Clegg, a clerk working for E.T. Dodge & Co. based in Lillooet, was sent to the Cariboo to collect some outstanding company accounts. Gold dust was a common currency back then, and Thomas collected about $10,000 or 50 pounds' worth that he carried in saddlebags secured to his favourite horse when travelling.

On his return trip to Lillooet, near Williams Lake, Clegg ran into an American acquaintance, Captain Taylor, and they travelled down the horse trail together. Clegg was happy to have a travelling companion because robberies frequently happened to solo travellers who carried gold.

They stopped together at 141 Mile (the distance from Lillooet, and about 20 miles from Williams Lake) and enjoyed a late afternoon dinner together. Clegg kept a close watch on the saddlebags, lugging them into Murphy's Roadhouse at 141 Mile and laying them at his side as they dined.

Two other men partaking there observed Clegg bring in his saddlebags and from how they were handled concluded that they contained something of considerable value. They left before Clegg and Taylor and headed down the road with the intention of robbing the two men.

Clegg and Taylor left soon after but instead of tying the saddlebags of gold on Clegg's horse, they secretly tied them onto Taylor's mule.

Down the road a few miles, the masked robbers jumped the two men, a struggle ensued, and Clegg took a bullet to the head from a Colt revolver. He died instantly. Taylor escaped with his mule and the gold dust, and he headed back up the road to Murphy's as fast as his mule would carry him to report the murder that he had just witnessed.

The two murderers quickly realized they had killed an innocent man for nothing and were now fugitives. They schemed to head south, into the US, travelling only at night.

Word quickly spread, and everyone between Williams Lake and Lytton was on the lookout for the murderers. Someone spotted them a few days later near Clinton, and in no time everyone along the Cariboo Wagon Road knew that they were somewhere in the area.

A nearby rancher on the Bonaparte River north of Cache Creek, Donald McLean, heard the news. A former Hudson's Bay chief trader, he made it his mission to capture the fugitives. Near his ranch, he tied ropes across the path so anyone coming down the trail at night would stumble in the dark and alert the farmhands who slept nearby and kept a watchful eye on the trail at night.

A few nights later when McLean himself was monitoring the ropes, the two fugitives skulked along the trail and tripped on the rope. McLean didn't see them but he fired several shots in direction of the noise. The murderers stumbled off into the darkness.

The next morning McLean discovered blood on the trail and knew a bullet had hit one of the murderers. The blood trail led toward the Thompson River. Apparently, reaching the Thompson, the fugitives had tried swimming across through relatively calm water above Black Canyon, three miles south of Ashcroft, and just east of where the great slide of 1897 later occurred.

The wounded man never made it across and drowned. His decaying body washed up the following spring on a gravel bar below Black Canyon. His partner, a better swimmer and not wounded, crossed without incident. However, a few days later some local men from the Spatsum Indian Band spotted and captured him near their reserve, about eight miles above Spences Bridge.

Chief trader Donald McLean escorted the fugitive to Lillooet, where he confessed to his crime. Judge Begbie presided at his trial, found him guilty, and sentenced him to death by hanging in Lillooet.

A certain pathos develops here. Nobody except a few very close friends knew the murderer's name as he…

> *…maintained an unbroken silence, but that he was of a good family in the Old Country is generally conceded by those who pretend to know about him. Mr. Elliott [the Judge who heard the original guilty plea] however, wrote*

to the man's mother, in accordance with a promise he had made, telling her that her son had been killed by Indians. Not the truth, of course, but the untruth—who would call it a lie?—at least saved a mother's heart from the awful pang and untold misery the whole truth would have caused. (Wade, *The Cariboo Road*, 160)

A well-dressed chief

11

A Handful of Characters

Chief Nicolas

*"A man so various that he seemed to be not one,
but all mankind's epitome."*—John Dryden

Many great Indian chiefs influenced the development and settlement along
the Thompson River. Purported to be one of the greatest, Chief Nicolas
(Hwistensmexe´qen) lived near the Thompson part of the year and the
Nicola River and Nicola Lake for most of the remainder.

By the time the first small parties of fur traders came to the area,
he was paramount chief of the huge Okanagan territory. His sphere of
influence extended from what is now Kamloops and the Nicola Valley in
the west to the large area stretching below the junction of the Okanagan
with the Columbia River, now part of the United States.

Nicolas was certainly "various." Not only was he a great chief, he
was a ferocious warrior, proficient hunter, skilled negotiator and trader,
expert guide, competent farmer, and one of the most valuable allies of the
Hudson's Bay Company men at Fort Kamloops.

The HBC's dependence on Nicolas's knowledge and influence is
noted throughout the company's Thompson River District journals.
When Archibald McDonald, his coworkers, and their families from Fort
Kamloops explored the Thompson River down to Lytton to determine its
suitability as a navigation route in July 1826, Nicolas was their guide and
intermediary with the indigenous peoples they encountered along the way.

Nicolas was born around 1785, probably at the Head of the Lake
(Okanagan Lake) near Vernon. He lived with at least 15 wives, chosen from
numerous Interior tribes, and fathered around 50 children. He usually

travelled with an escort of young men, but sometimes his entire family group journeyed with him as well. Semi-nomadic, they hunted, fished, farmed potatoes in the Merritt area in the summer, and travelled closer to Fort Kamloops or the Shuswap Lake area each winter, bartering their furs, produce, fish and game for wares, blankets, and assorted trade goods.

Nicolas displayed a character trait typical of great warriors of the time—the need for revenge if wronged. On November 20, 1822, the HBC post at Kamloops reported the arrival of Nicola's sister with the news that their father had been killed by a Lillooet chief while on a trading expedition for the HBC (Balf, Mary. *Nicola – A Very Great Chieftain*, Kamloops Museum Archives, 2).

Less than two months later, Nicola held a conference with four Shuswap chiefs at Kamloops, stating he was determined to avenge his father's death.

Rejecting the Lillooet chief's olive branches and gifts of appeasement, he prepared for battle for three months, assembling 500 mounted warriors from bands at Kamloops, the Shuswap, the Okanagan, Spences Bridge, and Lytton. According to James Teit, their retaliatory raid resulted in the death of 300 Lillooet Indians and the capture of many more; only then was Nicolas satisfied that justice had prevailed.

Despite his hostility toward the Lillooet tribe, Nicolas's friendship and conciliatory attitude toward the whites was legendary. His character was noted in an HBC journal entry in 1823 that confirms that he treated the whites very well but also noted that should he turn against them, they had lots to fear.

On February 8, 1841, a youth from the Shuswap band murdered HBC chief trader Samuel Black, a very good friend of Chief Nicolas. Black taught Nicolas how to till the soil and even lent him the HBC plow, a very precious commodity at the time, so he could grow potatoes. At Black's funeral, he delivered an impressive oration that was reported by Archibald McKinlay, a fur trader:

> *A mountain has fallen! The earth is shaken. The sun is darkened to us poor miserable Indians, but we can blame no one for it but ourselves… My heart is sad. I cannot look at myself in a glass… He was kind, just and generous to us; and I know he loved us. Wherefore did we kill him? He is dead and we shall never see him again. Our wives and children will weep and wail for him. Indian men do not weep, but*

their hearts will be sore for a long time. You, my friends of the Shushwap [sic] tribe, the murderer is one of you. Justice calls on him to die, and die he must. (Balf, 4)

Nicolas persuaded the Shuswaps to assist in the capture of the youth. One of Nicolas's sons was in the party that eventually tracked down the murderer. As he was being brought to the Fort where the intention was to hang him, he tried to escape while crossing the Thompson near Savona, nearly drowning the two men who were bringing him across. He was shot and wounded and upon reaching the opposite side, he was again driven back into the river where he sank to the bottom and drowned.

Nicolas showed remarkable tolerance and understanding during the events that unfolded with the influx of American miners in 1858. As unruly Americans waged an indiscriminate war against the Okanagan natives, killing many innocent men, women, and children, Nicolas successfully urged the young warriors under his influence to exercise restraint. Perhaps it was his old age—he died the following year—that tempered Nicolas's anger and thirst for revenge. Whatever it was, Nicolas was instrumental in averting a major war between a coalition of native groups and the looting and pillaging white miners.

A mining prospector who witnessed many atrocities and who kept a detailed journal of his experiences, Herman Francis Reinhart, recalled that Nicolas rebuked the miners in a manner that revealed the scope of his authority and influence among his people:

He blamed us for butchering the O[kanagan] Indians in cold blood and the O Indians had sent some messengers to him to avenge the death of his people, but he said he had better teachings from good men and priests, and good advice from Capt. McL[ea]n, head of the Hudson['s] Bay Company, and they advised him and his people to overlook the great crime. But…he had great trouble to quiet and calm down his young warriors, of which, with the Lake O tribe, he could have raised from 1800 to 2000 warriors, and could have surprised our command and cut them off to a man, utterly annihilating the whole of us, and taking all our animals and all our plunder. But he could not have told how it would have gone after, for he would have lost all control of his people, and the war chiefs would have usurped his power and carried on a general war against the whites, Americans, and English. Being the massacre had taken place in British Columbia, it would be the duty of the English queen Victoria to see justice done to her subjects, and he was right, no doubt. (Nunis, *The Golden Frontier: The Recollections of Herman Francis Reinhart 1851–1869*, 131)

Reinhart described Nicolas a year before his death in 1859: "He was an old man about 65 or 70 years old, wore a stove pipe hat and citizen's clothes, and had a lot of medals of good character and official vouchers of good conduct for many years" (Nunis, 129).

It is merciful that he died three years before the smallpox epidemic of 1862. He was also spared from seeing his people herded onto reserves while much of his favourite land was given to white settlers. "He was a great man, despite his [mistaken] belief that the white man and his justice were equally noble" (Balf, 9).

The Hanging Judge

Commonly known as the "Hanging Judge," Judge Matthew Begbie was an interesting and talented character whose legal decisions are legendary.

He arrived in Victoria in 1858 and the following spring headed into the Interior to get a first-hand look at the country and communities that he would later serve. He walked and rode hundreds if not thousands of miles, getting to know the miners and mining camps and judging cases everywhere.

History says that he was an unorthodox judge at times, applying common sense to his decisions when he needed to, and that he was a defender of the rights of First Nations people, who called him "Big Chief."

He was a very tall man, six-foot-five, with a deep baritone voice and a bearing that immediately commanded respect. Wherever he held court—in a courthouse, a barn, a tent, or astride his horse—he always wore the appropriate judiciary robes and always created the atmosphere of an English court of law. He had many talents and skills: he was a fly fisherman, an opera singer, a surveyor, an artist, an adventurer, and, of course, an exemplary judge.

During Begbie's era, if the accused was found guilty of murder, he had to be hung. The judge had no choice or say in the matter. Only 27 of

Begbie's 52 murder cases ended in a hanging; he even wrote to Governor Douglas about at least two cases that involved a native and alcohol, requesting leniency on behalf of the convicted murderer. "Leniency" usually meant a lifetime in jail.

Judge Begbie in a sombre, formal moment

Begbie's comments to his juries added to the longevity of his reputation as a hanging judge. In those days, the jurors were often lawless Americans who returned a not guilty or manslaughter verdict when the evidence clearly pointed to premeditated murder. This always infuriated Begbie.

In one case, where overwhelming evidence pointed to murder but the jurors came back with a manslaughter verdict, he harangued the murderer and the jurors with the following:

> *You deserve to be hanged! Had the jury performed their duty I might now have the painful satisfaction of condemning you to death, and you, gentlemen of the jury, you are a pack of Dalles horse thieves and permit me to say, it would give me great pleasure to see you hanged, each and every one of you, for declaring a murderer guilty only of manslaughter.* (Pettit, BCHQ, 145)

It was largely thanks to Begbie, with his reputation as a fair but strict enforcer of the law, that order was maintained during the difficult times in the Crown Colony of British Columbia's infancy.

Lytton's First Government Employee

For at least a decade that began in 1858, Lytton was strategically located and a place of great importance. It was the centre where various government officials resided and whose jurisdiction extended over practically the whole of what is now Kamloops, the Okanagan Valley, and the Nicola Valley.

Governor Douglas appointed an eccentric Frenchman named Captain Oswald Travaillot (first mentioned in Chapter 7) in June 1858, as revenue officer and gold commissioner for the District of Fort Dallas or Fork of Thompson's River.

His primary job was to issue mining licenses and collect legal fees from miners. Additionally, he was empowered to raise and maintain a "police" force of eight men for the service of government and to swear in as special constables everyone taking out a mining license for maintaining law and order.

Travaillot was one of Douglas's first appointees, and for a very short while, he was probably the most powerful government employee in the

Interior. And like many early gold miners, Travaillot was a colourful character with idiosyncrasies that stretched his personality beyond the commonplace.

One story that circulated about the good captain accused him of confiscating a lot of illegal whiskey, which often arrived with miners who came overland from south of the international boundary.

In the winter of 1858, a pack train arrived at Lytton that supposedly was laden with provisions, but whose cargo consisted primarily of kegs of liquor. Because regulations weren't complied with, Travaillot confiscated the entire outfit—cargo and animals.

In January, a party of miners arrived in Lytton. It took the party no time at all to sniff out the wholesale seizure of the "firewater." One of the smooth-talking miners suggested that they all, as a matter of courtesy, pay the gold commissioner a visit.

After some small talk, it was suggested to Travaillot that a great joke had been played on him and that the kegs of liquor that he seized were filled with water. Apparently, the good captain sat bolt upright, the picture of bewilderment, and the smile gone from his pleasant face, when he heard the news.

To prove the gossip wrong, a keg was brought in and Travaillot duly tapped it and drew off a sample glass. It didn't look like water, and it didn't smell like water, so the captain impatiently thrust the glass into the each miner's hand and encouraged them all to sample.

Soon every man had tested and sampled to his heart's content including the hospitable captain, who did not for one moment forget his duty as host. He set such a good example that, overcome by the potent fumes of the liquor, he became confidential, then overemotional, and finally had to be put to bed by the miners. It can only be speculated how much more of the liquor the miners tested as the good captain slept.

James Teit

James Teit is undoubtedly one of Spences Bridge's most eminent figures.

Teit left Scotland in the winter of 1883 at age 19, taking the same ship as John and Jessie Ann Smith on his way to Spences Bridge. Teit's uncle, John Murray, a well-established Spences Bridge businessman, needed an assistant to operate and perhaps inherit his many businesses, and Teit hoped to do just that.

Although Teit did work for Murray for a while, the older man had already given away or sold most of his business assets by the time his nephew arrived. Regardless, Teit settled into life in Spences Bridge, married a local native woman, and became a big game hunting guide. He soon acquired an international reputation.

James Teit and his native wife Antko

Thanks to his marriage with a First Nations woman and involvement with the community, Teit learned much about the lives, the grievances, the strengths, and the sufferings of the indigenous Thompson people.

In Spences Bridge in 1894, Teit met Dr. Franz Boas. Boas, a professor of anthropology at Columbia University, was researching First Nations peoples in the BC Interior, and Teit became his indispensable local associate.

For the next 25 years, working closely with Boas and other anthropologists, Teit chronicled the lives of the Thompson, Shuswap, Lillooet, Okanagan, and Carrier Indians and gained a reputation as one of the best ethnographers in the world.

The Thompson Indians of British Columbia was Teit's first major publication. Franz Boas edited and the American Museum of Natural History published this edition of Teit's fieldwork in 1900. Many other publications followed as his ethnographical work broadened and deepened in scope. He was the author of 11 books.

Besides recording in detail the lives of the First Nations peoples, Teit took thousands of photographs and recorded songs and legends. He collected hundreds of artefacts; most are currently housed in museums in Canada and the United States.

He also immersed himself deeply into First Nations politics, becoming a social activist and petitioning on their behalf. In both 1912 and 1916, he travelled to Ottawa with delegations of chiefs representing the Thompson, Okanagan, Shuswap, and Lillooet peoples. The 1912 group called themselves the Indian Rights Association of British Columbia. They aired their concerns directly to the Honourable R. Borden, premier of the Dominion of Canada, and his cabinet. Teit acted as interpreter.

By 1919, his primary focus became First Nations politics, and his writing and research declined. In 1920, diagnosed with cancer, his life took a turn for the worse. He passed away in Merritt on October 30, 1922, at the age of 58.

Krazy Arpat

Arpat Schneider always lived for the next adrenalin fix; his short life was a series of adventures.

I met Arpat in 1973, the first year that I offered rafting trips on the Thompson River. He stopped in at my Spences Bridge headquarters/office/living quarters (the 15-foot travel trailer) for a chat.

He was about 30 years old and wore thick glasses the size of coke bottle bottoms. His infectious laugh exposed braces on both his upper and lower teeth. His eyes sparkled when he told his stories, and when he laughed, he spanked both his thighs simultaneously for emphasis.

We had a good chat and he related at least a dozen funny and riveting stories of his exploits. I was convinced that he pushed life to the limit in order to have the delight of story-telling afterward.

By the time he left that afternoon, we agreed to paddle down the Thompson to Lytton together in my 15-foot Avon Professional River Runner raft, a raft so large that "it probably can't squeeze through the canyon on the lower Thompson," according to Arpat. Nevertheless, he was willing to give it a go the next time he was in the area.

I was impressed with his vast river experience, even if many of his exploits were on the edge of madness. In one of his stories, Arpat decided to follow in the footsteps of a 1960s British expedition that made the first modern-day descent down the entire Fraser River. He reasoned that if they could do it, he could too.

Krazy Arpat leads my first descent of the lower Thompson in 1973

And so, in 1970, he purchased a 15-foot Canova inflatable raft and a short time later launched it near the headwaters of the Fraser. Thus began his 800-kilometre descent of the entire Fraser River to Vancouver. He was alone when he started and alone for most of the journey.

A friend joined him for the ride through Hell's Gate, which he luckily completed without serious trouble. A few kilometres downriver, however, he flipped his raft in the huge swells of Sailor Bar rapid. Somehow, he and his friend managed to get the boat to shore, empty it of water, restart the outboard, and resume the trip.

A couple of days later, alone in the dark somewhere near New Westminster, Arpat was so sick that he was hallucinating. He made his way to a hospital, where he spent the next three weeks recovering from exhaustion and a variety of parasites. He had been drinking the untreated water of the Fraser during his two-week trip. "I almost died," he said, laughing. "I was so skinny that I could tread water in a test tube."

Arpat also rafted Hell's Gate during peak runoff in 1972, the highest water level since 1948. The first wave hit his tiny craft with such force that it propelled him out of the boat. He managed to grab an outside line as he went over and bobbed through the rest of the rapid, hanging onto the raft's safety lines. He showed me photos of the raft entering Hell's Gate, and I marvelled at the immensity of the waves and boils that dwarfed the little Canova.

The following year, Arpat swam through Hell's Gate in a wetsuit, nearly succumbing to exhaustion after being held in a back eddy immediately below the rapids for almost two hours. "I thought it was all over—then the river got tired of me and just spat me out into the current. I was almost dead by then and just floated all the way down to the Alexandra Bridge, where I was washed ashore like a floater."

For a few years, he owned and flew his own acrobatic plane. He had many narrow escapes with it and once flew under the bridge that spans the Fraser River at Prince George. "Almost lost my license over that one," he explained, always laughing as he told his stories. Then he flew to the Yukon, explored some northern rivers and lakes, and noted on a map the remotest lake that he saw. His plan was to go back to that desolate lake and shoot a sheep that would get him in the record books.

It was in late August 1973 when Arpat came back to Spences Bridge. Together with a few of my friends from Lytton, to whom I offered a free ride, we paddled down to Lytton. That was my first descent from Spences Bridge to Lytton, and remarkably, it went without incident.

Arpat led a few raft trips for me in 1974, but we both understood that he would be leaving in mid-July to head back to his remote lake in the Yukon. The plan included a drop off at Lake Desolation on August 1 and a pick up on October 1. His official reason for going was to prospect for gold (anyone not from the Yukon was required to hunt with a hunting guide), so he planned to take along his prospecting gear. His real intent was to hunt a sheep with record-breaking horns.

Kayaker about to enter the huge standing wave caused by Krazy Arpat Rock at high water

Arpat's raft-guiding days were cut short after a particular incident on the river, but he did not mind. A few weeks later, he was in his car on the way to the Yukon. On his way north, he stopped in Lytton for a brief visit and to say goodbye, and he left Lytton in his usual erratic style, driving south toward Vancouver when he really meant to head north. Just as I thought he'd messed up again, he laughed, his braces glistening and, slapping the steering wheel, did a U-turn on the Trans-Canada and headed for the Yukon.

That was the last time I saw Arpat. He was dropped off by a float plane at his beautiful lake on August 1, according to plan. The float plane that went to retrieve him on October 1 was unable to land because of a snowstorm. It landed three days later on skis, but there was no sign of

Arpat. His tent was found lying under three feet of snow. His sleeping bag was laid out inside, his rifle was propped up beside his bedroll, and everything was in perfect order, but Arpat was missing.

Whitehorse RCMP flew to the camp in a helicopter to continue the search. No sign of Arpat was found anywhere. His camera was in the tent; in the hope of learning something about his disappearance, the film was developed. The last photo taken was on September 21, a self-portrait of Arpat with a dozen dead wolves, each of them hanging by one foot in a circle around his camp. He had a strange look in his eye. Isolation most likely got the best of him.

What really happened to Arpat? No one knows. Some of his friends flew into the lake the following summer to look for clues but found none. He simply vanished off the face of the earth.

When I first heard the news, I fantasized that aliens had landed and whisked him away in their spaceship as a typical human specimen. The joke would have been on the aliens.

Original Jaws of Death wooden bridge in 1889

CPR Construction and the Role of the Chinese

To better understand the important connection between the Chinese and the Canadian Pacific Railway (CPR), it's necessary to have a look at what went on in British Columbia during the early years of the province.

In 1867, BC was a Crown colony of Great Britain, separated from the rest of Canada by the Rocky Mountains. The gold rush that began a decade earlier had ended, and the region had subsequently slid into an economic depression and was up to its colonial ears in debt.

US Should Take over BC

Conditions were so bleak that there was a yearning on the part of some people for British Columbia to be annexed to the United States. In 1867, the first of two annexation petitions circulated in Victoria. Addressed to the Queen, it requested that the British government assume the colony's financial burdens and establish steamboat service between the colony and Britain. Alternatively, BC should be permitted to join the United States. It is unknown how many signatures the petition gathered or if the Queen ever received it.

In 1869, a group of property holders and businessmen wrote a second requisition: The Annexation Petition. It was delivered to American president Ulysses S. Grant by the Alaska Indian commissioner. (Alaska had recently been purchased by the US, and some folks thought that BC was next on the American acquisition list.) The petition asked that the president begin negotiations with Great Britain for the transfer of British Columbia to the United States.

The petitions caught the attention of Canadian politicians, who pushed for BC to join Canadian Confederation instead of the United States. In 1871, prime minister John A. Macdonald promised to build a transcontinental railroad that would link the province to the rest of Canada. British Columbia took the prime minister at his word and, on July 20, 1871, joined Confederation.

Living conditions were especially tough the first few years

Work on the railroad was to start within two years of joining Confederation and to be completed within ten years. However, politics, finances, and scandal after scandal delayed the start. It wasn't until the premier of BC at the time, Amor De Cosmos, threatened to withdraw the province from Confederation and join the United States that the Canadian House of Commons finally approved the railroad construction on February 15, 1881. Ten years had passed since the initial promises.

CPR Receives Government Subsidies

The government gave the Canadian Pacific Railway Company, a private company started by a group of executives, $25 million in cash and almost 25 million acres of land suitable for settlement. Property used for railway purposes was to remain free of taxation forever. Equipment imported for building the railway was admitted into Canada duty-free.

The government passed laws that provided a virtual monopoly to the CPR for 20 years. It also agreed to look after the cost of construction of 342 miles of the western rail line—Port Moody (Vancouver) to Craigellachie near Revelstoke, the most challenging and expensive section of the entire line—and then donate it to the CPR.

The project contractor for the construction from Vancouver to Savona's Ferry was 37-year-old Andrew Onderdonk, the American engineer and construction contractor (whom we first heard about in Chapter 7 in the story of the *Skuzzy*) who was the front person for a group of wealthy American financiers. Onderdonk entered into five separate contracts with the Canadian government that covered the construction of the 215 miles of main line.

Onderdonk's Contract #63, from Junction Flat (a few miles north of Spences Bridge) to Savona's Ferry, was signed on December 15, 1879, more than a year before the government in Ottawa passed the railway act formally approving the construction of the railway. In fact, all four of his contracts to build the railway from Yale to Savona were signed prior to February 15, 1881, the date that royal assent was given to the bill outlining the terms and conditions of the railway. Tunnel blasting began at Yale late in 1879, more than a year before the bill was passed in the House of Commons.

It's interesting to speculate on the outcome had Parliament not approved the railway construction in 1881. Approval was not a *fait accompli*, as passage of the bill in the House of Commons required over two months of bitter debate.

As things turned out, the Canadian taxpayers paid for most of the construction of railway in western Canada. Not only did taxpayers pay for the construction, they donated the land, provided the CPR with huge amounts of cash, and approved a 20-year-or-until-sold tax-free status to the railway for any land removed from the land grant and sold. Then, upon completion of construction, the government donated the government-financed portion of the railway to the CPR.

Onderdonk in a Dilemma

As work on the railway progressed, Onderdonk knew his contracts with the government were below his own cost estimates to build the railroad from Vancouver to Savona. The shortfall was more than $1.5 million, and he had to find ways to save money.

He had initially promised the Canadian government that he would first employ surplus white labour from BC and the rest of Canada, then French Canadians, then First Nations from Canada and the US, and lastly, Chinese.

That promise placed Onderdonk in a dilemma. He knew that he could not make up for his shortfall without hiring Chinese workers, who would accept lower wages than other labourers. He petitioned the federal government and told them the railway simply could not be built unless he was allowed to use Chinese labour. The cost-conscious federal government approved his request, much to the chagrin of the BC government.

Although the province already had a sizeable Chinese population following the gold rush in the late 1850s, racism toward the Chinese was widespread. Most newspaper articles and editorial illustrations of the time repeatedly portrayed the Chinese in a degrading way. The Chinese culture was repugnant to white Canadians, who made no effort to understand the virtues of their practices.

Onderdonk Imports Chinese

Between 1881 and 1884, as work on the railway progressed, more than 15,000 Chinese came to Canada. Several thousand travelled north from coastal areas of the US, where they had helped build the American transcontinental railroad. These were experienced railway workers—just what Onderdonk needed. However, he needed many more to meet his business objectives and fatten his bottom line.

In 1882, Onderdonk chartered ten sailing ships and conveyed around 6,500 men from the Guangdong and Fujian provinces in southern China to Canada. Recruitment companies in China advertised the job opportunities and arranged passage on ships. The miserable voyage in crammed holds below deck cost each worker $40, payable once work began. Workers also paid 2.5% of their wage to the recruitment company.

Workers, mostly uneducated, unskilled, and unmarried, came from a country devastated by two wars that had claimed millions of lives. In the mid-1800s, starvation and poverty were the norm. Most came from rural areas in the two provinces, where they rented their small farms from a handful of wealthy Chinese who owned most of the land. Crippling high rents and taxes consumed the farms' profits, forcing many peasants to borrow money just to feed their families. Given the opportunity to gain financial independence, Chinese labourers eagerly boarded ships by the thousands and headed to Onderdonk's railway in Canada.

Onderdonk later built 1200 log cabins for the Chinese workers

Women did not emigrate at first, mostly because of historical tradition and societal norms that expected women to be caretakers of family and ancestral roots. A $50 head tax later prevented migration of the women who wanted to marry those Chinese labourers who remained in Canada after the railway was built.

Three-masted sailing ships took workers from Hong Kong to Victoria in two or three months, depending on the weather. On board, they endured extremely crowded conditions, the men below decks slept in closed hatches with poor ventilation, and food and water were scarce. At Victoria, the ones who survived boarded jam-packed ferries to cross the

Georgia Strait to New Westminster, where they transferred to smaller boats for the journey up the Fraser River to Yale.

At Yale, the voyage by water ended. The Chinese were divided into groups of 30 men. Each group had a cook, an assistant cook, a Chinese record keeper who kept track of work hours and other details, and a white supervisor who dealt directly with the record keeper. The Chinese labourers paid for their own work utensils, camp equipment, and cooks.

Once the groups were created, they slowly trekked along the Cariboo Wagon Road to a railroad camp near Lytton. As they trudged along, the wagon road often disappeared because of blasting or other railway construction already underway. They continued their march to Lytton along narrow trails, carrying their supplies suspended on shoulder poles or in large packs on their backs.

The Lytton to Savona's Ferry section of the railroad was built using primarily Chinese labour. Chinese, white, and First Nations labour, both from Canada and the US, worked on the section from Boston Bar to Lytton, while mostly white labour worked on the section from Yale to Boston Bar, the first section that Onderdonk began in May 1880.

Discriminatory Wage System

Onderdonk's discriminatory wage system paid Chinese workers less than white workers, who were paid $1.50 to $2.50 per day. The Chinese wage of $0.80 to $1.00 per day was barely enough for survival. As part of their contract, the Chinese workers were required to buy their supplies at CPR company stores, where prices were often inflated. After paying for food, clothing, equipment, and shelter, there was usually little or no money left over. White workers, on the other hand, had their camping gear and cooking gear supplied for free.

During the three winter months when construction came to a standstill, the labourers were forced to whittle away at their meagre savings that on average amounted to $43 per worker per year. Since many had borrowed money for passage to Canada, the savings often went to the agents who had loaned them the money for their fares.

For a dollar a day, the Chinese undertook the dangerous, backbreaking jobs. Using simple tools and manual labour, they built roadbeds, bridges, and tunnels along a route that spanned deep canyons and rivers and cut through hard granite mountains. They moved an unimaginable amount of rock and gravel in pushcarts and on shoulder poles. They worked under extreme conditions, sometimes clinging to the side of a steep mountainside or being suspended in the air by harnesses in the skeleton of a partially built bridge. They were unaccustomed to working in the cold and often found it nearly intolerable.

Hard-working Chinese labourers with a white foreman

On October, 4, 1883, *The Inland Sentinel* newspaper summarized the treatment that the Chinese received this way: "The poor Chinamen were treated much after the manner in which the worst class of slave-owners in the Southern States used to care for their unfortunate 'chattles.'"

Chinese Die by the Hundreds—or Thousands

Onderdonk admitted that more than 600 Chinese died in work-related accidents. Others estimated that several thousand died, some from malnutrition and diseases like scurvy. The exact number of deaths is unknown, as Chinese deaths were not reported by Onderdonk's company.

Safety measures to protect Chinese workers from injury or death were almost nonexistent. During blasting, in particular, workers were crushed by collapsing tunnels and rock slides; Chinese were often required to use volatile nitroglycerine instead of the more stable TNT dynamite. One incident occurred in 1883 in which a Chinese worker had his head blown off because the work gang was not given adequate warning of the blast. The white foreman dove into the river to escape the remaining angry workers, who attacked him with their tools and rocks.

Deaths and train wrecks were frequent, especially in the early years

Families in China were often not notified when someone died, nor was compensation paid as promised by the agents. Usually the bodies were simply buried next to the tracks so work could resume as quickly as possible. In 1891, the bones of more than 300 men from graves in the Thompson and Fraser Canyons were collected by the Chinese Consolidated Benevolent Society and returned to China for burial.

The Chinese: Honest, Hardworking, Dutiful

Generally, the Chinese were considered honest, hardworking, and dutiful. However, they reacted strongly to defend themselves if they felt the railway contractors had treated them unfairly, especially if they were exposed to unnecessary danger.

The worst incident occurred on May 10, 1883, at a Chinese camp three miles south of Lytton. After a white supervisor was assaulted by the Chinese for firing a Chinese worker and refusing to pay him for the work he had already performed, the white workers retaliated. *The British Colonist* in Victoria reported the event three days later:

> *An inquest is being held here [in Lytton] today on the body of the Chinaman, Ah Fook who died from the effects of the assault made on the Chinese camp by white men last Tuesday night.*

Great difficulty was met in obtaining the requisite number of disinterested jurymen. The inquest opened at 4 p.m. and a few witnesses were examined.

> *From the evidence it appears that a number of the Chinamen belonging to camp 37 assaulted their foreman Tuesday morning and that at about 10 o'clock the same night a body of about 20 white men marched down to the Chinese camp armed with clubs and as the frightened Chinese left their houses they brutally assaulted them. One man died from the wounds received and some seven or eight others are seriously injured. The houses were then set fire to and the white men left. It is expected that some assailants will be identified by the wounded Chinamen; but so far no clue has been found as every effort has been made by white laborers along the line to screen their guilty comrades. Supt. Todd, who is conducting the inquest, is using every endeavor to discover the perpetrators of this the most unmanly and cowardly affair that has yet occurred in the country. The inquest will probably be brought to a close tomorrow morning.*

Two Chinese workers died in the attack. The body of one was found in a hole near the Chinese camp and another seriously injured man was taken by his friends to the Chinese joss house in Lytton (described in Chapter 7), where he died of his wounds.

The following day the inquest resumed, but as it was impossible to identify any of the murderers, no charges resulted.

Chinese Work Camp at Kumsheen Rafting Resort

Chinese work camps consisted primarily of canvas structures and were quite portable, but Onderdonk also constructed 1,200 log cabins for them along the line. They moved along as work progressed. It made sense to be as close to the job site as possible. Major camps were established at Lytton, Spences Bridge, Ashcroft, and Savona, with satellite camps in between.

I discovered the remains of a Chinese work camp on the Kumsheen property when developing the resort in 1994. As I levelled a campsite for our guests in the Back 40 camping area, I unearthed a stash of bones. My first thought was that I had disturbed a gravesite. However, I then found a number of long, perfectly preserved boar tusks. Most people don't have tusks attached to their skulls.

I quickly realized that I was dealing with a Chinese encampment when I discovered the scant remains of cooking pots and several depressions in the ground. This had obviously been the location of a Chinese cookhouse, and as the bones of the pigs were emptied from the pots after making a broth, they were unceremoniously dumped into a hole behind the cookhouse. (Not a scrap of pork was wasted. Pork was a Chinese delicacy and considered nutritionally essential. Onderdonk occasionally supplied the workers with pigs to supplement their diets after deaths caused by scurvy during the winter.)

It has been estimated that Onderdonk's plan to import Chinese railway workers reduced his cost of building the railway by 25 percent, a savings of between three and five million dollars. Onderdonk, the Canadian government, and the CPR benefitted from their labour. Because of the Chinese labourers, the railway construction progressed, and British Columbia wasn't annexed by the United States.

Thousands of men were forced to ride the rails during the Great Depression of the 1930s

13 The Iron Horse Arrives

Although the Chinese played a pivotal role in constructing the western portion of the CPR, apparently none were invited to the driving of the last spike that literally and symbolically linked the western and central divisions of the railway and Canada as a nation.

During a ceremony on November 7, 1885, at 9:22 a.m., the western and central sections of the transcontinental railroad were officially linked at Craigellachie, a small settlement not far from Revelstoke, BC. The simple "Last Spike" ceremony of driving a spike into the last rail section to anchor it in place marked the completion of a monumental task. Symbolically, it still stands as a symbol of national unity.

The direct construction cost of the CPR to Canadian taxpayers was about $52 million (an economic cost of approximately $68 billion in 2013), *plus* lost taxation revenues, lost duty revenues, lost land sale revenues, and myriad other less obvious lost returns for Canadian taxpayers.

The impact of the CPR line on Canada generally, and on the Thompson River specifically, was significant. As the Last Spike ceremony was taking place, 6,000 Chinese were already out of work and many were starving. To make matters worse, in BC anti-Chinese sentiment hit the highest point as many ragged workers wandered about as if in a stupor, ill and homeless.

Many of the newly unemployed had survived the harsh winter of 1883–84, when Onderdonk temporarily laid them off for three months with no pay, no accommodation, and no food. A traveller along the Thompson River reported seeing hundreds of men dug into holes just to find some warmth provided by the ground below the surface. The Spences Bridge area absorbed 2,000 men that winter. Many survived by collecting and consuming dead salmon found along the river, and a few resorted to theft of food from neighbouring farms. Miraculously, most survived.

After the completion of the railroad, a few who could afford the journey left Canada and returned to their homeland in China. Some found their way to Vancouver and Victoria or to eastern Canada, where they picked up any work available. Others stayed in the Interior and worked as merchants, in sawmills, as general labourers, in market gardens, as laundrymen, as cooks, or as domestic servants. Still others became permanent CPR employees, working on gangs maintaining sections of the track. Many became placer miners along the Thompson and Fraser Rivers, working for themselves or for wages of $1.00 a day.

Chinatowns along the Thompson

Many of these immigrants congregated and clung together in Chinatowns. Lytton and Ashcroft had sizeable Chinese communities after the completion of the railway. Generally, the men supported one another and could work and live within their isolated enclaves in relative safety and security. Many developed or worked in market gardens or farms, and others, identifying the need for supplies and equipment, opened merchandise stores to supply their own people as well as the white population. In Ashcroft, a Chinese man opened a store in 1886, and three years later, there were four Chinese businesses. This typified the entrepreneurial spirit of the Chinese and their culture of supporting one another.

Prostitutes imported from China eased the burden on the single men who dominated the Chinese communities by a ratio of 1 to 82. In 1885, only 160 Chinese women were listed in all of BC. Of these, 70 were listed as prostitutes, many of them living as concubines since it was an accepted cultural practice for Chinese men to support a concubine or two.

Most remained bachelors because in 1885 the Canadian government levied an expensive head tax of $50 for any Chinese coming to Canada. Few families in China could afford to send their daughters to Canada to marry those who remained here, whether or not they had been previously betrothed. The tax mushroomed to $100 in 1900 and $500 two years later. So much for gratitude to them for accepting lower wages and inferior working conditions while building the railway.

It wasn't easy for the Chinese to live and work in a country that no longer wanted them. Attitudes toward them had changed significantly from the early 1860s when they enjoyed the same legal rights as British subjects in the colony of BC.

Chinese adapted well and many became successful merchants

An article in *The British Colonist* in 1861 stated: "We have plenty of room for many thousands of Chinamen…there can be no shadow of a doubt but their industry enables them to add very largely to our own revenues…"

Although times were tough for them in BC after 1885, they were tougher still at home in China. Men originally came to BC to work a few years to earn their fortune with the hope of returning to China with at least $300 in their pockets. A man with that much money was considered wealthy in much of China at the time. Unfortunately, very few realized their dream of returning to China and financial independence.

Communities Transform

With the completion of the railway in 1885, communities along the Thompson River between Savona and Lytton instantly grew. Immediately hotels sprang up in proximity to the train stations. At Savona, most of the town was relocated from the north side of the lake to the south side close to the railway by skidding buildings across frozen Kamloops Lake.

Lytton's first railway station changed the town

At Ashcroft, the Thompson River Hotel was built next to the reaction ferry down by the river in 1883. No community existed at the time—only two farms owned by John Barnes and Oliver Evans—and the area was known as St. Cloud. Being located close to the railway station was considered the ticket to economic success.

Then, the post office that for 20 years had served the area at Ashcroft in the valley to the west of the Thompson was moved to St. Cloud, and the community grew around the railway and the post office. The name of Ashcroft was transferred to the new town in 1885. Ashcroft became the gateway to the Cariboo, and the BC Express Company (BX) moved its main depot to Ashcroft to service the Cariboo region. Huge stockyards were constructed in Ashcroft to hold the cattle that were driven down from the Chilcotin to the CPR for shipment across Canada and the US. The railway brought instant prosperity and jobs to hundreds of residents in Ashcroft and the surrounding area.

Residents Enjoy Instant Mobility and Find Employment

Probably the first major change that locals noticed was the relative ease of getting into neighbouring towns, visiting friends up or down the Thompson, or even visiting family who lived thousands of miles away. Suddenly, instead of riding a horse or taking a BX stagecoach from Lytton to Spences Bridge, a trip that could easily take half a day or more, it could now be done in less than an hour. Travel time took on a completely new dimension. Although not every hamlet had a train station, spaced judiciously along the tracks were flag stops where folks could disembark from or board the train by simply raising a flag or waving down the train during the day and waving a lantern at night.

One of Onderdonk's earliest steam engines (1884) pulled a car of firewood to fuel the boilers

During blasting and rail-bed construction, much of the Cariboo Wagon Road had been obliterated by the CPR. The railway made little or no effort to restore the road since it wanted everyone to buy a ticket and ride the train. In many cases, this caused great inconvenience to local residents, who were forced to walk on rough trails between the sections of still usable road. It wasn't until the construction of the Fraser Canyon Highway in the 1920s that a practical, relatively high-speed road transportation alternative to the CPR was available.

Locally, employment opportunities became available with the railway hiring employees to maintain the line and to work as station attendants, as conductors in passenger cars, and in various other positions created by the new railroad.

The earliest locomotives, especially the ones used during the construction period, heated the engine's boilers with cordwood instead of coal. Many indigenous people harvested wood and sold it to the railway by the cord. Old photographs show barren hillsides stripped clean because of firewood harvesting.

Annie York, a Thompson First Nations elder from Spuzzum, talks about cutting firewood:

> *Indians used to cut wood for the CPR engine. They cut it from way up on the bench across the highway. Cut it for seventy-five cents a cord. Old Bill said, "We used to work from dawn," and he meant it. He said, "The stars were out when we began, and they were out when we were through."*
>
> *Pretty near every man cut wood, and some women helps [sic] their husband cutting wood. And all along there you see they cut from the other side of the track right up. You can still see the remains of some of the stumps. They did that for a living in the fall and spring as soon as the snow went— they go up there, and they cut it....*
>
> *And the first man that has a saw, you see, he asks another fellow to work with him, and they have a double saw, you see, a man on each end. They share a profit. But the man that had the saw, he has a little more than the fellow that didn't have it. Finally the fellow puts that money aside, and he goes to the beach, and he washes some gold, and he saves the money, and he buys a saw. He goes to Yale, and*

he buy it. And he says after a while…you see a fire [and everybody] there at lunchtime. They're making their teas, here and there, all the way up.

That was the main food, dry salmon and bannock. That's what they have for lunch. They say they works [sic] so hard at it like that—bring it down and split it in long lengths, and then they pile it all along the track, and the train picks it up. All those old work trains were wood burners. That was their main thing, to save enough money to buy a saw, a broadaxe, and a wedge. (Laforet, *Spuzzum: Fraser Canyon Histories, 1808–1939*, 91)

Earliest Steam Locomotives

Early steam locomotives also needed a constant supply of water so reservoir towers were stationed along the line at regular intervals. Generally, the larger locomotives were coupled to a tender car that carried the water and wood (later coal rather than wood). Smaller steam engines had a bunker on the locomotive itself that needed refilling more frequently. The smaller locomotives ran shorter routes.

A work crew kept the water towers full and maintained them. The Lytton CPR station had a large water tower, and not far up the Thompson near the Jaws of Death rapids was another one. To this day, the area—the highway section specifically—is called Tank Creek, named after the water tower that captured water from a nearby creek and fed it by gravity into the water tank and from there into passing steam locomotives.

Later, coal was used to heat the water that generated steam that powered the trains. Coal bunkers along the track stored coal that was brought in by railcars. Like the water, it was loaded into the tender car or into a storage bunker next to the engine firebox. Men were needed for every job so Lytton, Spences Bridge, Ashcroft, and Savona quickly grew in size.

The spinoff employment, created by the railway's marketing efforts, was commendable. The railway benefitted, of course, by selling seats on its passenger trains. The CPR took advantage of recreation opportunities along the line and produced brochures advertising activities such as fishing, hiking, and hunting. For example, Spences Bridge became famous for its large, fighting steelhead. Fishermen from BC, other Canadian provinces, the US, and even Europe came to catch Thompson River steelhead. The Spences Bridge Hotel became a famous inn on the CPR line and a gathering spot for fishermen.

Farmers and especially ranchers along the Thompson and farther in the interior of BC now had a means of shipping their produce to market. Stockyards were built, and Ashcroft became the shipping centre for Chilcotin cattle that were brought down in long, overland cattle drives. Suddenly, new markets were available since there was now a relatively quick and easy way to ship cattle and fruit and vegetables to major cities previously not accessible.

Spences Bridge was famous for its apple farms; Ashcroft was renowned for its disease-free potatoes, sweet tomatoes, and pumpkins that were exported widely. In Lytton, one of the first fruit farms in BC, across the Fraser River from town, shipped apples from its 300 acres of fruit trees. Earlscourt was a famous Interior farm that benefitted from the arrival of the CPR by expanding its markets. Because the farm was upstream and across the Fraser from the CPR, boxes of fruit were stacked on a scow on which a sail was rigged. When the wind was blowing hard upriver (it seldom stops!), the sails were set and the craft sailed and drifted to Lytton to deliver its fruit to the CPR station on the east side of the Fraser.

However, there was constant complaining that the railway was charging too much to carry freight and local produce. Often it was cheaper and faster to continue using horse-drawn freight wagons than rely on the railway to move commodities to market. Wherever the CPR had no competition, it was common for it to charge exorbitant freight rates.

Environmental Impacts

The environmental impact of the CPR construction along the Thompson River corridor was significant. Deforestation, soil excavation, the effects of blasting, and fish and wildlife overharvesting—all affected the previously unspoiled waterway and the surrounding environment.

South of Ashcroft, landslides caused by ranchers irrigating their fields above the railway tracks brought tons of material directly into the river and shoreline. One slide resulted in a lawsuit between the farmer who owned land above the railway and the CPR, which filed the petition demanding that the farmer stop irrigating his land. The CPR lost the Supreme Court decision before going to the UK and petitioning the highest court in the Commonwealth. It's unclear whether the farmer was represented in England, but the British court ruled in favour of the CPR.

The influx of thousands of railway workers and settlers, during construction and after completion of the railway, affected both fish and wildlife populations. To the First Nations and then early settlers, hunting and fishing was not only a way of life, it was life itself. With the increase in population came an increase of pressure on the wildlife and fish resources.

Derailments continue to be a problem along the river

Fish and wildlife numbers were affected in several ways. First, indigenous peoples were encouraged to hunt for wildlife—elk, deer, bear, and grouse—and sell the meat to the railway workers. Many Thompson natives pursued game for resale, significantly affecting wildlife numbers and in the longer term negatively influencing their own ability to sustain their traditional way of life.

Second, a staple in the diets of both the Thompson First Nations and the railway workers was salmon, caught primarily by natives. For a few cents a fish, natives caught and delivered salmon to the workers' camps by the hundreds. Often, supplying fish in exchange for payment took precedence over drying and storing fish for their own sustenance.

Third, the problem was only exacerbated when the CPR began to advertise hunting and fishing as recreational opportunities along the Thompson Valley. While there were benefits to people engaged as fishing and hunting guides and outfitters, and other spinoffs to hotels, equipment suppliers, and so on, the game harvested by imported hunters and fishermen added still more pressure on fish and wildlife.

Jaws of Death

Blasting the rail bed and tunnels along the Thompson in 1884 created a relatively minor environmental impact when compared with the blasting in the Fraser Canyon between Yale and Boston Bar. The exception was an infamous section of railway about 7.5 miles from Lytton, now known as the Jaws of Death. It was a construction challenge. The engineer in charge proposed to build an expensive 400-yard tunnel to bypass the difficult terrain, sheer canyon walls, constant water erosion, and falling rock.

Because of budget overruns, the Canadian government (a.k.a. Canadian taxpayers), which was footing the bill, did everything possible to reduce construction costs. The engineer responsible for building the railway along the Thompson scaled down his ambitious scheme and built a shorter tunnel closer to the edge of the bluff. Unfortunately, the tunnel was too unstable and collapsed with Chinese workers inside, so drilling and blasting stopped. A new engineer was summoned. His solution was to build a 200-foot tunnel under the existing one, load it with 30 tons of black powder, and blow 80,000 tons of rock into the Thompson. This was BC's largest dynamite blast up to that time.

The new blast created a new rail bed except for one short section where a wooden trestle was built. Then, about 15 years later, a beautiful stone-arch bridge replaced the wooden structure. To this day, the original granite masterpiece carries millions of tons of freight every year without swaying an inch. This arched bridge at the Jaws of Death is a reminder of the Chinese who lost their lives when the tunnel collapsed and of the largest dynamite blast in BC history.

Today, it's difficult to imagine the Thompson River without two railroads and a highway straddling it. Fortunately, the river goes about its seasonal business, ignoring them as best it can. However, occasionally during spring flood it flexes its muscles and erodes and undermines the rail bed to remind the Iron Horse that the river was here first, that the Thompson River Valley is its home, and that it doesn't need to be restrained by ribbons of steel if it doesn't want to be.

While the negative environmental impact and permanent change to the First Nations' way of life cannot be denied, the blasting of 80,000 tons of rock into the river at the Jaws of Death helped to create the most exciting whitewater rapids along the Thompson.

The arrival of the CPR changed the Thompson Valley forever. From the earliest Chinese labourers who came to build the railway in order to improve their lives and stayed because they could not afford to return to China, to the railway itself, nothing was the same after the Iron Horse arrived.

The Jaws of Death stone arch bridge replaced the first wooden one

Most rapids received names after hair-raising rides through the Devil's Gorge in 1974

14 This and That

The Naming of the Thompson River Rapids

As we've seen in the first five chapters, all of the rapids on the Thompson from Savona to Lytton have names. Some are good names, some are interesting, some are revealing, and some are just plain dull.

The boring ones were probably named by some surveyor 150 years ago or more. Others are named after a nearby geographical or railway feature; the remainder are names that I came up with from the dark recesses of my mind.

While early cartographers named features on maps because of political expediency or to honour someone dead or alive, my names invariably came after a hair-raising experience running a rapid, usually during high water when the Thompson is the most dangerous. Most were named in 1974.

In 1974, the Thompson River flowed at near-record flood levels. My largest raft was a used 18-foot German-made, military-surplus Canova raft, so that was what I used on every high-water trip. Although I had two identical rafts, to save what little money I had, I often routinely and foolishly operated single-boat trips. Just thinking about the consequences had I flipped a raft with no other raft to assist in a rescue still makes me shudder. Every run down the swollen, aggressive river was a different experience, and every rapid seemed to have a personality. Thanks to some skill and lots of luck, I never flipped a boat, nor was I swallowed by a whirlpool or devoured in the Jaws of Death.

Each name that I doled out reflected how I felt about a particular rapid at some point during that summer. A few names I simply borrowed from a local feature or landmark and applied them to a nearby rapid.

Readers already know about The Frog, a gigantic piece of rock that often looks like a bullfrog about to leap out of the water, or the Jaws of Death, a name that originated with the CPR.

By 1975, I discovered the benefits of larger motorized rafts

When I co-authored the guidebook *Rafting in British Columbia: Featuring the Lower Thompson River* with Doug VanDine in 1984, we put the names into print. Name standardization followed, and anyone descending the river in a raft or kayak thereafter referred to them by the names in the book.

The names are now etched firmly into Thompson River traditions.

Formation of the Thompson River

The Thompson Valley is at least 50 million years old. Geologists speculate that for much of this time, the river flowed northeast and not southwest. Its headwaters lay somewhere between Boston Bar and Hell's Gate, and it collected all the drainages in the vicinity, including the Stein River, and then headed northeast toward the ancestral Peace River.

It's also possible that for a time, the Thompson flowed in a northwest direction through the Cariboo Plateau to the Quesnel area, where it joined a much larger river that also flowed into the Arctic Ocean. This northwest or northeast trend may have lasted for 50 million years, up until the Pleistocene epoch two million years ago.

Geologists also conjecture that for some time, until very recently, the Thompson flowed east and then south into the Columbia River and not southwest into the Fraser drainage.

Thompson Valley Glaciations

The last glacial period along the Thompson Valley began about 21,000 years ago and lasted for roughly 11,000 years. The ice was thickest 18,000 years ago; it was more than two kilometres deep in places.

The Frog rapid at extremely low water has bedrock exposed

Kokanee salmon fossils discovered on the banks of Kamloops Lake were carbon dated between 18,000 and 21,000 years ago, precisely at the time when glaciers filled the Thompson Valley. Scientists guess that sockeye salmon initially migrated up the Columbia River (some of it wasn't affected by glaciers), then up through the Okanagan and the glacial melt-water of the Thompson River into glacial Lake Thompson, and were trapped there by the ice that later blocked their return to the Columbia and the ocean.

Envision a gigantic glacier that filled the Thompson Valley from Lytton all the way past Kamloops. It also had fingers up the Nicola Valley from Spences Bridge to Merritt, and the Bonaparte Valley near Ashcroft up to Cache Creek and Loon Lake. It filled the Deadman Valley northwest of Savona and the North Thompson Valley directly north of Kamloops.

Then, as the climate warmed, the ice sheet slowly melted and contracted (downwasted); the valley between Kamloops and Chase to the east opened first. Slowly the ice decayed or shrivelled from Kamloops down in the direction of Lytton.

Eventually, all that remained was a large piece of ice that choked the valley about eight kilometres south of Spences Bridge. Above it, all the way past Kamloops, two long lakes—glacial Lake Thompson and glacial Lake Deadman (in the Deadman River Valley a few kilometres north and west of Savona)—formed from the glacier's melting ice.

Although these were technically two lakes, for practical purposes imagine one lake that started just south of Spences Bridge and extended up the Thompson, filling all the interlocking valleys with glacial water instead of ice. It was a long, ribbonlike lake and ranged from 50 to 140 metres in depth. Kamloops Lake is a remnant of this glacial lake.

Typical of glacial lakes, the water was silt-rich. Over a few thousand years, the silt settled out of the water and onto the lake bottom, forming a layer of silt and sand that is clearly visible today between Savona and Spences Bridge. It is more than 100 metres thick in places. It is recognizable because of its fine texture and dull white color. The silt layer's instability when mixed with water accounts for many of the slides along the Thompson, especially between Ashcroft and Spences Bridge.

Ice Dam Breaks Free

Roughly 9,500 years ago, a catastrophic event occurred: the ice dam south of Spences Bridge at Skoonka Creek suddenly let loose. About 20 cubic kilometres of water drained from glacial Lake Thompson and glacial Lake Deadman into the Fraser River and down the Fraser Canyon out into the ocean. The lake's water level dropped immediately, and glacial Lake Thompson eventually morphed from a lake into a river again. However, this time it flowed into the Fraser watershed to the west, not to the east and into the Columbia.

In geological terms, the Fraser *pirated* the water of the Thompson. The floodwaters reached the ocean, 250 kilometres away, and deposited exotic muds with microfossils that were identified in drill core samples in the Strait of Georgia and the Saanich Inlet on Vancouver Island. The mud samples from the Interior provide strong evidence that supports the theory of a catastrophic drainage of glacial Lake Thompson and other interconnecting glacial lakes in the valley.

For the next 3,000 years, the ancestral Thompson incised through valley fill down to solid bedrock, to within a few metres of the current river level. Since then, it has continued to erode, but now it happens at a snail's pace compared with the first 3,000 years after the ice dam broke free.

David Thompson's River

David Thompson never laid eyes on the river that now bears his name. It was all a mistake.

Simon Fraser thought that explorer Thompson was upstream discovering and mapping the headwaters of the Thompson River when Fraser arrived at the Great Forks (Lytton) on June 19, 1808. In fact, at the same time that Simon Fraser was shaking hands with 1,200 Thompson natives at Lytton, David Thompson was exploring the headwaters of the Columbia River.

However, it is only fitting that the legendary Thompson River shares a name with one of the greatest unsung heroes in Canadian history. "Thompson's cartography, his endurance, his consistent respect for Aboriginal peoples, his pathfinding, his versatility in at least six languages and his prodigious literary legacy qualify him as the most under-celebrated hero in Canadian history" (Twigg, *Thompson's Highway: British Columbia's Fur Trade, 1800–1850*, 65).

A fleet of Kumsheen rafts on David Thompson's river at Spences Bridge

Thompson explored and mapped the main travel routes for about 1,200,000 square miles of Canada, and 502,000 square miles in the United States. To accomplish this feat, he travelled more than 80,157 miles, much of it on foot and the remainder by canoe or on horseback. He produced detailed, astoundingly accurate maps that other explorers used for over a century.

Simon Fraser wrote the following in his journal when in Lytton in 1808:

> *These Forks [of the Thompson and Fraser Rivers] the Indians call Camchin, and are formed by a large river, which is the same spoken of so often by our friend the Old Chief. From an idea that our friends at the Fort des Prairies department [referring to David Thompson] are established upon the source of it, among the mountains, we gave it the name Thomson's [sic] River.* (Lamb, *The Letters and Journals of Simon Fraser, 1806–1808*, 88)

David Thompson may be the unacknowledged hero of Canadian history, but his river is revered and admired by thousands of travellers who visit and interact with his azure waterway every year.

Bat Attack

During the summer of 1980, we stopped as usual for lunch in Pitquah Gorge. A short and steep rocky trail led us to a flat bench above the river, from which the view was spectacular.

Guides prepared the lunch table as guests relaxed in the natural beauty or explored the remains of the old CN section camp nearby. On this particular trip, a number of German tourists were along who especially enjoyed the remote wilderness experience.

Suddenly, an uninvited guest appeared at our lunch. Materializing out of nowhere, a bat was suddenly fluttering among the rafting guests—brushing against them, then flapping a short distance away, then returning, again and again.

Most of the guests ran from the bat in fright or swatted at it when it came too close. One German man did neither. He simply froze, likely paralyzed from fear, allowing the bat to inspect him. I looked on as the bat quivered close to the man's head, fluttered in a circle above it, flapped away, and then abruptly returned to him and latched itself onto his ear. Shocked, our German guest immediately pulled it off and threw it at the ground. The bat escaped into the distance.

At that moment, it struck me: rabies. Why would a healthy bat be flying around in the middle of the day? It must have been rabid. We quickly field-dressed the small puncture wound, packed our luncheon supplies, and rushed downriver to the hospital at Lytton.

Lytton had no rabies treatment available; Vancouver was the closest supply. The man and his family immediately left for Vancouver, and as he was returning to Germany a day or two later, we lost contact with him.

A few days after the episode, a small article appeared in *The Vancouver Sun*. It described the rabid bat attack and stated that although the bat had eluded capture, making analysis for the rabies virus impossible, medical staff assumed it to be infected. Healthy bats do not act erratically and bite people in broad daylight.

The treatment consisted of a dose of immune globulin and five doses of a relatively painful rabies vaccine, which continued over a 28-day period. In this case, the treatment began in Vancouver General Hospital and continued in Germany.

Bats or no bats, the view at Pitquah was spectacular. We continued using the picturesque luncheon spot for a few more years and were never attacked by another bat.

Telegraph Poles

In the early days of the railroad, section gangs lived in humble, railway-supplied accommodations beside the tracks, usually in remote locations.

Section houses, simple living quarters with tool sheds, functioned as work locations for the railroad crew. Each gang was responsible for the maintenance and upkeep of a specific section of track. They also looked after the telegraph poles that paralleled the tracks in their section.

The gangs also intercepted Morse-code messages destined for trains passing through. The message was interpreted and written out in longhand, then clipped to a peg or hoop at the top of a long wooden pole. When approaching the section gang camp, the engineer slowed the train, reached out the window, and inserted his arm through the hoop. The message was quickly retrieved and the peg thrown out the train window.

Many telegraph poles still stand along the railway right-of-way, although some have rotted and collapsed and others have been removed. All played a part in the history along both the CN and CP tracks.

Collectors still find colourful glass insulators in remote areas that can fetch up to $100 for the right colour and brand.

Telegraph poles, wires, and insulators were state-of-the-art electronics not that long ago

Flag Stops

The construction of the CPR along the Thompson River in the early 1880s destroyed much of the Cariboo Wagon Road. This forced many residents to depend on the railway instead of being self-sufficient in their travels.

Residents of small villages or remote areas near the tracks caught the train at flag stops or flag stations, which served as a primitive alternative to permanent stations. The use of flag stops allowed seldom-used stations to remain open because of their efficiency and minimal expense. They were usually little more than unmanned huts with a bench or two pushed against the wall and a timetable tacked up near the door. Some of the larger ones boasted small pot-bellied stoves so passengers wouldn't freeze to death during the winter.

Trains often slowed but did not come to a complete stop if no one was waiting. Sometimes they wouldn't bother to slow down at all, roaring through at full speed.

The 1906 CPR Annotated Time Table identified five flag stops between Savona and Lytton: Penny, Spatsum, Drynoch, Thompson (at Nicomen), and Gladwin. Many other flag stops had already been abandoned. When the Canadian National Railway began operating in 1914, it also operated flag stops; they were located on the side of the Thompson opposite the CPR.

Today, railway flag stops no longer exist. However, buses stop when flagged in remote areas. Need a Greyhound bus ride home from the Kumsheen Resort? Stand on the highway at the entrance to Kumsheen and flag down the next bus. It almost always works.

Pit Houses

Very different from the relative luxury that most of us live in today, the semi-underground dwellings that the Thompson First Nations inhabited from December until March each year were well adapted to the climate conditions and to their lifestyle.

Pit houses served as cozy winter homes for the Thompson natives

These winter homes, also known as kekuli houses, were usually located on benches in the valley bottom near the Thompson River. Each cluster of three or four lodges was inhabited by related families (usually between 15 and 30 members); occasionally, a single large home accommodated everyone. Each round pit house was between about 25 and 40 feet in diameter. The size depended on how many family members would be living together.

The winter homes were quite warm because they were essentially below ground. The women of the family group would excavate the soil to a depth of about three feet with root-digging sticks and wooden scrapers with sharp, flat blades. By hand, they scooped the earth into large baskets and then emptied them near the hole.

The roof consisted of log rafters laid side by side and then thickly padded with pine needles or grass. The excavated earth, spread over the roof and stamped down with their feet, served as insulation. An entrance hole was left in the centre of the roof.

A notched log ladder, with a groove on the back to serve as a grip, protruded through the centre opening. The cooking fire was located at the base of the ladder (always on the north side), separated from it by a slab of stone so the smoke could curl up and out.

When entering the dwelling, it was customary to shout the warning, *"A´la!"* to give the women who were cooking time to protect the food from dust and dirt. The houses were very warm, so the residents were usually scantily attired when inside.

The last pit house in the area went out of use among the Spences Bridge band around 1890. Many depressions along the Thompson are reminders of the winter homes that once existed here.

"Indian Hunting Grisly"

The Interior Salish peoples were very competent hunters. They hunted a variety of big game, including deer, sheep, goat, elk, and black and grizzly bear—mostly with a bow and arrow.

Killing a black bear was not a particularly great achievement. Killing a grizzly, on the other hand, was big news. If a hunter killed a grizzly, he was held in very high regard by the other hunters and by the women and children. So, to pad their own egos, young men, being young men, often went out to search for and hunt grizzlies.

James Teit, in *The Thompson Indians of British Columbia*, relates a fascinating story called "Indian Hunting Grisly" about a native hunter who specialized in killing grizzly bears. The hunter used a highly unorthodox hunting technique, with two weapons that were equally unconventional:

> *Stories are related of an Indian who lived a couple of generations ago [early 1800s] and hunted the grisly [sic]*

with weapons peculiar to himself. One of these was a bone, which he held by the middle with his hand. It was sharpened to a point at both ends. His other weapon was a stone club. When the grisly opened its mouth and stood up to fight him, the Indian shoved the hand holding the bone (with points up and down) into the animal's mouth. When the beast closed its mouth, the sharp points pierced it, causing it great pain: then, while the bear was trying with its paws to take the obstruction out of its mouth, the Indian clubbed it. (Teit, 249)

Teit does not comment on whether the "grisly" hunter lived to a ripe old age or whether he met his guiding spirit early in life. You be the judge.

Double-Headed Snake

A double-headed snake lives in the sagebrush and rocks along the Thompson River. Fortunately, it is very friendly and likes people although it looks very ferocious when curled up in a ball, with a scarred tail that resembles a head moving back and forth menacingly.

This snake, the Pacific Rubber Boa, is a relatively common snake but because it is nocturnal and spends most of its time hidden under logs, brush, and in cracks in rocks—anywhere that snakes can slither into and hide—it is seldom seen. It's non-poisonous with skin that is relatively smooth, thick, and shimmering brown on top. Its belly is a yellowish-brown. It is about 40 centimetres long on average, but can grow to 60 centimetres under the right conditions.

Perhaps it's their laid-back, calm nature, that allows some rubber boas to live to be over 50 years old. The average life expectancy is 25 years. Their good nature makes them ideal for handling by children and anyone trying to overcome a fear of snakes. They never use striking as a defence mechanism. If handled too roughly, they simply spray the holder with a smelly musk from their vent.

A unique characteristic of the rubber boa is how it gently wraps around the holder's wrist for an hour or more before wanting to crawl around and explore more than the wrist.

They hibernate from mid-October until mid-March. In the spring and fall, they lie in the warmth underneath logs and other debris, regulating their body temperatures. During summer, when it is hot, they spend their time underground in rodent tunnels or rock fractures to keep cool and moist.

The boa's favourite meals are baby mice, voles, or shrews. The snake slithers into the rodents' underground homes and looks for the babies. Using its tail as a decoy for the mother, it curls around and crushes the babies. Then it chews and swallows them as it deflects the mother with its tail. The scars on its tail are the result of these attacks and help create the "double-headed" look that is the trademark of the Pacific Rubber Boa.

Ashcroft Manor

Well educated and relatively wealthy, Clement and Henry Cornwall left England in April 1862 and decided to settle on the flats a few kilometres west of the current town of Ashcroft. These brothers, both Cambridge graduates, were innovative. They constructed a sawmill to manufacture the boards and timbers needed to build their ranch house and outbuildings. Next, they built a roadhouse and a water wheel. When no longer needed to cut lumber, the sawmill was converted into a gristmill, the second one in the Cariboo. The water wheel was installed in the Bonaparte River to power the gristmill.

However, the brothers' bread and butter was their ranching operation. They eventually purchased 6,000 acres, ran as many as 1,500 head of cattle, and operated a large vegetable garden and a roadhouse known as Ashcroft Manor, named after their family home in England. The manor became a popular stopping place for travellers between Spences Bridge and Kamloops, in large part because of the friendliness and hospitality of the Cornwalls, but also because of their friendly saloon.

Three years after establishing their ranch, the brothers hired a young manager, Charles A. Semlin, to oversee the operation. (Semlin later purchased his own ranch and became the premier of British Columbia for a short while.) With Semlin at the helm, they turned their attention from working seven days a week to having a social life. They imported an Arabian stud, built a racetrack behind the manor house, and advertised regular races on "Cornwall Flats." Their "Ashcroft Hunt" was an adaptation of the English foxhunt, chasing coyotes instead of foxes on horseback.

Clement Cornwall had also studied law in London before settling in Ashcroft, and in 1867, he became district magistrate and postmaster. Both the court and post office were originally located at the manor and afterward moved to the present town of Ashcroft. Later, he became a member of the legislative council (when BC was still a Crown colony) and still later was appointed lieutenant governor of BC. He married into the well-known and well-connected Pemberton family and raised five children.

Buffalo George

During the railway construction in the 1880s, the timekeeper always needed to record a name for each worker. First Nations people were often hired, but some of their names had no English equivalent.

To solve the problem, some natives provided the name of their village and this became their timesheet name. Others adopted common names like Johnny, Joe, or Tom.

Sigurd Teit tells a story that illustrates the complexity of the practice:

> *Two brothers who hired out together were given the name George and to distinguish them one was called Little George and the other Big George. When another brother hired on later, he was the largest of the three and was called Buffalo George."* (Lean, 43)

Thompson Indian Burial Customs

It has always been important to the Upper Thompson First Nations to look after their dead carefully and properly.

Before the arrival of Europeans, Upper Thompson people followed a variety of burial customs when dealing with the body of the deceased. They are a reflection of the primitive practices that were abandoned soon after contact with Europeans. James Teit, unquestionably the authority on the Thompson people, describes their customs:

> *If the deceased had dogs, one or more of them were killed, and their skins were also hung up near the grave. Sometimes dogs were taken to the grave, strangled with a rope, and hung to a tree or pole. Horses were sometimes shot or clubbed near the grave, and left there. If the deceased had many slaves, some of them were either killed at the grave and their bodies thrown in, or they were forced into the bottom of the grave, and buried alive. After a sufficient quantity of earth had been covered over them, their master was put in and buried on top of them.* (Teit, 328)

An elaborate native grave in downtown Lytton around 1865

The Reverend George Grant also provided a detailed description of a gravesite when he travelled into Thompson country in 1872:

> *Whatever these poor people can accomplish in the way of architecture or art is reserved for their dead. A house better than they live in is built, or a good tent erected, and in it are placed the valuables of the deceased,—his gun, blanket, food; in front hang scalps, or bright shawls, and white flags; his canoe is placed outside, and beside it the hide of his horse or mule over a wooden skeleton; rude painted images representing the man, woman, or family as the case may be, are arranged in front.* (Grant, Ocean to Ocean. Sandford Fleming's Expedition through Canada in 1872, 310)

Golden Eagles

Every spring, I look forward to seeing a pair of golden eagles in Black Canyon. Because they return to the same area and usually to the same nest year after year, I always expect to be greeted by the pair circling in the canyon thermals or sitting on their nest. For almost 40 years, they—and now their offspring—haven't let me down; they've appeared soaring on the wind in Black Canyon.

Their first task in the spring, after they have returned from their winter in the southern US or Mexico, is to repair and refurbish their gigantic nest. This means adding more sticks, grass, and other material from the vicinity. When the nest is egg-worthy, the female lays one or two (sometimes even three) and sits on the nest for the next five or six weeks.

While she incubates the eggs, papa eagle hunts. He is in charge of finding enough food for the two of them. With his incredible eyesight, he spots rabbits, gophers, marmots, fish, and a variety of other birds and rodents, which he kills and brings back to the nest. (Golden eagles also take young deer and antelope, calves, lambs, and young goats, as well as carrion and reptiles.) I've noticed that he often has his eye on a large flock of rock doves that nest in the canyon with him.

Golden eagle with a fish for the family

Once the chicks have hatched, they are very vulnerable and require nearly constant attention and protection. Both parents share in the rearing responsibilities. The chicks hatch a day or two apart, and, interestingly, the first-born chick will often bully its sibling by pecking at it relentlessly. The elder chick will also eat most of the food that is brought to the nest. The adults never intervene in the fights, and usually, after a month or two, only the strongest eaglet is still alive.

Sometimes the younger chicks tire of the bullying and fly from the nest a wee bit too early. Unfortunately, they end their short lives by drowning in the Thompson River 70 metres below the nest—they have not yet received their swimming lessons.

Eventually, the surviving chick learns to hunt on its own, taking a lot of pressure off its parents. In the fall, the whole family heads to Montana, where they congregate with other golden eagles from all over the continent. Before long, like many northerners, they all migrate farther south to spend the winter in the sun.

Osprey

Also called fish eagles or white eagles, osprey are raptors—birds of prey like eagles, hawks, and owls. They resemble a bald eagle, with the one major difference being their white belly.

When fishing, osprey dive at 50 kilometres per hour and hit the water at 80 kilometres per hour, their outstretched talons ahead of their noses and aerodynamic body. After impact, they completely disappear under the water. Sometimes the osprey wins and the fish loses, but more often the fish wins and the osprey flaps its way out of the water without a fish in its talons. Persistent, they keep fishing until they win.

Osprey were endangered in the 1960s because of the effects of DDT and other pesticides, and in 1973 when I first started rafting the Thompson there was only one osprey nest along the river between Ashcroft and Lytton. Now there are dozens.

Mating for life, an osprey pair returns to the same nest every year to raise their young. On average, each adult needs to catch 2.3 kilograms (five pounds) of fish a day to feed themselves and the two or three youngsters waiting with gaping mouths in the nest.

Again, like many Canadians, the birds head south for the winter. Flying nonstop from their summer nests on the Thompson to their winter tanning grounds, males and females take separate vacations. The young travel on their own when they head south. They don't follow their parents, but work on pure instinct, staying over land as long as they can before flying over water at the Gulf of Mexico.

Eventually they arrive at the Florida Keys, Mexico, the south eastern tip of Cuba, or other choice vacation spots in Central America, where they spend the winter.

Osprey numbers have increased significantly along the river

The Roaring Landslide of 1880

The wife of Bishop Sillitoe, the first bishop of New Westminster, visited the Cornwalls at Ashcroft Manor in October 1880. Her visit coincided with the big landslide that occurred 11 kilometres below Ashcroft. Although the manor was six kilometres (as the crow flies) from the slide location, she could hear the roar of the debris letting loose and crashing into the Thompson.

Here is her first-hand account:

> *Whilst we were sitting in the drawing-room one evening during our stay at Ashcroft, an extraordinary noise was heard. Some supposed it to be an earthquake, but we finally came to the conclusion that it was nothing more than the moving of some chairs or tables overhead. The next morning, however, we heard that the sound had been caused by a tremendous landslip three miles distant from where we were, and which had dammed up the river until it should have forced its way through this immense dam. However, in company with our hosts, we drove to the river to judge for ourselves. We found that the dam was half a mile long and eighty feet high. The river above had already risen forty feet over its usual level, and was almost dry below. As it had still forty feet to rise before it could carry away the only bridge by which we could cross, we decided on continuing our journey to Cook's Ferry [Spences Bridge], where we were able to cross safely. It was painful to see the salmon—some floundering in shallow pools, others lying dead in the dry bed of the river.* (Gowen, 25–26)

Horse Ferry

Horse ferries were the original powerboats and an indispensable conveyance for shuttling people across lakes and large rivers.

Humans had been struggling with long, heavy oars for a few thousand years ago and sails had been used a thousand years before that, but records show the first horse-powered craft in North America in 1790.

The boat's design utilized the power of a horse or several horses to drive a propulsion device (for example, a paddlewheel) that was attached to the side or back of a barge or boat. The horse (or as many as eight horses) walked on a treadmill that in turn was connected to a shaft that rotated the paddlewheel.

Other propulsion devices (like propellers) were experimented with over time and other methods besides treadmills used for transferring the power from the horses to the water craft, but horses were always the engine that powered the craft.

A Savona horse ferry could have shuttled people, livestock, and supplies across the lake near the outlet of the Thompson River. Quite possibly, it could also have shuttled passengers from Savona along Kamloops Lake to Fort Kamloops.

Horse ferry use peaked around 1850, and according to my early research, one operated at Savona from 1858 to 1862. However, my diligent sleuthing found no official record of the craft's design, no photographs, and no information whatsoever, except several references that referred to it as a "one-horse ferry."

Turns out, it was all a matter of mistaken research. A one-horse ferry was not necessarily a ferry that was powered by one horse, and the one-horse ferry that operated at Savona was not a horse-powered ferry at all; it was a reaction ferry with room enough to be able to transport a saddle horse and rider across the mouth of the Thompson River.

A 16-year-old cowhand driving cattle to the gold fields noted in his diary in 1861 that he and his horse crossed the Thompson at Savona on a small ferry while the cattle swam.

Oops! I almost led you astray.

Kamloops Lake Salmon Fossils

The relatively recent discovery of fossilized salmon in Kamloops Lake has geologists rethinking some of their theories about the last glaciation.

Conventional thought has the Thompson River Valley buried solidly in ice for at least 10,000 years. The glaciers filled the valleys about 20,000 years ago and remained there for 10,000 years, with the thickest ice being firmly entrenched 18,000 years ago. The salmon supposedly arrived after the glaciers melted.

But fossilized, land-locked sockeye salmon (kokanee) found along the south bank of Kamloops Lake throw a wrench into the spokes of this thinking. The fossils are 18,000 to 21,000 years old, forming precisely when the glaciers were supposedly scouring the Thompson Valley bottom. So how did the kokanee get there, and how did they survive?

Several possibilities emerge. Either the ice melted earlier than previously thought, the glaciers moved in later than theorized, or several stages of glacial melting and freezing occurred. For fish to live in Kamloops Lake for three or four thousand years, there must have been a period of glacial melting.

288

Since the Columbia River remained glacier-free throughout the last ice age, and with the Thompson flowing east and south into the Columbia, salmon could have migrated up into the Thompson melt water and into glacial Lake Thompson.

Then a blockage of either ice or sediment occurred, isolating the salmon from the Columbia and the ocean. These land-locked sockeye salmon remained in glacial Lake Kamloops until their demise, probably caused by the freezing of the lake.

Much evidence supports the theory that the last chunk of ice to break free and drain glacial Lake Thompson occurred about 9,500 years ago, just south of Spences Bridge.

What took place for the 10,000 years prior to that is speculation, supported by an increasing body of geological evidence. Large pieces of the puzzle are still missing, however.

A Desert Climate

A desert is an area that receives less that 25 centimetres (10 inches) of precipitation per year. Applying this simplistic definition, the Thompson Valley is a desert.

In fact, the lower Thompson River Valley is one of the driest and hottest regions in all of Canada. Annual precipitation is usually less than 20 cm in places like Savona or Ashcroft and about 25 cm near Lytton and Kamloops. (Compare that to Vancouver and the Lower Mainland, which often get more than ten times that amount.)

The average of daily and nocturnal temperatures during July and August hovers around 22° Celsius (71.6° Fahrenheit). However, daytime temperatures are usually over 30° C. (86° F.), and extremes as high as 42° C. (107.6° F.) are common. The area basks in more than 320 blue-sky days every year.

Deserts are often windy and the Thompson Valley is no exception. Wind gusts of over 100 km/h occur, and 80 km/h winds are a common experience.

Even the vegetation is typical of desert climates, as we saw in Chapter 6. Growing along the Thompson are sagebrush, rabbit bush, ponderosa pine forests, bunch grasses, saskatoon bush, prickly pear cactus, balsamroot, and a host of other plants that have adapted to little water and extreme temperatures.

One of the key benefits of the desert climate to recreational river users is the sun's warming effect on the water. At Kamloops, the top few feet of water are warmed in Kamloops Lake before flowing out of the lake at Savona. The water continues to warm as it flows 117 kilometres through the desert from Savona to Lytton. By early August, the river temperature is usually a balmy 20° Celsius, creating perfect rafting conditions.

The desert climate keeps the river warm all summer

Conclusion

When I began this book, my goal was to expand your understanding of the Thompson and enrich your experience with my favourite river. By sharing some of my stories and broadening the book to include the stories of many other interesting people and events that have played a role in defining the majestic Thompson, I hope I have come close to accomplishing my goal.

Perhaps you didn't read every chapter of the book; if so, I understand that. Not everyone is interested in reading about the Kokanee fossils of Kamloops Lake or a horse ferry that never existed. Nevertheless, I hope that you were absorbed enough to read most of the stories and tales. If you're a rafter, kayaker, or angler, I hope you found the KM-by-KM guide to be motivating and informative.

I wanted to infuse in you some of the awe, respect, and enchantment I felt when I began my relationship with the Thompson more than four decades ago and that I continue to feel today. The best way to gain an understanding of this magical feeling, besides reading this book, is to immerse yourself in the river and experience it first-hand.

You can accomplish this in many ways—but, of course, I'm biased. My first total immersion in the river was by whitewater raft. I'll never forget the excitement as a monstrous wave broke over us, the sun sparkled through the azure water for an instant, and then every pore of my body was underwater. Pure exhilaration is the best way to describe the emotion that overwhelmed me.

My desire to share that exhilaration grew from that first intense whitewater experience. From Bernie's Raft Rides the first year in 1973, to founding Kumsheen Raft Adventures Ltd. the next year, to creating the Kumsheen Rafting Resort in 1994, sharing that feeling found only in the whitewater of the Thompson was always my primary goal. The Kumsheen Resort is far more luxurious than the VW van and the 15-foot house trailer I had parked beside the highway in June of 1973, but the rapids haven't changed at all since my first day on the river back then.

I still venture down the Thompson every year, whether it's on a fishing trip or because of a special request from someone who has been with me many times in the past to be their rafting guide. For example, I was thrilled when, in 2012, Hazel Amos turned ninety, and to celebrate the occasion she and three generations of her family rafted the Devil's Gorge with me. She said it was by far the most fun and the best run through the rapids she'd had in the more than twenty-five times she had been down the river. I think she may have said that after every trip, but each time, she meant it.

If your appreciation and understanding has broadened because you held *British Columbia's Majestic Thompson River* in your hands, then I'm pleased that I shared my thoughts and experiences with you. If, after reading this book, you are motivated to experience the river, then I'm especially thrilled because that means we'll both know the same thing about the Thompson—that it is no ordinary river.

Bibliography

Anderson, Nancy M. *The Pathfinder: A.C. Anderson's Journeys in the West.* Victoria, BC: Heritage House Publishing, 2011.

Balf, Mary. "Nicola, a Very Great Chieftain" Part 1, Kamloops Museum.

Bancroft, Hubert H. *History of British Columbia 1792–1887.* Vol. 32. San Francisco: The History Company, 1887.

Begg, Alexander. *History of British Columbia: From Its Earliest Discovery to the Present.* Toronto: William Briggs, 1894.

Cheadle, Walter B. *Cheadle's Journal of Trip across Canada 1862–1863.* Edmonton: M.G. Hurtig, 1971.

Cockfield, W.E. Canada Department of Mines and Resources. *Geological Survey, Memoir 249; Geology and Mineral Deposits of Nicola. Map-Area, British Columbia.* Ottawa: King's Printer and Controller of Stationery, 1948.

Fandrich, Bernard and Doug VanDine. *Rafting in British Columbia Featuring the Lower Thompson River.* Surrey, BC: Hancock House, 1984.

Gosnell, R.E. *The Year Book of British Columbia and Manual of Provincial Information.* Victoria, BC: Legislative Assembly and Bureau Statistics. 1897.

Gowen, Herbert H. *Church Work in British Columbia: Being a Memoir of the Episcopate of Acton Windeyer Sillitoe, First Bishop of New Westminster (1899)*. London: Longmans, Green, and Co., 1899.

Grant, George M. *Ocean to Ocean. Sandford Fleming's Expedition through Canada in 1872*. Rutland, VT: Charles E. Tuttle Co., 1967.

Gunn, John C. *Gunn's Household Physician, Or, Home Book of Health*. 1901.

Howay, F.W., *British Columbia from the Earliest Times to the Present*. Vol. 2: Vancouver: The S.J. Clark Publishing Company, 1914.

Huck, Barbara, Heidi Henderson, and Philip Torrens. *In Search of Ancient British Columbia*. Vol. 1: Southern B.C. Winnipeg: Heartland, 2006.

Laforet, Andrea and Annie York. *Spuzzum Fraser Canyon Histories, 1808–1939*. Vancouver: UBC Press, 1998.

Lamb, Kaye W., ed. *The Letters and Journals of Simon Fraser 1806–1808*. Toronto: The MacMillan Company of Canada, 1960.

Lambert, M.A. *Fishing in British Columbia with a Chapter on Tuna Fishing at Santa Catalina*. London: Horace Cox, 1907.

Lean, Pat, ed. "A Year in the Life of James A. Teit–1910." *Teit Times*. Vol. 1. Merritt: Nicola Valley Museum Archives Association, Summer 1995.

Lyons, C.P., and Bill Merilees. *Trees, Shrubs and Flowers to Know in British Columbia and Washington*. Edmonton: Lone Pine Publishing, 1995.

Lyons, C.P. *Milestones on the Mighty Fraser*. Vancouver: J.M. Dent & Sons, 1950.

"Lytton: A Story in Pictures." Compiled by the Lytton & District Centennial Society, 1966–67.

Lytton Museum and Archives Newsletter, Issue 3, Vol. 5, Nov. 2004.

MacKinnon, Kershaw, Owen Arnason, and Karst Hammersley-Chambers. *Edible and Medicinal Plants of Canada*. Edmonton: Lone Pine Publishing, 2009.

McDonald, Archibald. *Peace River: A Canoe Voyage from Hudson's Bay to Pacific in 1828*. Ed. Malcolm McLeod. Edmonton: M.G. Hurtig, 1971.

Mouat, A.N. "Notes on the *Norman Morison*." *British Columbia Historical Quarterly*. Vol. III. 1939: 203–213.

Nunis, Doyce B. Jr., ed. *The Golden Frontier: The Recollections of Herman Francis Reinhart 1851–1869*. Austin: University of Texas Press, 1962: 108–145.

Pettit, Sydney G. "'Dear Sir Mathew': A Glimpse of Judge Begbie." *British Columbia Historical Quarterly*. Vol. XI. 1947: 1–14.

——. "Judge Begbie in Action: The Establishment of Law and Preservation of Order in British Columbia." *British Columbia Historical Quarterly*. Vol. XI. 1947: 113–148.

Ramsey, Bruce. "Those Cariboo Camels." *Pioneer Days in British Columbia*. Vol. 2. 1976: 60–69.

Rickard, T.A. "Indian Participation in Gold Discoveries." *British Columbia Historical Quarterly*. Vol. II. 1938: 3–18.

Robinson, Noel. *Blazing the Trail through the Rockies: The Story of Walter Moberly and His Share in the Making of Vancouver*. Vancouver: Vancouver News-Advertiser, 1914.

Shewchuck, Murphy O. *Cariboo Trips & Trails: A Guide to British Columbia's Cariboo Gold Rush Country*. Markham, ON: Fitzhenry and Whiteside, 2008.

Smith, Dorothy Blakey. "The Journal of Arthur Thomas Bushby, 1858–1859." *British Columbia Historical Quarterly*. Vol. XXI. 1957–1958: 83–198.

Smith, Jessie Ann. *Widow Smith of Spences Bridge.* Ed. Murphy O. Shewchuk. Merritt: Sonotek Publishing, 1989.

Teit, James. *The Thompson Indians of British Columbia.* Merritt: Nicola Valley Museum & Archives Association, 1997.

Thomson, Duane. "Hwistesmexe´qen (Nicola, Nichola, Nkwala, Nickilush), Indian chief, warrior, hunter, trader, guide, farmer." From the Royal BC Museum website: http://www.livinglandscapes.bc.ca/thomp-ok/river-post/nicola.html.

Twigg, Alan. *Thompson's Highway: British Columbia's Fur Trade, 1800–1850: The Literary Origins of British Columbia.* Vancouver: Ronsdale Press, 2006.

Wade, Mark S. *The Cariboo Road.* Victoria, BC: The Haunted Bookshop, 1979.

——. *The Thompson Country: Being Notes on the History of Southern British Columbia, and Particularly of the City of Kamloops, Formerly Fort Thompson.* Kamloops: Inland Sentinel, 1907.

Walkem, W.W. "Edward Stout: Gold Rush Pioneer, 1858." *Pioneer Days in British Columbia.* Vol. 3. 1977: 30–35.

West, Willis J. "Staging and Stage Hold-ups in the Cariboo." *British Columbia Historical Quarterly.* Vol. XII. 1948: 185–209.

Zuehlke, Mark. *Scoundrels, Dreamers & Second Sons: British Remittance Men in the Canadian West.* Toronto, ON: Dundurn Press, 2001.

Photo Acknowledgements

Colour Images | *Courtesy of the following photographers:*

Andrew Fandrich
Front cover, pages 96, 114, 116, 118, 127, 242, 265, 292.

Bernie Fandrich
Pages 15, 17, 19, 20, 21, 23, 24, 26, 37, 44, 45, 49, 50, 51, 53, 56, 57, 59, 62, 63, 71, 74, 77, 78, 85, 86, 87, 100, 106, 108, 112, 122, 124, 126, 127, 128, 131, 133, 136, 137, 139, 140, 189, 205, 271.

Don MacGregor
Back cover, pages 36, 42, 52, 55.

Harry Kublik
Pages 74, 92, 129, 135, 141.

Kumsheen Resort Staff Photographers
Pages 35, 41, 46, 66, 69, 76, 94, 95, 99, 102, 109, 121, 274, 186, 240, 268, 270, 274, 284, 286, 290.

Archive Photos | *Courtesy of the following organizations:*

Library and Archives Canada
Page 6: C-002774 detail.

Lytton Museum and Archives
Page 142: 1545 detail / 145: 251 / 149: 1099 / 154: 294 / 158: 1062 / 161: 603 /176: 0715 detail / 178: 405 / 187: 1618d / 204: 0737 / 220: 0595a / 230: 01279 / 251: 1047 / 260: 0323 / 278: 0665 / 283: 0312.

McCord Museum of Canadian History
Page 163: VIEW-1746 / 173: I-69931 / 202: I-69926.1 / 215: I-69929.1 / 241: VIEW-2135.

Royal BC Museum, BC Archives
   Page 83: A-00347 / 147: B-00693 / 166: B-07265 / 168: D-09299 /
   169: D-03185 / 170: D-03168 / 191: A-01622 / 193: A-00144 /
   196: A06645 / 212: A00348 / 216: D-02450 / 218: A-00566 / 220:
   bottom A-09854 / 221: I-58408 / 235: C-04848 / 246: D-04712 /
   249: I-30869 / 252: A-00724 / 259: B-05526 / 261: I-30869.

Vancouver Public Library, Special Collections
   Page 244: VPL-2135 / 256: VPL-30956 / 267: VPL-463.